# Haunted Cars and Highways

## The definitive account of paranormal events on Britain's roads

# Haunted Cars and Highways

## The definitive account of paranormal events on Britain's roads

Antony Milne

EMPIRICUS
BOOKS

Cambridge, England

First published in Great Britain 2019
by Empiricus Books
The Studio
High Green
Great Shelford
Cambridge CB22 5EG

www.januspublishing.co.uk

ISBN  978-1-85756-894-3

Cover Design: Barry Small

Printed and bound in Great Britain

# Contents

# Author's note

The many events listed in this book in bullet-point form have been derived from Britain's numerous county paranormal databases, which can be found on the Internet, and are hence without reference notes. Reference notes throughout this book indicate other sources for the events described.

# Preface

As so often, I decide to turn a recurring theme or observation from an earlier book into another work – a new book – that looks at the earlier subject from a different and perhaps more important angle, or singles it out for special treatment.

In two earlier works on the subject of 'orbs' and Ufos, it became clear that – being an outdoor phenomenon – motorists, as they travelled along the highways of Britain, would be more likely to report the existence of strange aerial phenomena either on the road itself, or manoeuvring not far above it, either to the police or to the media. In researching for further evidence of orbs I was introduced to women's monthly *Fate* types of magazine in which 'spiritual orbs' were often referred to, and photos were included in the letters to the editor about this spooky phenomenon. These letters and other features would often refer also to dreams and premonitions – omens in a sense – of future car accidents on road journeys the writers were planning to make, and even describe the warnings in their heads while driving along the road with their families: uncanny messages that told them to pull over before being struck by another vehicle.

These two important themes – Ufos and premonitions – are combined in this present book, which includes other paranormal incidents experienced on the road, such as cars mysteriously vanishing from view.

This book also relies heavily on the various paranormal databases that are held – perhaps to the surprise of many – in the archives of Britain's county headquarters, and which can be found on the Internet, most of which have been vetted by local historians for their veracity and provability. This 'road ghost' archive material is immensely interesting, and although undoubtedly made use of by local 'ghost hunter' historians, I don't believe much of it has yet been collated and categorised, county by county, and presented in a single volume.

All combined, the story of haunted cars travelling along our haunted roads, I hope you will agree, is an extremely riveting one.

# Chapter 1

## Britain's Haunted Roads

Of all the strange road episodes listed in this book vanishing is the main phenomenon – people, hitchhikers, road victims – most of them uncannily disappear. People who are run over by cars are never seen again, with the shocked driver screeching to a halt to search in vain for the body of his victim. Cars heading towards drivers who fear the inevitable head-on collision just vanish from sight before impacting. Contrary to the laws of physics, anything and everything can dematerialise if the circumstances somehow seem right, but which we can never understand. While most of the literature dealing with ghostly apparitions refers to dead people, it is the reports of strange events on the highways that confirm the suspicion that perhaps even large solid objects – cars and lorries that exist in the same real world as we do – are not quite as real and solid as we thought. Transport disaster scenes seem to be strangely embedded in the landscape itself. What were prehistoric trackways now seem to be chock-a-block with spectral coaches, mischievous spirits, desperate suicidal maniacs and evil witches.

Roadside ghosts have a peculiar menace of their own, and have plagued drivers of all vehicles large and small, private and commercial. The strangeness of Britain's haunted highways, especially the many tales of menacingly dangerous tailgating vehicles, are not the conventional mysteries of the paranormal. Stories involving cars forced to a grinding halt, with their engines simply cutting out, even with ghosts wanting to climb in beside the driver, are extremely unnerving.

The bizarre and uncanny entities and unknown forces that many drivers come across are peculiar and hardly believable. In fact it is incomprehensible – evidence of an unpleasant stalking pathology. Nothing is rational in the world of the occult: madness seems to reign in its alternative reality. In West Wilton, Yorkshire, in Church Lane near midnight on 18 September 2010, a driver got out to retrieve his son's teddy bear that had been thrown out of the car window. Stooping to pick it up, he was stunned to see a 'shadow' throwing a ring-like object which clattered onto the road, but was amplified by other clanging sounds that came from nowhere.[1] In Coundon, on the B4098 road in the West Midlands, a car's bonnet was unaccountably struck by a fall of apples on 12 December 2011 (known as 'Fortean phenomena').

The numerous researchers who have delved into the subject of haunted highways, and the police who have often had to visit the scenes of various untoward events – especially those involving people alleged to have been run over – say the events described to them are absolutely true. There is a curious overlap with other ghostly occurrences reported in the occultic literature, such as the 'woman in white' scenarios, an integral feature of the road-haunting legends in Britain and America. There are horrible stories of unknown and unearthly creatures haunting local roads at night, causing many a car to crash.

# The Truth about Haunted Cars

The title of this book makes an extraordinary assertion – cars can be *haunted.* But can cars and car drivers travelling along haunted roads be equated with machinery and transport technology like Tube trains, overground trains as well as lorries, ships and planes? How can they be part of the occultic, mystic world? Can any form of transport *have* ghosts, or could they themselves take on the characteristics of unreality that people associate with the paranormal?

The answer must be Yes – cars *can* be part of the paranormal. The faltering car which seems to have acquired a worrying tapping noise could have been affected by the same 'gremlins' – an oft-used expression for mischievous entities in English and North American folklore, and often known to affect machinery and technology. Too often mechanical or electrical faults happen to a car on a particularly notable journey that has already displayed alarming anomalies. Many motorists in Chipping Campden, Gloucestershire in November 1998 were annoyed and surprised to find that their remote control keys, for some reason, didn't work.

Ghosts could in fact exist parallel with living things, in the same way cars could be counterparts to this parallel world. Ghosts haunt *places,* and cars travel though these places. That's why, one could argue facetiously, ghosts never quite get it right, and explains why there are doubts and misinterpretations about strange and uncanny events. But both – the ghosts and the haunted cars – should be analysed according to their destructive or distressing potential. A car driver senses a sudden change in atmosphere or temperature, just as ghost hunters exploring haunted houses experience unaccountable patches of cold in certain rooms. But just as often the driver who sees a Ufo hovering over his vehicle will experience intense radiation-type heat. (see Chapter 20 ). Not only do drivers have spooky experiences on the road, the victims have strange night visions in their own homes. An exhausted driver once had an unnerving experience while out driving for a considerable time along the motorway at night, and witnessed weird poltergeist effects when he returned home.[2] Uncanny things occurred one morning in a man's kitchen that were somehow attributed to the hitchhiker he picked up who later disappeared from the back of his car, a subject that I will return to later in this book.

Jenny and Lyndsey hinted that an unpleasant experience was connected with their car trip to the Lake District. They booked into a small hotel, but didn't like the sullen staff and the general negative atmosphere of the place. On top of that they had a drugged sensation, and fell asleep on their beds. They packed their bags and got out quickly the next morning. On driving back home Jenny had a hazy recall of a black silhouette leaning over her bed in the hotel bedroom. Lyndsey stared at her, wide-eyed. 'What the hell just happened?' Lyndsey gasped. Neither of them could remember much, and the two girls drove home in silence. Despite going back later to look for the hotel, they couldn't find it.[3]

Jenny's and Lyndsey's hotel was part of the paranormal, the 'paraphysical' (i.e. what is beyond the present understanding of Newtonian physics), and their joint experiences are connected with many aspects of contemporary industrial and urbanised life. Frightening experiences are often all linked up in some way. Ghosts are definite entities – interacting not only with each other, but somehow also with the living. Parapsychologists are uncertain as to whether the agent – or the 'percipient' – himself produces an internal object-moving energy, or whether he makes contact with outside sources. Take the residual nature of some hauntings. Ghosts can easily enough ignore us and go about their familiar routines. Sometimes they are referred to as coming from portals from another world – or our own world from our own past. Rich Newman refers to several hauntings like this – the ghost story is part of a documented historical event. Sometimes, an entire army can be seen marching off to battle.[4]

In January 2013 Alison, 52, had borrowed her husband's second-hand Peugeot to go to the shops. But it suddenly sped across a roundabout as if it had a life of its own. The car also started to move off after Alison parked it outside her friend's house in Taverham, Norfolk. But, as she ran frantically after it, she noticed that the steering wheel moved by itself as it managed to weave in and out of street obstacles. Inevitably the spooked car soon hit another vehicle. Her husband Dominique was a medium, and sensed that an entity had taken control of the car. He believed an old man had once owned the Peugeot and didn't like women drivers, and indeed the log book showed that a previous woman owner had sold the car after just a few months. One day, at the shops, the door locks went down by themselves, trapping Alison inside, and the alarm went off. She phoned for help, and soon the doors unlocked themselves as if by magic. The car was soon sold![5]

Deborah Kent, 47, was living in an attractive thatched cottage which was involved in a concatenation of weird events which included, among other things, inexplicably huge electricity bills which the energy company couldn't explain. The dreaded gremlins often seemed to plague Deborah's home. She had failures in her love life, a fire occurred in the shop next door, she experienced poltergeist activity and she had a car accident. Deborah's mother told her that she heard that the previous owner suffered from peculiar experiences, such as things moving by themselves, and inexplicably haemorrhaging utility bills. Deborah believed some kind of negative energy in her cottage was due to entities or alien creatures, or other ghostly phantasms which were entering and leaving her cottage and actually draining the electricity from it. The late German paranormal researcher Hans Binder said that supernatural agents do in fact tap into electrical supplies in some way, especially to move heavy furniture.[6] Electronic and electrical devices in the home or in the car too often seen to have a destructive potential. They show that they cannot act benignly with human life.[7] They break down, and they cause accidents and deaths, such as fires in flats, or collisions on the road.

But Deborah suspected the house was on a ley line (see Chapter 2). A medium she called in to check over the house said he sensed 'demonic creatures' using the house as a doorway from the underworld, and that they had been doing so for 'hundreds of years'. The medium also employed the services of another healer who could channel in 'white light' to close the portal that the aliens were using while Deborah was out of the house. But a little while later she heard a loud banging on the front door, preceded by the sound of hooves crunching up the gravel path to the front door. Closing her eyes in fear, she had a vision of a demon-like figure with hooved feet, with a red face and scaly tail, tapping its tail in anger, and telling her in the vision that they were angry that the healer, or mystic, had closed their portal. 'We didn't want to go but you made us,' he said in a growling, deep, but human-sounding voice.[8]

A Welsh lorry driver named Gordon was on his way home from work on his motorbike in June 1994 when he lost his life in a collision with another vehicle. On that same the night his widow experienced paranormal events. Burglar alarms went off and couldn't be silenced except with the brute force of a carpenter's hammer. There was a phone in the house that started to ring, with no one at the other end. Indeed, the phone did ring without any connection to a power source. The widow suggested that Gordon was trying to send her a 'sign' that 'he was still with me'.[9] The phone, it was surmised, could instead simply be playing a cruel trick on Gordon's widow.

The common link, obviously, is death – not specifically murders or suicides but tragic and fatal accidents on British roads, and many more in the US and other countries. British road deaths in 2013 were 1,700, declining from 3,400 in the year 2000 – a welcome statistic. But between 1951 and 2006 there were some 309,144 deaths, and 17.6 million people were recorded as seriously injured.[10]

The ghostly tales of those unfortunates who have been killed in bizarre accidents, annotated and discussed in this book, add to the cumulative total of others who have tragically died in road accidents. It is not surprising, then, that many roads and highways around the world are haunted.

One could, in the meantime, ask about the whereabouts of the missing wraiths of the thousands who have met their deaths on the road over the years. Although ghostly road experiences seem to accumulate over time as more roads are built or are used, they are not as numerous as the more traditional haunted spaces in the sense of yielding more ghostly spectres. But you can never get the true ghost toll in any event because of 'our modern mixture of fear, disbelief and cynical amusement' on the subject, wrote John Harries.[11] Even the ghost hunter can get cynical about the related tales repeated so often in ghost books.

## Car Experiences: Uplifting and Frightening

Nevertheless, some inexplicable events involving car journeys can be uplifting. George, who ran a thriving business, was invited to an afternoon gathering by his old friend, Alan, who had helped George in the past. At the party George noted that everyone was well dressed and elegant, except for one ageing man who looked unkempt and dishevelled, and was huddled in a corner. Yet, oddly, as he was introduced to him, he noted that the man smelled of lavender soap. Alan said the man's name was Thomas, and as the guests began to leave he asked George if he would drive Thomas back to his care home. George, put off by the man's appearance, declined, and 'Alan and I parted company that evening with a stilted handshake and pursed lips'.

The following day when George was driving in his brand-new Porsche he became aware of a strong smell of lavender in his car. It reminded him of Thomas. For the next few days the lavender scent would accompany George in his car.

Alan normally ferried Thomas on his various journeys, and phoned George and asked him to do to him a special favour and take over these duties for a short period while he was on his holidays. George, largely to please Alan, this time reluctantly agreed. Eventually George got used to the strange Thomas, even though their conversations on the various car trips were rather desultory. One day Thomas expressed his gratitude to George in a whimsical way, saying how he thought people like George only thought of themselves and making money. 'I was wrong,' he said. 'That will teach me to judge others by the way they look.' George felt guilty at that, because this was precisely the way he had judged Thomas.

Alan later explained how Thomas was once a surgeon, but was severely injured in a cycling accident which so impaired his physical abilities that he had to discontinue his profession. Soon he went into a decline. He had no living relatives to take care of him, and wasn't able to look after his bodily functions well, and used bottles and bottles of lavender fabric conditioner on his clothes to mask any unpleasant smells.

George was overcome with sadness when Thomas died in the late 1990s, as his lavender scent was indelibly inscribed in his senses. Thomas taught George that angels can appear in many different guises. 'I still don't know why my car smelled like him before he had even got into it,' he said later. 'One thing I do know is that the scent of Thomas taught a man who was a critical case of hardness of heart to open his heart and his mind. That man was me.'[12]

But more frightening events greatly outnumber George's experience. Here is a strange encounter that would normally be an explicable, if disturbing, incident, but had several intriguing aspects to it that were clearly suspiciously paranormal.

Bob Warren explained how he was driving along the road leading to the bypass late at night in the winter of 2008. He had a girl with him in the car, and she pointed to something moving, but told him not to stop. But Bob, curious, did stop, got out and encountered a naked man. 'I didn't like the look of this geezer one bit. I said to him what are you doing mate? He just looks at me as if I'm not there, but he seems to smile like he's noticing the lady in the car, and she's screaming at me now, get in the car mate! get in the car! I want to go!' Bob was more alarmed at the screaming woman than the naked man. Then the man seemed to vanish but reappeared in the back seat of his car! 'The lady turned round and screamed at him so loud it would wake the dead, and it seems he's smiling at her then, like he's really happy to see her!'

Bob, angered, got a jack out of the boot of his car to 'smash his face in'. Then he noticed the screaming had stopped, and both the man and the girl had disappeared from the car. Bob then got scared, thinking this was a kind of set-up: 'Maybe the geezer and the lady are working together or something, because you hear about things like that … where the bloke gets robbed.' He jumped back into the car to drive off, but seemed to hear the girl's screams from a distance. 'Sod this, I drive off and I don't look back, and I never drive that road again. I often wonder what happened to the girl though.'[13]

## Ghosts Who Grab Steering Wheels

Bob Warren's story of the screaming kidnapped woman was indeed salutary. Many lady drivers, especially, are often frightened when travelling along British roads, or have premonitions or forebodings about future journeys. Indeed, very many women, young and old, feature in the following chapters; unfortunate females involved in car accidents, murders and suicides, the latter often resulting from romances going wrong (see Chapter 13). A number of premonitions and dreams involving potential or actual road accidents seem to refer to women. Many of these premonitions are cited in women's occultic and 'Fate' types of magazines and books. Other cases involving female passengers or drivers can be found on the Internet.

Take the following frightening story. A lady driving between King's Lynn and Boston was suddenly plunged into a fierce struggle to regain control of her steering wheel, as an invisible pair of hands wrenched the car to the right, forcing her into the oncoming traffic stream. She nearly lost her life as the car finished upside down in a dyke.[14] Later the woman took a paranormal investigator, a man called Michael Sadgrove, to the scene of the incident. The psychic said he was able to contact the spirit of a man of about thirty who said he and his young family were killed in their car on the same road, and that in the afterlife he was acting out of vengefulness towards other drivers because he said his death was not his fault.

Other spiteful steering wheel-grabbing ghosts were detected when Michael went further into the strange event. One pestering menace was said to be that of the malicious ghost of a 70-year-old illiterate farmhand alive at the beginning of the 20th century, whose wife had been killed by one of the earliest motors.

Florence, aged 28, was driving on a lonely road from Postbridge to Two Bridges across Dartmoor in Devon, in failing light, when her car seemed to develop engine trouble. She pulled over to the side of the road. She then felt unnaturally cold, and sensed she was being watched. She looked up and saw a pair of disembodied hairy hands moving across her windscreen. Frozen with fear, she was unable, for some reason, to scream. She learned later that the disembodied hands were a cursed legacy dating back to the 1920s, with pony traps overturned, cyclists thrown off their bikes, a motorcyclist nearly killed when his engine was unaccountably torn off, and an army officer complaining of giant hairy hands covering his own on the steering wheel.[15]

In 1921 there were strange press reports of invisible hands taking control of an army captain's steering wheel while he was travelling along the B3212 in the Dartmoor region. He had to fight for control of the wheel, and was forced into a verge.[16] In recent years drivers in the small town of Bromyard in Herefordshire complained that an entity would grab their steering wheel with such force that they could not turn corners. This alarming syndrome was caused by the apparent ghost of a woman who died struggling with someone in her car as she drove at speed.[17] Once again in the Devon town of Postbridge, near the hamlet of Two Bridges on the B3212, hairy hands grabbing at the handlebars once made a motorcyclist crash.[18]

There was a horrible pit disaster in 1910 at Platt Lane, Lancashire. Some 344 workers and others died. Motorists have seen 'eyes peering from hedges, and ghostly miners trudging alongside cars, or pulling coalwagons behind them'.[19]

In another suspected case of supernatural influence, a motorcyclist in Kent felt his mount careering out of control, and actually yelled at a policeman on point duty that he was unable to stop. The policeman was knocked down and the biker was seriously injured in the resulting accident. But his speed was not excessive, and nothing – it turned out – was wrong with the bike. Publicity about this event encouraged other motorists to complain of having accidents after inexplicably losing control of their vehicles, with accelerators or brakes suddenly failing to work properly.[20]

Then there are strange compulsions that some drivers experience out on the road. A motorist felt a need to repeatedly turn off the motorway at a junction, and drive back to the previous junction and start all over again. On each occasion when he belatedly approached the place where he had just turned off he knew that an accident had occurred, with the police just arriving.[21] And its's not just a British phenomenon. In the summer of 1929 more than 100 automobiles had mysteriously crashed on the newly opened highway between Bremen and Bremerhaven, Germany, with some drivers dying. The highway was marked out with numbers carved onto stone headers. Most of the accidents seemed to happen at the one marked 239, and survivors said they experienced a 'tremendous thrill' as their cars reached this marker, and then some force seem to drag them off the road. In view of the weird sensations drivers had reported – a kind of exhilaration – a local dowser, a Carl Wehrs, got hold of the police accounts and suggested that a mysterious force was operating on the cars from a powerful magnetic current generated by an underground stream. When his steel dowsing rod was snatched from his hand at a certain point on the highway – where most of the accidents happened – he believed his theory was correct. Indeed, when he buried a box full of small star-shaped pieces of copper at the black spot for a week, no accidents happened, but they resumed when the box was dug up.[22]

Other compulsions, while on the high road, have been commented on. For example, on a road in Eaglesham in East Kilbride on 4 March 2005, two friends were coming close to some hospital grounds at half past midnight. They both felt an uncontrollable urge to lift the cover of a main storm drain that they had just passed. Inside the drain they thought they could hear the sound of a woman sobbing which turned into a distressing wail. Staring at each other, they looked into the drain again and could see an eerie mist coming upward towards them. They rushed back to their car and drove off in a hurry.[23]

Kirsty Richardson, on 7 January 2016, took a picture of the aftermath of a car crash on a trunk road near south Manchester. She took it on her iPhone and sent it to her boyfriend, who often drives the same model of car that crashed, and it was in his neighbourhood. Yet the picture contained a strange hooded figure on the grass verge, which had not been seen by Kirsty herself.[24]

# Chapter 2

## Liminal Places and Sacred Borders

Time warp apparitions – where the passage of time seems to behave oddly (see Chapter 20) – occur with both the ghost and his surroundings revealing themselves to each other. People claim to have been suddenly plunged into historical settings. They see nothing that is totally bizarre or absurd, such as we get in dreams, but houses and ordinary people. Indeed, so realistic can these scenes be that they actually see living actors moving about, dressed in their ancient costumes, and can even converse with them. These witnesses have their own 'present' which becomes divorced in a sense from a new present that was formerly a past, but a past belonging to others. The apparent oddness arises when the physical surroundings are obviously different or substantially altered to reflect an earlier time, where the landscape has subtly changed. When it comes to roads and byways this phenomenon can cause serious accidents, when drivers go to turn off onto roads that aren't there.[1]

Liminal places are the borderlands or transitional or marginal spaces between one region or place and another ('limen', denoting 'threshold'). There have long been reports of 'elemental forces' traversing routes across the countryside's 'spirit paths'. Books on county ghosts often mention them.

The liminal effect is assumed to apply to the Oldnall Road in Kidderminster, Worcestershire, where the ghost of a young girl has been seen.[2] The Oldnall Road runs along the parish boundary. A folklorist called Jeremy Harte said that most spooky road events do occur within a tenth of a mile of parish boundaries.[3] Perhaps, he suggests, parish boundary roads tend to be busier.

Sean Tudor, whose writings will be discussed later, raises the question of what constitutes a haunted 'place', which usually is a building, a house or a churchyard, with clearly defined boundaries. 'But a road is an open feature. Which perhaps makes it harder to comprehend how the same figure (i.e. the ghost) could manifest miles away from its supposed "centre".' He then admits that a non-material entity could pass through walls or anywhere or be seen anywhere.[4] The haunted road, in a sense, becomes a *notional* boundary, but at the same time it is not a *real* boundary, and often, being haunted, is a *tricksterish* boundary. These invisible boundaries also hint at a connection between mind and the environment, or even the boundary between the life and death of the road accident victim. And road ghosts at junctions are also customarily associated with human intrigue and tragedy – another boundary line.

These liminal thresholds are extraordinary considering how they reveal topographical realities; the scene is literally transposed from the past to the physical present. On many highways and A roads in Britain, apparitions occur near junctions or road bridges, as well as near railway bridges. These bridges can sometimes seem to alter in appearance, so obvious is their spooky nature. Ghosts are in some kind of limbo between earth and the spirit world, but which is actually marked out in the physical world, and where road ghosts are often seen. Ghosts are the residents of the liminal: they include the spatial, notional and symbolic. The liminal features could alone be the cause of road ghosts – a state of crossing over in twilight, and this includes over bridges and under bridges, and motorway turn-offs and slip roads. There are lonely roads, junctions, fords, hills, caves, cemeteries, stiles and gateways – all notional boundaries between one geographic feature and another, as if they were spiritual council districts – where the nervous hurry past after dark.[5] Throughout the world there are fearful spots where travellers meet supernatural entities which suddenly vanish. Crossroads were often feared as designated haunted spots, often serving in the early 19th century as burial places for executed murderers and suicides.

Some researchers like John Huffam suggest the relentless on-and-off road works and earth-moving programmes for new bypasses and motorways have shaken up the spirit world, or annoyed its inhabitants. A common theory about hauntings decrees that sacred burial grounds, of long-standing residences, where ghosts once lived as persons, have given rise to ghostly activity.[6] Many eerie sightings on roads that have experienced road deaths are often related to the building of bypasses that slice through hillsides and perhaps graveyards. Susan Kew of Derbyshire wrote to ghost hunter Philip Solomon of *Fate and Fortune* magazine to remark on a mysterious spate of accidents in Brimington, Derbyshire, outside the town's crematorium. She was wondering whether some spirits may have been disturbed when part of the crematorium car park was dug up. Philip replied that a disturbance can happen when bodies interred are 'drawn back to the other side'. People sensitive to spirits may see orbs or white mist, causing them to swerve their cars.[7] The spirits come back to a particular roadway to relive the ordeal or trauma of the past, or somehow deal with it or rectify it. A monk might have been buried in unhallowed ground and re-emerges to appear among other wandering spirits.

Twyford Down, Hampshire, now an area of the M3, seemed to develop a 'curse' in the year 1992. Apparently the building of the motorway disturbed the graves of three men who had died while working on it, and the graves of some fifteen others who died later, or prematurely, as a result of the curse, although the county paranormal database is not entirely clear on this point, or where the other graves were located.

Anecdotes suggested that a woman had been killed by a car along a stretch of road in the Blue Bell Hill area of Kent (see Chapter 14), which has all the hallmarks of liminal boundaries – human, spiritual and geographical. The Blue Bell Hill area is a mid point between north Kent towns, district cross-overs, such as the section of the A229 between the M2 and M20 motorways. These intersections include burial grounds, bridges, a hill and road junctions. Often ghostly encounters take place between 11 p.m. and 1 a.m., at the turn of a new day.

Leagram Hall, a stately home in Chipping, North Lancashire, had fallen into such a state of disrepair by 1963 that it had to be demolished. But rumours persisted that the ancestors of the estate had been 'upset no end' when the coffins of deceased occupants – dating back aeons – had to be removed from the family chapel attached to the home into new premises, to be later buried in a distant churchyard. This caused hauntings and other spooky events, including strange sounds. Cars, even from the first year after demolition, had stopped inexplicably in the lane which skirted the estate, and would not restart. Ghostly figures leapt straight in front of moving vehicles, and 'went right through' them.[8]

The car itself could propel its driver into an historic ghost scene. A husband and wife were approaching a level crossing at Utterby Halt in 1985, over which used to run the line between Louth and

Grimsby, Lincolnshire, but which the driver, a Mr Hewitt, thought was still used three times a week for freight traffic. But the car stalled half way across. A gust of wind suddenly hit the vehicle, but the couple felt like it was a fast oncoming train bearing down on them, one which in fact seemed to actually pass right through their car. Getting out of the car, Mr Hewitt realised that the track could not even have been use for freight, because it was totally derelict, with weeds growing, something that mysteriously had not been seen at the time the car stalled. A railwayman had apparently been killed near the crossing when the line was in regular use, and it was suggested this might have been the phantom train that the Hewitts had experienced.[9]

There are cases of phantom roads leading drivers astray, as we have seen, looking like extra turnings off the highway, but which do not in fact exist. Car drivers seem to realise this when they seem to miss a turning which they know they would not have normally, or when they seem to be misdirected. For example, Mr Pike and his wife Sally were travelling home after a Ufo sighting at Starr Hill, in Warminster, Wiltshire. 'At various points along the highway,' said Sally, 'the road suddenly shot off to the right – yet we both knew it should be perfectly straight at these sectors.'[10] A Mrs Babs Davison, on more than one occasion in the 1970s, experienced this while driving on the Sevenoaks bypass, and suggested this might be the cause of several road accidents in the area.[11]

Roads, then, are the links between one place and another, even at the borders of one county and another, particularly across landscapes. They are liminal places, and are similar to 'ley lines', which are kinds of spiritual pathways. They form continuous routes across England that connect up various other-worldly events. Unusual phenomena are associated with the ley lines: phantom animals, spectral lights, the flights of witches, phantom underground tunnels.[12] They are associated with earth energies which prehistoric people knew about. Paul Devereux, as well as writing about 'earthlights' (mysterious lights in the sky), also used the word 'Earthmind'. He referred to 'Dragon paths' and 'The Dragon Project', as they all meander, apparently disliking straight paths. They are also known as feng-shui.[13] There is evidence from all over the world. In Germany they are called *Geisterwege* (spirit ways). In Holland they are known as *Doodwegen*, the roads of the dead.

Hence, it is unknown how many unexplained accidents on the road, or sudden swerving into ditches, have happened because the driver has literally ploughed into an invisible wall or barrier. These events can be attributed to the 'stray sod', a patch of soil on which fairies have placed a spell. Once you venture accidentally onto this path on foot you will have great difficulty in getting off it, or you will find yourself inexplicably walking in the opposite direction. There are enormous circles of stones, mounds of earth and cromlechs, all of which look like ancient graves. Occult writer John Michell said twenty-two leys were connected to fifty-three megaliths in Cornwall. Their energies became enhanced when buildings and erections were done above ancient tracks on or near sacred sites such as standing stones at certain nodal points.[14]

A bridge near the Finchale Abbey Campsite in Durham was haunted back in the 1970s by a club-footed monk, known as Slewfoot, who would haunt the location and the abbey ruins. The bridge over the river which cars and people used was subject to a time-slip phenomenon, transporting individuals back into history. The bridge sometimes changed shape, and a nearby phone box would turn into a cottage![15]

# When Street Scenes Totally Change

Early owners of cars in the First World War also had their own weird time warps. One night in October 1916 Edith Oliver was driving from Devizes to Swindon. She stopped her car to get a closer look at what seemed to be a village fair in progress, amid much fun and laughter. Yet it was dark and raining heavily, and no one seemed to have umbrellas or be wearing appropriate clothing – indeed, from what she could make out in the gloom, the clothing looked rather odd. Miss Oliver later learned from a guidebook that the village fair, once an annual occurrence, had been abolished as long ago as 1850. Hence the image she saw was of a summer evening in the sunlight, and not a rainy night.[16]

There are strange events that occur in the actual reality of outdoor life. Teenager Pamela Goodsell accidentally fell down a 20-foot shaft in 1978 while walking through a park near the site of the old Crystal Palace in south-east London. She seemed to have ended up, injured, at the site of an historic train disaster, with the broken ruins of a train carriage and skeletal remains of victims. When she reported this the next day, London Transport officials said it was extremely unlikely that any underground train accident had happened there, or that any bodies would have been left to moulder. The Tube authorities assumed any disaster would have been relatively recent, say during the post-war years. But there was long a rumour in the area that there was indeed an abandoned Tube train under the park; an early model dating back to about 1870. It was possibly an experimental train involving compressed air technology.[17]

A man from Wimbledon had a time-stopping experience while out walking. Everything continued to move, and the cars and buildings looked the same except that 'the past and the future no longer had any significance'. A subdued effect came over him, and the bright sunlight became diffused. He had the impression of being a lone observer of a timeless scene.[18]

Bold Street in Liverpool has a reputation for having out-of-time scenes. Anthony Peake, in his book *The Labyrinth of Time*, refers to a weird experience of a man in July 1996, who felt that the street had become unusually subdued and muffled, and had a leaden feeling in its atmosphere. Then a small van, with the upright contours of the 1950s, rushed by, honking its horn. It had 'Cardin's' written on its side. The man then made his way to Dillons bookshop and a similar experience overcame him. It seemed to have become, virtually overnight, 'Cripps', and dealt with women's handbags and shoes. People around him seemed to be wearing 1940s apparel. The shop miraculously turned back into Dillons within just minutes, but in doing so revealed another aspect of time warps – both the shops in Bold Street, and various customers and pedestrians on the pavements, were all in their own confused state of time. The man in question spotted a girl wearing contemporary 1990s clothes, grabbed her arm and asked if she had seen anything odd. She said she had entered what she thought was a shoe shop to discover it to be a bookshop. In other words, Cripps did actually exist in the 1990s, but alternately switched places with Dillons. But, and this is significant, both Cardin's and Cripps were trading businesses in the 1940s, and Mr Cardin did own a fleet of vans. Hence the man and the girl were caught in a peculiar situation, made more so because of the fact that they remained in the 1990s while other people, and other buildings and vehicles, apparently flipped about within a 50-year period.[19]

There were more obvious signs of liminal places, sometimes known as 'bilocations', often involving ancient battle scenes. In Northamptonshire, for example, there have long been rumours of building and landscape apparitions and battlefield sounds, which some attribute to the ancient Battle of Naseby. At Tibenham in Norfolk, where there is a disused RAF base, echoing voices from a non-existent public address system are often heard, barking orders to RAF crew, accompanied by sounds of a bomber warming up, although no specific dates have been given. At Marston Moor in Yorkshire, there are local reports of battle sounds – probably from the 1644 battle – on foggy nights. Another strange case of bilocation is reported from Frith Park, in Sheffield, Yorkshire, of a vanishing fish and chip shop, which occurred in 1990. This was surprising, because it was relatively new and had new lights, and customers were seen inside. But within a few days it had gone – vanished. In Church Street, York, in the Davygate area, two women saw a re-enacted battle between Roman troops and 'barbarians'. A van driver momentarily witnessed this scene, until it suddenly vanished.[20] In Dunwich, Suffolk, famed for its 18th-century flooded coastline and sunken churches, there were still phantom events pertaining to the flooding disasters that afflicted this town long afterwards, right up to the last ghostly event in 1924, when church bells could he heard ringing out from the sea.[21] In Aberdeenshire, in the late 20th century, a cottage literally disappeared in a town called Woodhead – and there were apparitions of earlier submerged buildings.[22]

Jade Jackson, as a 14-year-old schoolgirl in 2004, suddenly found her familiar terrain had altered. She too had been plunged into a time warp. She was walking her usual route to her school in Camborne, Cornwall, but she was startled to note that the old-fashioned red phone box was now some yards away from where it was usually located. Then she realised that a gate at the end of the lane was no longer there, but instead there was an unknown new road. As she stared in shock, a whole crowd of people walked past, all seemingly dressed alike and indistinguishable from each other. 'It was if they were part of a parade – but there were no local or national events going on,' she wrote in the magazine *Chat It's Fate*. 'It was 8 a.m. on a weekday, in a Cornish back street!' She realised something odd was occurring – the atmosphere felt oppressively silent – a common phenomenon in many similar events.[23]

Jade's experience is proof of the locational nature of time warps: buildings vanish or get moved. In 1978 a Mr P. J. Chase once took a walk down an unfamiliar road in Wallington, Surrey. He paused to admire two pleasant thatched cottages with attractive flowers in the front gardens. He mentioned the cottages to someone at work the following day, who said that no such cottages were to be found at that place, only two brick houses. When a puzzled Mr Chase revisited the scene he found to his amazement that this was so. But an old resident told him that the two cottages on the site had been demolished some years earlier.[24]

At Tendring in Essex, in the winter of 1974 at around 7 p.m., two cyclists spotted a large gothic-style manor house where they knew a bungalow should stand.[25] At Horning, in Norfolk, a recurring event happens on 21 July, every five years. The village is said to revert back to how it looked several hundred years earlier.[26]

Ivan Sanderson and his wife were once travelling through Haiti when their car got stuck in a mud road at night. They knew they were deep in the country, yet they had the eerie impression of being in a street full of European houses which Sanderson recognised – from earlier studies – could have been French, built in a style dating back some 500 years! The vision lasted some 15 minutes before disappearing.[27]

Similarly, in 1997 an Australian woman motorist suddenly felt a change in the air, which became 'denser somehow', and was transported back to about 1950. The tarmacked road became a dirt road, and the trees had gone. Then an old black car crossed an intersection in front of her, and the driver 'was looking back at me in total astonishment before he accelerated'. From what she could see he was dressed in 1950s fashion, complete with hat.[28]

A couple were driving across the Isle of Wight at night in January 1969. The area was quite rural and lonely, and they thought it strange to see 'bobbing coloured lights' strung across neighbouring roads and fields as if an agricultural festival were under way, although it was the dead of winter. They approached an inn but were alarmed to see another set of vivid lights, plus people wearing leather jerkins and carrying 'torches', and moving about. They drove rapidly away from the bizarre scene, but curiosity made then return a few hours later. The scene was completely normal, and they surmised that they had viewed an apparition of a medieval festival of some sort.[29]

Sarah Johnson, 55, while riding in a relative's car some years ago in Hertfordshire, seemed to have been plunged into a time warp when she came cross a sign with the intriguing name of 'Clusterbolts'. They decided to visit it, failed to find it, but drove instead through a very attractive village which looked extremely ancient, and was virtually deserted. When they got home they checked Ordnance Survey maps in search of the quaint Clusterbolts. There was no trace of it. But Sarah's father checked with the Hertford records office and found there had once been a village of that name – way back in 1348! All its inhabitants had been killed by the Black Death, as were many of those in the villages in that area at the time. The only remaining place with the name of Clusterbolts was a modern housing estate. Had Sarah and company actually driven through the original Clusterbolts as it was centuries earlier?[30]

A married couple got lost while on a motorbike trip through rural Suffolk in 1948. Soon, however, they came across a 'magnificent' village church that was particularly ornate. The wife thought she saw people coming and going from the building, but the husband did not. Later the couple, having located more or less where they were at the time, sought out the church, but no church resembling it could be found.[31]

During the early 1930s in Nazi Germany, a reporter, who became J. Bernard Hutton when he moved to Britain, had a weird time warp experience when he went to do a story on the Hamburg-Altona shipyards, accompanied by a photographer. By late afternoon the two men left the place. Suddenly they heard the drone of aircraft, and in a short while the inferno of anti-aircraft guns drowned out all other sounds. They hurried into their car, and headed back to Hamburg city centre. After a brief period they stopped on a hill, and got out to look back at the shipyard scene. Everything looked perfectly normal. When the editor got to hear of their story he accused them of being drunk on the job. However, just before war broke out Hutton left Germany for England. There, in 1943, he read newspaper accounts of the RAF raids on the Hamburg shipyards. Probing further into the details of the attack, he was alarmed to note that what he had witnessed in the spring of 1932 had been real after all.[32]

Sometimes myriad weirdnesses occur at the same time – strange night visions, time lapses and wristwatches malfunctioning. Take the experiences of the Christian Aid group that was touring through Salen Forest on the Isle of Mull in the Hebrides. The date was 8 October 1981. A strange mist descended and seemed to attach itself to their car: the driver could not seem to accelerate through it. Slowly, however, as he gained speed a vortex sensation seemed to make the car drift. Ahead the group could see undefined shapes, with the road oddly devoid of noise (the typical silencing that we have seen is reported in many travel-ghost stories) and, unusually for the time of year, devoid of traffic – there was not another vehicle in sight. They got out of the car and found the boot open and its contents lying in the road. More alarmingly, they soon realised that they had entered some kind of time-vacuum. A lapse of several hours had occurred, and the group later found that their quartz watches and the car's electrics had been interfered with.[33]

# Chapter 3

## The Legacy of Haunted Landscapes

Phantom people and their horses, travelling along above or just below the modern surface, is just one weird aspect of it all. Nothing looks or feels right somehow – not only do motorists experience time warps but the apparitions look larger or smaller than they should, with the feet of the ghost sometimes touching the ground or seeming to go beneath it. Ghosts of the ancient past can only be seen on the ground as it once was, at the level it was at the time. Ghosts seem to walk dangerously along highways which of course did not exist hundreds of years earlier.

In Linton, Buckinghamshire, near the Old Bell pub, an Elizabethan gentleman was seen during the renovation of a local road. But the man's legs appeared to be cut off at the knees, because the new road was 2 feet higher than before.[1] On a by-road five miles outside Worcester, at a town called Littleton, a phantom horse-drawn carriage can be seen by motorists. It moves over a road that vanished long ago, and is seen traversing tracks and bumpy overgrown woods. The carriage turns towards the River Teme and stops as if to allow the horse to drink. Then the apparition fades away.[2] (Other horse-drawn coaches have been heard – but not seen – along the Pershore high street.)

At Milton Keynes, Buckinghamshire, Roman soldiers were once seen moving, but with the lower half of the legs covered by the tarmac, following the height of the old Roman road.[3] At Ilmington, Warwickshire, during the 20th century, on local roads, there was a year-end reoccurring vision of a spectral vehicle suddenly veering off across fields.[4]

A teenage workman by the name of Harry Martindale saw Roman ghosts while working in the cellar of the Treasurer's House in York in 1953. But he couldn't see the lower half of their legs – the soldiers seemed to be walking through the floor. He described them as each having a round shield, all with the same sort of embossed emblem in the centre. He noted that they were wearing helmets and leather skirts, and not all were clean-shaven. This was, however, disputed by historians who claimed to be experts on the subject of the Roman occupation of Britain. But two archaeologists, interviewed years later, said they had witnessed the same apparition while in the cellar, and saw the soldiers carrying the same round shields as described by Martindale. At the time the Sixth Legion moved out of York in the 4th century, it had been reinforced by auxiliaries who carried similar shields, they said. What was startling about this episode was the fact that the sartorial aspects of the soldiers would have been known only to historians of that period – and exceptionally specialised ones at that – and not known about by any layman. Telepathy or ESP – in regard to Martindale being somehow able to communicate his vision to the historians – could also be ruled out.[5]

In another example, a ghostly monk at a Cambridge college was only seen from the waist up, 'the body jerking along the paving stones'. The ground level had been raised, and the ghost was still walking on the original surface.[6] Sometimes only part of the ghost can be seen. Near the village of Little Haldon, on the A380 road to

Teignmouth, the ghost appears of a monk who was thrown down a well in the 14th century by a robber whom he had disturbed. The monk died shortly after he was hauled out. But the ghost appears as just the head and shoulders of the monk, struggling to extricate himself from a well that no longer exists.[7]

Motorists, when travelling along the A1 towards Duffield in Derbyshire, say they see a horse and highwayman on the roadside with its legs vanishing at the knee. Both the ghost and the horse vanish if approached.[8] At Littleton in Herefordshire, motorists often have a vision of a coach travelling over lumpy fields and overgrown woods, where a road possibly existed in the past.[9]

The solid materialising of phantom armies can definitely interfere with road traffic. One witness in a taxi in 1960, on a road near Otterburn, Northumberland, a Mrs Dorothy Strong, said the engine died and the fare-meter 'went haywire', and the taxi felt as if it was being forced against an invisible wall. 'The soldiers seemed to close in on us then fade into thin air,' an event which has happened to other witnesses. One girl, walking in a wood, sensed a phantom army she could hear but not see; there was an invisible barrier of sorts which she could actually touch. She was trapped for hours behind it. She could see the search party sent out look for her, but they could neither see her nor hear her shouts.[10]

Jayne Bicker went to her sister's house in Snape in Suffolk with her boyfriend, Alan. Both were members of a spiritualist church in Felixstowe. They drove down an unfamiliar road, and Jayne experienced apparitions of people who lived 350 years earlier. She herself had turned into a 12-year-old girl, and she was aware of panicking people fleeing from armed men on horses. Frightened by the experience, Jayne pulled the car over to the side and burst into tears. When she related her experience, Alan told her the road had a reputation for bad accidents. But on a later trip to Snape, the same experience happened, and Jayne this time knew her name from an earlier life, and saw the wooden shack where she used to be 'Elizabeth'. Later return trips filled in even more of the memories of the past life, including the knowledge that Alan was her father! But Alan himself believed that in an earlier life he was a female witch, and later concluded, with horror, that the people on horseback terrorising the village were a posse set up by the 'Witchfinder General', Matthew Hopkins, and had come to prosecute witches, among them Alan.[11]

On the B roads surrounding a Cheshire country house known as Cleve Court, scenes are said to move back in time. A local doctor once saw a modern road replaced by a rough track, with ruts of cart wheels showing, along which was walking a caped man carrying a hunting whip.[12]

The following story is another indication of the how the landscape itself can be altered by unknown forces. In this case it involved strange changes in the street lighting along a dual carriageway, and the nature of the roadway itself. Mrs T was driving with her young son towards the village of Tarleton in the Lancashire mosslands. It was 7 p.m. on a dark evening in the winter of 2015. They were heading westwards along the Southport New Road, the A565. They had reached a stretch of dual carriageway with fields on either side. All of a sudden Mrs T could see, as she looked up to her left, an arc of clear white light coming down towards them from a what looked like a crescent moon. It seemed to be beaming down to the roadway and the surrounding fields. A hedge was dividing the two lanes of the carriageway, and Mrs T and her son could see that the street lights and the headlights of the oncoming cars, as they flickered through the hedge, all seemed to be arcing downwards as well, and all the lights had a somewhat unrealistic sharp border to them. Mrs T then overtook a car which had two ladies in it. But when she looked in her rear-view mirror the overtaken car had vanished. In fact there were no cars at all behind them, and the nearest in front of them was some way ahead. Mrs T then realised that the moon was to the right of them in the sky, and all the other cars and street lights had gone as well. She and her son did a return journey at around 10 p.m. on the same day, and soon realised that the street lights for the road were down the *middle* of the dual carriageway! But both mother and son were convinced that the street lights – on the outward journey – were originally along *each side* of the road, not down the centre. And where was the hedge that ran down the centre of the road, through which glimmering lights could be seen? *It was no longer there.*[13]

In the early 20th century at Great Clacton, Essex, at the junction of the London Road and St John's Road, a ghostly horse would cross the junction.[14] In Battlesden, Bedfordshire, in the autumn of 1982, two cyclists saw a disembodied pair of arms throw a small log over a hedge. At Clophill, in Bedfordshire, in 1969, a hooded monk was seen on horseback holding a lantern early one morning. He passed straight through a car. At Honeydon Road, in the Camworth district of Clophill, in the late 1980s, five occupants of a car saw a car in front of them, just yards distant, disappear around a winding road, but there was nowhere for it to turn off or pull over.[15]

## Celts, Norsemen and Fairy Forts

Belief in the afterlife of people living in northern Europe was derived probably from the harsh underworld. These Teutonic ghosts, as John Harries put it, 'ranged the earth seeking out recruits for their forces among the dead and the dying'. Harries, in his *Ghost Hunter's Road Book*, says the ghosts in the north of England can be the most frightening and vicious because for centuries the north 'was a bloody arena' of battles and civil wars, and had many legends of witchcraft and even werewolves with glowing teeth. Britain was the cloudy land across the misty sea, where the 'Islands of the Dead' live, according to Nordic tradition. English spirits do often resemble the Arthurian legends of idyllic love affairs and gallant victories, but at the same time possess an underworld of miserable forlorn ghosts, hideous wraiths who had met violent deaths, constantly seeking a resting place.

Both the Dutch and Norsemen in their longships, and other northerners, arrived in the north and east of England. The Teutonic tribes who came after the Roman empire declined also had their ghostly legends, perhaps even more unfriendly than the ethnic British ghosts.[16] The Celts and the Norsemen had bequeathed a haunted 5,000-year tradition to the British Isles, with the Roman and Nordic death cults merging with the existing Celtic spirits.

The fairy legend investigator W. Y. Evans-Wentz wrote about the haunted paths of Ireland and Brittany which ran along straight lines between ancient hilltop forts inhabited by the 'Little People', and folk are warned about building houses on the routes lest they experience unpleasant supernatural effects, even death.[17] Indeed, Ireland's haunted roads are attributed to bad luck caused by disturbed areas that have strong connections with fairies. They are known as 'fairy forts'. There is a dip in the N22, a major road between County Kerry and County Cork. According to Irish politician Lucian Danny Healy-Rae, the dip just before Kerry Way had been repaired several times, but the dip had mysteriously disappeared every time. Healy-Rae said he shared the belief in the fairy fort legends, and the legends of this apparently cursed road.[18]

Fairies, of which I shall have more to say in Chapter 16, are also common in Welsh folklore, older people putting out a saucer of food for them in midsummer nights. The country's phantoms are said to be these little people, normally harmless and friendly, but dangerous when riled or thwarted. There are stories of screaming souls in torment, and grotesque faces appearing out of nowhere.[19] Welsh ghosts of heavily armoured soldiers from medieval times leading pack ponies along a lane from Llambedr are common. So are the 'orbs', strange balls of light in the air (see Chapter 19) that were often seen over the ground between the village of St David's, Dyfed, and the Welsh coast.

## Which Is the Most Haunted Highway in Britain?

There is no definite answer to this, as *so many* are indeed haunted, some for only small segments. John Harries in his *Ghost Hunter's Road Book* tells of roads in Britain being 'chock-a-block with spectral coaches, supernatural hounds, mischievous sprites, good fairies and evil witches'. Indeed, such was the belief in such stories that in 2007 the construction company Tarmac undertook a survey to find Britain's most haunted motorways. There are multiple reports of apparitions affecting restaurants and their roadway surroundings. People often experience hauntings when they visit cemeteries by car, especially Redditch, Worcestershire, and Hereford, Herefordshire.

According to Tony Simmons, sightings coordinator for the survey, he said he believed most of the apparitions would apply to many A and B roads. He said it would be logical that the M6 – formerly the A6 – one of Britain's longest roads, running some 230 miles from Carlisle to Rugby and passing through many counties, would have a longer ghost-ridden history.[20] The M6 is also mentioned by

*Autotrader* magazine and a car insurance company called 'Car Hire Insurance'. And Mike Brooker also singles out the M6. He describes himself as a psychic medium, and says drivers see phantom lorries and Roman soldiers between Junctions 16 and 19 in Cheshire, and also – a subject that will be dealt with at length later – plenty of vanishing female hitchhikers. There is a 'real negative energy' in the road, he alleges. He suggests that the appearance of Roman soldiers might be due to the built-on Roman site in the area, or that the road was the site of the slaughter of a Scottish army.[21]

The A75 Kinmount Straight is also alleged to be the most haunted road in in Scotland. On the website trucknet.com under 'Britain's most haunted roads', the most haunted road is the A75 from Annan to Dumfriesshire. One lorry driver gave up after his experiences on this road; one where drivers have seen 'screaming hags, eyeless phantoms and ghostly animals'.[22]

Various other haunted roads have been listed on websites: the A50 Warrington to Knutsford, Cheshire; the A58 in Yorkshire; and the B3212 at Moretonhampstead on Dartmoor, where hundreds of cars were once forced off the road by unaccountable powers, and ghostly sightings were common.[23] Roman centurions, and phantom lorries going the wrong way, are often seen.[24]

There were ghostly hauntings on A roads in the West Midlands, and on a B road between Halesowen and Stourbridge, where drivers swerved to avoid mowing down children in Victorian dress. And there is a man and woman on the site of an old farm by the roadside, all of which disappear. There is a tradition of Roman spectres at Bleaklow Head, Pennine Way, Derbyshire, that gradually disappear, drifting out of time. In the above-mentioned survey conducted by the road company Tarmac, the most haunted roads were: Drews Lane, Birmingham (phantom cars often swerving or overturning);

the B1403, Doncaster (ghostly soldiers); the A9 in the Highlands (phantom horsemen or coach and horses); the B3313 in Cornwall (jaywalkers); the M4 motorway (various hauntings); the road to Devoudin, Wales (warning voices); Gloucester Road, London (laughing children); the high street, Great Yarmouth (strange dogs), possibly 'shucks' (see Chapter 18); and Platt Lane, Westhoughton, Lancashire (pit disaster ghosts). According to the BBC News website, one of the most haunted roads is the A23 London to Brighton road. A small girl with no hands or feet is often seen. Another figure is dressed in white cricketer's clothes, or is wearing a white trench coat. The area close to a local nature reserve in Cheshire, on the rubble of an ordnance factory that was demolished in the 1970s, is said to have the ghosts of people lost in the bleak mosses of the area. The Gorse Covert Mounds is encircled by a network of meadows, ponds and small wooded areas.

There is the notorious Stocksbridge bypass, on the A616, north-west of Sheffield, formerly part of the M67 motorway. The ghost stories about this road started during the actual construction of the bypass. Security guards claimed they saw children dancing beneath pylons. In the moorland region near Sheffield there were local variations of road hauntings. Stories in a Sheffield newspaper, with the 'Friend of a Friend' stories and repeated elsewhere, added to the apocryphal nature. 'Terrified' police, travelling on this highway, said they saw a dark-clothed torso actually gliding by the side of their police cars, and other officers witnessed a Victorian figure next to their car in 1987. Their vehicle was also struck by unseen objects.[25]

At Salford, Greater Manchester, in July 2009, a driver saw a figure standing in the road at 11 p.m. He was featureless and had no legs, and was possibly from the Cavalier era, with a light-coloured but bloodstained tunic. He moved across the road and disappeared into bushes.[26] In Keswick, in Cumbria, along the A6, in the early 20th century, a cyclist heard the thump of horses and coach wheels passing him. It was later revealed that there was a legend of a murdered couple in a coach who were shot dead by the father of the woman.[27]

The frequent encounters of road ghosts just after midnight is also a liminal phenomenon between one day and the next. A sighting by a motorist coming down the A13 in the direction of rail crossings – where there was a local boundary – was of a liminal nature. Lone drivers in an 'auto-pilot' state of consciousness, with the unconscious mind steering the car – could be classed as another liminal boundary.[28] There are continual re-enactments of history itself, of embedded time warps, where the present collides with the past. But the visible and the audible are not always synchronised.

# Chapter 4

## Landscape Ghosts

The Pilgrim's Way from Winchester, Sussex, to Canterbury in Kent is a boundary running parallel to the A20 between Hollingbourne and Charing. Here, a ghostly horseman can be heard galloping by motorists and walkers, but he is not seen. He is alleged to be nicknamed Duppa, and hundreds of years ago lived in a nearby large country house. He was known to occasionally show off his trick riding skills, but alas this behaviour brought about his own and his horse's death when he tried to leap over the wrought-iron gates to the grounds of his own mansion. As a result, when Duppa's ghost is seen during the day, with his unusually wide-brimmed Cavalier hat and ornate silver spurs, he and his and horse look crazed, with the hapless animal wheeling and rearing, but this time the vision is not accompanied by the sound of either hooves or harness. But, as a convivial character, when he deigns to slow down his horse, Duppa has a tendency to accompany walkers along the way and even chats politely with them![1]

Some claim to have seen the ghost of Anne Boleyn in a coach on the anniversary of her death on 19 May 1536, near the National Trust property of Blickling Hall in Norfolk. Old maps from Tudor times show that the land in that part of Norfolk was not enclosed, and the present-day hedges did not exist, and neither do the few remaining streams have the bridges which they had then. As a result Anne Boleyn appears only fleetingly and chaotically over existing roads. She seemingly plunges through hedges, as her coach originally went over bridged streams and long-disused tracks in the area that vaguely correlate with existing routes.[2] The ghost of King William Rufos (1056–1100), the third son of William the Conqueror, can be seen often on the nights of 22–23 July, the night of his death in the Gregorian calendar, walking, with his head bent, along the road from Stoney Cross to Winchester, Hampshire.[3]

At Easter in 1965 Eva and Alick Knight were driving from London a for a brief holiday, and to do some renovation work at their semi-derelict farmhouse which they had bought for their impending retirement. As they passed Enchmarsh, Shropshire, at about 3.30 on a bright sunny afternoon, they had to travel along a single -track lane for the last couple of miles to their farmhouse.

Just then, however, they came across a large black horse with its rider, stuck right in the middle of the track. The rider had a wide-brimmed large-plumed hat, and a cloak and breeches that were characteristic of noblemen of long ages past. But he didn't look real somehow, almost as if he was in a film, and the surrounding scenery was a kind of backdrop. Yet there he was, sitting motionless and staring steadily to the west, and with his clothes gently rippling in the hilltop breeze. Mrs Knight slowed the car to a halt, and both she and her husband watched, silent and fascinated by this intriguing encounter. Both the horse and rider, of course, situated in the English landscape of 300 years earlier, were unaware of the Knights' car of the 20th century barely yards from them. The rider then spurred his horse to leap into the field on the left-hand side of the track. The horse turned sharply and galloped southward parallel to the roadway.

On arriving home Eva and Alick both agreed that the horse and rider had appeared in monochrome – greys and blacks (which would be typical of a ghostly encounter), as they also agreed that the scene, even with the horse galloping away, was totally silent. But what was the weather like? They had the vision, as we noted, at Easter, which is in the spring, but they didn't mention whether the greenery and foliage of the landscape indicated the horse and rider were also in the spring, or instead in their own version of a high summer. And did the hedge the horse leapt over actually exist some 300 years earlier? Nevertheless there was no suggestion of the supernatural, just perhaps an historical film being made in the neighbourhood, or the rider was practising for a pageant. But the following morning the Knights' enquiries drew a blank: no one could identify either the horse or the rider from their description.[4]

In 1924, an archaeologist, R. C. Clay, was returning by car from a dig in at a Bronze Age village in Salisbury, when he saw a lad in a flowing cloak from an earlier era riding a pony bareback without stirrups or bridle, and waving a sword. The rider was heading across a field straight into the path of the road and Dr Clay slowed down, fearing a collision. The rider then strangely abruptly changed direction and rode alongside Dr Clay for a short while before vanishing.[5]

## The Civil War Ghosts

So often in haunted road literature the description is given of Cavaliers, but are these mere guesswork, based on a sketchy knowledge of English Civil War history, where the only definite thing known about the war is that there was a battle between 'the Roundheads and the Cavaliers'?

Cavaliers were soldiers of King Charles I (1600–1649), and participated in the Civil War which ran from 1642 to 1651. The

Roundheads were the Parliamentary soldiers who wore tight-fitting metal helmets, while the Cavaliers were 'Kingsmen', or Royalists, who wore large hats with feathers as their uniform headdress. But there was considerable similarity in both factions in regard to the rest of their clothing – similar breeches, doublets of woollen cloth, linen shirts and huge collars, and long leather boots. Some would have protective leather tunics or metal breastplates. Some historians say that the Cavaliers were a little more dressy in their more expensive clothing, but the officers of both armies tended to go for more elaborate clothing – lace collars, plumed hats, velvet and silk shirts and vests.

Across England, the two sides had their geographical strongholds, largely aided by the fact that any perceived enemies were silenced or fled. The Royal troops, the Cavaliers, were more likely to be found in the countryside, the shires and the poorer parts of northern and western England. Most of the industrialised parts of the country were Roundhead areas.

Civil War skirmishes between Cromwell's troops and Royalist Cavaliers reveal their ghostly remnants on the road between Hook and Basingstoke, and the figure of a Royalist soldier holding what looks like a broken sword – probably the victim of a violent death – can be seen near the Basing House, which the ghost of Oliver Cromwell is supposed to haunt. Det. Con. Roger Ryder, driving alone along the A456 to Hagley, Worcestershire, on a summer night, saw a lit-up pub after hours, and assumed a party was going on. A man ran out by the car park in an old Cavalier costume, with wig, hat, boots, red uniform and a sword – was this, wondered the constable, a fancy dress party?[6]

On the A640, in 1968, there occurred the strange case of an officer in a police car who happened to be cruising between Huddersfield and Saddleworth on the Yorkshire–Lancashire border. He dropped in at the Huddersfield Divisional HQ for a chat and tea. Talking with the other cops, he came to the conclusion that many of the weird incidents reported to them were true events. He himself noted the smell of pipe tobacco in a friend's old house, although no one smoked. The cop then says he resumed his patrolling duties, travelling to Buckstone Moor in the Pennines to a village called Denshaw. By then it was late at night, but he saw four horses and three riders and accompanying packhorses. They were in ancient dress, with rough clothing, neckerchiefs, leather doublets, swords and pistols. Was this from the King Charles epoch, he wondered? They seemed unaware of the police car. Curious, the officer then turned his car around to follow the riders and perhaps question them. It is unclear from that point whether he got out of his car to approach them on foot, because the newsletter that reported this incident said that one of the riders acknowledged him with a touch to the brim of his hat. At this moment, though, the policeman lost his nerve and 'drove off in fear'. The local newspapers on the following days failed to report any fancy dress parade or sponsored rides. And the incident was never apparently repeated.[7]

Unmounted spectral horsemen in Cavalier costumes with wide-brimmed hats were once seen in pre-war years in the road near Marston Moor, the scene of 17th-century battles involving Cromwell's troops and the Royalists. Today the area can be reached along the A59 York to Skipton road. A motorist in 1932, a commercial traveller with a passenger, on his way to Harrogate, could see the men walking ahead of his car in the middle of the road. The driver slowed, but was alarmed to observe a bus heading towards him and the soldiers, whom he assumed to be real people in period costume, but the bus seemed to pass right through them. He stopped and searched the verges of the road, but could find no trace of anyone. The Cavalier troops were obviously mere apparitions.[8]

At Buckstones, Yorkshire, on the A640 in 1968, a policeman in a patrol car saw a small group of horsemen in Cavalier clothing. Not believing his eyes, he returned three times to check this out, and saw them again each time.

Two police officers were travelling towards Solihull, responding to a crime in progress, in the early hours of a morning around the year 1988. The unlit road was straight and surrounded by countryside. They had reached a village called Catherine-le-Barnes. The driver saw a man on horseback and instinctively realised that it was a ghost, as the rider was very dated-looking, wearing a black flowing gown and matching floppy hat. There were no field entrances or gates the rider and horse could have passed through.[9]

In Hassop, Derbyshire, the paranormal archives refer to a phantom Cavalier corps travelling along the roadside of a narrow village lane, although no date was given.

At Laleham, Surrey, on a date in October 1982, a passenger got out of his friends' car to check into a strange light in the woods. It was after midnight. Suddenly he saw a tall figure with a cloak and old-fashioned boots and hat – the typical 'Cavalier' phantom. The figure paused, saw the witness, and walked towards him, but passed straight through him! Terrified, the witness ran back to the car, and his friends said they saw the same phantom walking through a wall.[10]

Ghosts were seen outside Banbury, Oxfordshire. At Edgehill, Warwickshire, there were rumours of Civil War ghosts going back to the 17th century. They are still sometimes seen, but more often heard – fighting, cannons and horses' hooves. There are stories of galloping horsemen and a headless soldier haunting lanes between Market Bosworth and Hinckley, Leicestershire.[11]

At Hook, Hampshire, on the south side of the A3, a figure with a long cape and wide-brimmed hat was seen some time in the 20th century at an unknown date. It was thought to be a Civil War ghost, complete with a metal sword in his hand. Also, on the road between the Crooked Billet and Hook House, a figure in a cape and tricorn hat was seen – and considered to be a bad omen.[12]

In January 1974, 22-year-old Geoffrey, together with some young friends, was driving towards Manchester to watch United play Ipswich. About 11 a.m. they stopped at the Keele service station on the M6, when Geoffrey and one of the others, named Francis, went to the men's room. But they soon realised that the man standing between them at the urinal was dressed in what appeared to be a theatrical costume. He had a wide-brimmed hat, a broad white collar, buff-coloured clothes and calf-length boots, in typical Royalist garb. Intrigued, the two men hurried out after him only to find that he had vanished. This seemed impossible, because there was nowhere he could have gone without being noticed, especially dressed like that. None of the others in the car saw him actually leave the men's room. All this was odd, and left Geoffrey suspicious and puzzled. The theatrical figure looked so solid and real. Further, said Geoffrey, 'I noticed particularly the very coarse stitching of his clothes, and the fact that the material seemed well-worn and shabby.' It hardly seemed likely that any theatrical costumier would go to such lengths to create historical authenticity. But this was not the first time that Geoffrey had been plunged into a Civil War time loop, which might have been due to his wife's family connections to Colchester, Essex.[13]

At Marston Moor, in November 1932, a ragged figure in very historical garments crossed the road in front of a car. Local historians said the clothing, described in detail by the driver, could have been what soldiers were wearing at the Battle of Marston Moor in 1644. And at Guisborough, Yorkshire, in 1988, four persons in a car saw a monk with a hood in the road. At Doncaster, off the B1403 at Common Ball Lane, a couple in a parked car late at night in September 2005 saw a marching soldier pass by, but no sartorial descriptions were given.[14]

# Chapter 5

## Phantom Stagecoaches and Horsemen

Phantom coaches and horsemen are often seen in the grounds of large houses or estates, or when approaching the driveways of buildings, in all counties. Ghostly large dogs (shucks) and large black cats (which will be discussed later in this book) the size of panthers, plus walruses and other odd creatures, are all referred to in the county paranormal databases from which most of the material in this book is obtained. At Dunwich, Suffolk, in the early 20th century, herds of invisible animals were once heard or sensed along roads, as well as 'will-o'-the-wisps', a kind of flickering orb light (discussed in Chapter 19). These apparitions apparently stopped in 1924.

### Phantom Horsemen and 'Highwaymen'

The ghost of a highwayman, said to be Dick Turpin on Black Bess, is seen on Watling Street, on the long stretch between Hinkley, Leicestershire, and Nuneaton, Warwickshire. He wears a tricorn hat and has an unusually visible red coat with his sleeves, apparently, illuminated. Harries reckons, however, that Dick Turpin probably had a hideaway in Woughton on the Green, connecting Newport Pagnell, Buckinghamshire, with Bletchley. If so, he is probably the cloaked figure seen moving haphazardly about on the B488 at night, as if waiting for something to happen, anticipating perhaps a patrolling posse about to arrest him.[1]

And south of Waltham Cross on the A11 through Epping Forest, Essex, is another galloping highwayman, and the accompanying suggestion is that he was the overworked Dick Turpin, galloping along the verge with an aged and skinny woman hanging down, whom he had robbed at her home in the vicinity of Loughton, and who he was dragging to her death.[2]

- At Rockfield, Gwent, at Anere Hill, on an unknown stormy night, a phantom coach and horses crashed into a wall. At Nefyn in Gwynedd another phantom coach is sometimes seen.

- On the famed Hogs Back near Guildford, Surrey, on the A231, on 8 January 2007 at 10.40 p.m., a driver watched a horse-drawn box carriage with a dim lamp cross the road right in front of him, but there was no slip road or gap that it could have emerged from.

- A phantom coach and horse travels at night between the Buckinghamshire villages of Radnage Bottom and Bennett End.

- At Coombe in Wiltshire on an unknown date, there were reports of a phantom coach.

- A phantom horseman with a bloodied face and galloping on a white horse can be seen on the A688 towards Hamsterly Forest, where there is more than one 14th-century castle, in the Bishop Auckland area. The horse and rider gradually disappear into the ground.[3]

- In the 1960s three friends travelling by car through the Castleshaw, Pennines, area of Greater Manchester, saw a Roman soldier riding towards them, and thought perhaps it was someone in fancy dress. But the figure passed right through the car.[4]

- At Hemel Hempstead, Hertfordshire, on 19 April 2009 at half past midnight, a driver saw a caped figure with a wide-brimmed hat cross in front of his car, and vanish from the driver's rear-view mirror.

- At Clifton Down, Bristol, in the south-west of England, at 11 p.m. on an unknown date, but said to be in the year 1977, a driver and his passenger saw a dark figure in the road with long arms extended. This was apparently the ghost of one Jenkin Protheroe, a 'highwayman'.

- At Broadwindsor in Dorset, on the B3163 to Drimpton on an unknown date, a hearse pulled by four black horses was followed by a crowd in dated clothing.

- At Buckland Newton, Dorset, another phantom coach and horse was seen.

- At Stoke Abbot, a phantom coach was driven angrily over a local road and an adjoining field.

- At Purse Caundle another invisible team of horses was heard travelling along local lanes.

- On New Year's Eve, reoccurring, at Stourton, a headless horseman is seen.

- At Stone, Buckinghamshire, on the local road to Thame, in 1994 in the late summer, a driverless stagecoach was seen.

- The same in Beverley, Yorkshire: a coach and headless horses.

- In Long Compton, Warwickshire, the coach and headless horses were weather-dependent.

- At Westcott, Surrey, on the road to Dorking, at 2.30 a.m. in 2007, a headless horseman.

- At Cantley, Norfolk, on an unknown date, a headless horseman was seen.

- At Skipsea, on local roads, the same headless horseman, this time with a headless horse, was seen. At Thirsk, a lad on a vanishing horse was seen.

- At Charley, Leicestershire, along Abbey Road in the autumn of 1997, a car passenger saw a figure on the grass verge with a long coat and hood, but with no face. The driver saw nothing, but stopped and both got out to check. They found nothing.

- At Tavistock, on the road to Plymouth, a black headless horse was seen, said to be one of those pulling Sir Francis Drake's hearse.

- At Colwall, Herefordshire, a woman cyclist in February 1940 encountered a procession of cowled monks carrying a body, accompanied by a ghostly horseman.

- At Midhurst, Herefordshire, in October 1999, a man was seen in a tricorn hat. As the bemused driver slowed to get a better view, he realised to his horror that the man was actually transparent (a real phantom, or a spectral vision) and disappeared into nearby trees.

- At Bramshot, Hampshire, on village roads in December 1991, a 'Cavalier' phantom highwayman was seen, together with, or at other times, 'a small group of Tudors'. At Petersfield, on the A3 leading towards the town, near a major service station, a lorry driver reported a figure in the middle of the road, seeming to signal for help. Police were called, but found nothing. Also at Portsmouth, over a narrow railway bridge on St Mary's Road, a driver saw a man on the bridge, although there was no pedestrian pathway or access. The year was 2002. The driver said the figure 'didn't look right somehow'. Indeed the figure 'evaporated' from his rear-view mirror.

- On a local road in Enchmarsh, Shropshire, in April 1965, two men in a car encountered a 'colourless' horse and rider dressed in 17th-century garb.

- At Cannington, Somerset, on the A39 near a roundabout on 21 November 2016 a driver saw a 'cloudy' horse jump into a hedge.

- At Beckhampton, Wiltshire, in the mid 20th century, there was the phantom highwayman as well as the coach and horses.

- At Bridgewater, Somerset, on the A39, a ghostly highwayman called Pocock was seen, causing several accidents by his lurching appearance.

- On the road between Trimsara and Llanelli in Dyfed in January 2011, a slow-moving ghostly coach was seen.

- Motorists in Oare on the A345 to Marlborough, and at West Kennett, were visited by phantom coaches and their horses, with or without their headless driver, often in the dead of night, and often just disappearing through hedges.

- At Hungerford, Berkshire, a ferociously galloping horse pulled a coach which didn't overturn in the process.

- At Moneygrow Tree, in Berkshire, a racehorse is sometimes seen, but is mainly heard galloping by.

- At Slapton, Buckinghamshire, circa 1986, a well-dressed horseman was seen on the road between Ivinghoe Aston and Slapton.

- At Bunbury, Cheshire, a ghostly horse and rider carrying a lance vanishes.

- At Fifehead Neville, Dorset, at a T-junction, there is often a phantom horseman.

- At Nuneaton, Warwickshire, on the A5 towards Hinckley in the 1990s, a phantom man was sometimes seen on a horse. In 1979 the same figure was seen 'shimmering'.

- At Loders, in Dorset, along Yellow Lane, a coachman is seen with no head, apparently having been decapitated when he hit a branch. No date is given for this.

- At Uplyme, Dorset, on the road to Yawl, a white horse and its rider is sometimes seen at midnight. At Minchinhampton, Gloucestershire, in the 19th century, a phantom horseman is seen.

- At Trawsfynydd, Gwynedd, a phantom coach and horse was seen along a village road on 30 December 1979.

- And at nearby Tremadog, approaching a roundabout on 20 July 2012 at 5 p.m., a group of phantom horsemen went 'charging across'.

- At Stow-on-the-Wold, Gloucestershire, on the A429, along the Fosse Way to Warwick in September or October 2005, a horseman wearing a long black cape was seen by a woman driver in her rear-view mirror, just feet from her car.

- In Denton, Leicestershire, in January 1967, a horse and rider stood in the way of oncoming traffic. But in this case only the driver of a car could see him, and not the car's passengers. Other drivers said they could only see the man, but not the horse.

- At Horsford, in Norfolk, along the Halts Road in the early summer in the 2000s, a disappearing phantom highwayman was seen. Not far away in Stratton Strawless at the same time there was yet another ghostly highwayman.

- At Exmoor, ghostly sightings and the hoof thuds of horses were once reported, dating back during the 20th century.

- At York, along the A558 at the 'Hellfire Corner', a phantom horseman apparently struck a car, and the area became an accident black spot, probably because it was a recurring hazard.

- At Barford, Merseyside, on 19 April 1985, on Walton Road which lies between Barford and Kimberly, three ancient figures were seen by motorists. The same three were seen again at 1.15 a.m. on 1 September 2013, seemingly oblivious to oncoming traffic, causing a driver to dangerously swerve.

This driver the following day made enquires to check whether a fancy dress event had occurred, on the suspicion that drunk partygoers were making their way home and got lost.

- At Hungerford in Berkshire, along the A338, in 1957 a woman on a white horse crossed the road and vanished.

- At Orlingbury, Northamptonshire, a phantom coach was said to belong to Lord Wolfage. At Whitby in Yorkshire a coach charges over a cliff.

- At Shepley in Yorkshire a night-time phantom coach with its four horses often travelling at 'breakneck' speed, and invariably every winter, and invariably also along the same roads around the same memorial.

- More 'charging' horsemen and their coaches were alluded to at Bungay in Suffolk, this time in the 20th century at some unknown date, rushing towards oncoming traffic and turning away at the last moment.

- At Matlock, Derbyshire, along the Bakewell Road in February 2001, a woman passenger saw a 'dark man' on horseback, with his long cape and large floppy hat. In Polstead, Suffolk, in a summer of the 1990s, at 4 p.m., a Mrs Hackford, a passenger in a car, could clearly see a horse and carriage containing an old lady and two males, all dressed in Victorian clothing. She craned her head to look behind as the phantasm passed, but could see nothing.

- At a town in Bedfordshire, on some date in the 2000s, a glowing ghostly knight was seen descending a nearby hill; it was seen both by a driver and by soldiers at a nearby barracks.

- At Chesterfield, Derbyshire, on the M1 close to Junction 29, a passenger in a car saw a tall man dressed in a purple hooded coat standing in the road at 10.15 p.m. on 10 December 2011, who then vanished. At Stoney Middleton, in the 1960s, a driver saw a cloaked figure with a hood pass through a stone wall.

- At Beaconsfield, Buckinghamshire, in the 1920s the sound of coach wheels along the road from Gerrards Cross could be heard.

- At Chalfont St Peter, Buckinghamshire, an old-fashioned stagecoach was often seen on misty nights being pulled by ghostly horses, and would vanish at the Greyhound Inn.

- At Marlow, along the Finnemore Road, a phantom coach driver was once observed whipping his horses.

- At Peterborough on the Sutton Heath Road, in about 2007, a driver saw a horse and carriage with a figure emerge from the right-hand side of a grassy bank and cross the road. A phantom coach and horses were also seen at Bennett End.

- At Tickhill, Yorkshire, along Wong Lane in the late 19th century, a ghostly coach was often encountered.

- In Cheshire at the town of Delamere Forest on 14 February 2006, a driver saw a small horse and carriage dimly lit by lanterns.

- At Mevagissey, Cornwall, in the 20th century, a driver saw an 18th-century coach driven by four horses appear and vanish.

- At the Ladybower reservoir on the A6013 in Derbyshire in the middle of the 20th century, a motorcyclist saw a horse and cart being led by a man with a large whip before it vanished.

- In Askham, Cumbria, a phantom coach was seen around the St Peter's Church area in the late 19th century.

- In the Devon town of Salcombe, in July 2004, a witness heard, late at night, the heavy breathing of running horses, although strangely there was no accompanying sound of galloping hooves. But something odd also happened: a hedge glowed briefly as the sounds increased. In Torbay in 1938 the landscape suddenly appeared totally changed.

- At Uplyme in the 1970s a 'phantom' coach was seen, pulled by four horses. There is a significant point to be made here: although the term 'phantom' was used, normally indicating a colourless ghostliness, this coach gave the appearance of being quite solid and very real, because the colours of the coach – red and black – were clearly discernible.

- The phantom coach seen at Letton in Norfolk in the 1830s was illuminated and was pulled by invisible horses. Another coach, probably driven by the ghost of 'Old Hutch', was seen at Long Stratton.

- In Norfolk, at the village of Weybourne, yet another ghostly coach pulled by the usual four horses – plus the headless figure driving – vanished into a church wall.

- Along the A9 towards Falkirk, and heading for the far north, an ornate coach and horses can be seen at times, complete with 'bewigged footmen walking alongside'.

Christine Sharp was driving her mother, Jill, 77, along roads in Brixworth, Northamptonshire, when she saw something big and black with two swaying lights ahead in the road. Just as she was about to overtake it and get a better look, it suddenly vanished. The object seemed to hang around the Brixworth area, because a family member later said she had seen it too. But a few weeks later Christine and her mother were out driving towards Lathbury, Buckinghamshire, when they decided to stop at a graveyard, as Jill said she had vague knowledge that some members of the Sharp family might be buried there. They pulled up and went over to the graveyard. Jill stopped at a gravestone with the name of Arthur Williams on it, who, it said, was from Headington, Oxford, and who had died at the age of 17 in a drowning accident on 29 June 1878. 'My gran came from Headington,' exclaimed Jill, 'and her maiden name was Williams!' They later checked out the details of Arthur's story at the records office in nearby Milton Keynes. They found to their surprise that young Arthur was indeed related – he was her mother's grandmother's brother, and thus Christine's great-great-uncle. They then checked into old newspaper accounts and found that Arthur was once a footman on a stagecoach, but had later drowned in the River Ouse. So Christine and Jill concluded that the dark object with the swaying lights that they had seen on the road was a phantom stagecoach that the late Arthur used to be sitting on![5]

## Frightening Headless Men and Horses

A number of headless apparitions appear in Dorset – women, horses and coachmen. Indeed, headlessness is a dominant feature on our haunted roads – animals, jaywalkers, highwaymen and headless coach drivers flogging on their teams of headless horses.

- Headless coachmen and horses have long been careering about Britain. Various headless people, some on horseback, are recorded. In the 1970s a car driver saw an old coach and horses bearing down on him outside Bungay in Suffolk. Queen Boadicea was seen driving her chariot along the old Roman road Ermine Street as it passed through Cammeringham in Lincolnshire.[6]

- A spectral coach can also be seen on the A386, and is said to be the coach of Sir Francis Drake, who has haunted the Plymouth, Devon, area for decades, as he once had a home in Buckland. The coach meanders only periodically into the visible range, as it takes the physical route of the earlier pathways across hedges and streams. Drake was said to have been involved in black magic practices at the headland overlooking Devonport, rituals designed to conjure up storms to disperse the Spanish fleet. After his death, imps and demons who were his black magic servants would not let his soul rest in peace. On the nights of raging storms, said to be Drake's doing, his black coach pulled by a headless horse races along from Tavistock to Plymouth. At the front of the coach headless hounds – said to represent the beheaded Drake – run wildly and improbably in front, with devils keeping up the rear.[7]

- At Bossington, Shropshire, in the late 19th century, a headless horseman driving a phantom coach and horses. At Brockley the exact same phenomenon – horses, headless horseman and all – possibly coming over from Bossington, but this time charging recklessly into the horse and cart traffic, usually at midnight. This type of apparition went on for years in

Shropshire. It happened once or twice in Cutcomb the A396, on the road to Timberscomb in Somerset.

- In Forest Road, Binfield, Berkshire. in October 2007 a motorist on the A321 spotted a galloping horse and rider in woodland to the side of the road, looking like a 'centaur' with a human head instead of a horse's, or the rider was headless.

- A coach and headless horsemen were seen once at West Lulworth; clues indicate this occurred in the 18th century.

- At Woodrising, Norfolk, in earlier centuries, a glowing coach with lamps and headless horses was seen.

- At Tenby, Dyfed, Wales, a headless team of horses along with its headless coachman disappeared in a 'loud explosion' at the Sampson Cross crossroads. This was said in the Database to reoccur every night, but there was no indication that spectators were drawn to witness this; neither has there been publicity in the press or paranormal literature.

- In Chettle, in Dorset, a coach and headless horseman is recorded in the paranormal archives. This time there was the familiar syndrome: he had not only carried his head under his arm, but had his hat on! Further on in Lytchett Matravers, on the A350 heading towards Poole, headless pall bearers were seen before vanishing into a hedge. At Marnhull, at midnight on various recurring dates, a black horse-drawn carriage and mourners took to the road. Prior to 1940 another coach and headless horse was seen at Oakley Down.

- In Essex, at Audley End, along the B1383, another headless coach driver was seen. At Geldeston, Norfolk, on the road to

Bungay, another headless coachman was seen perched on a coach pulled by four horses.

- At Bradfield, Essex, on the Southend to Cock Lane road in the 2000s, a father and daughter in a car saw a horse and rider emerge from a hedge and vanish.

Two patrol officers encountered ghostly figures in December 1994 while travelling near to Stocksbridge and its notorious bypass, north of Sheffield, South Yorkshire. There were already reports of dark shapes, musty smells, uncanny presences and eerie sensations. One of the officers said he felt cold, because of an inexplicable lowering of the temperature inside the car. When he turned his head he had the impression of a shadow somehow attached to the car. But when he moved his head sharply it disappeared. The other PC saw the torso of a man dressed in 1820s costume, right next to the car, before it vanished. Both policemen searched the area but found nothing. They drove further but heard loud thumps as if something was in the boot. The story soon reached the *Sheffield Star*. Six years later a TV documentary was made about the event.[8]

Motorist Paul Ford, 28, and his wife, Jane, also saw the apparition. Driving to Stocksbridge on New Year's Eve 1997, they could have been killed trying to avoid a figure on the road: 'a frightening experience'. Paul thought someone was trying to cross the road, and when he got closer the figure seemed actually to be hovering over the road, and had no face. 'There are so many accidents on the Stocksbridge bypass,' said Jane. 'People could get killed.'[9]

Hugh Reid, a lorry driver, at 10.45 p.m. one night in October 1957 in or near Gretna, Scotland, at a bend in the road near a junction, saw a middle-aged couple simply strolling along the centre of the road. They looked like they had just come from a fancy dress event, with the man wearing a top hat and frock coat, and the woman in a crinoline ankle-length gown. Mr Reid brought his lorry and trailer to a halt, jumped out with the intention of remonstrating with the couple who could have caused an accident. But, of course, they vanished. There was no way they could have jumped clear of the vehicle, and there were impenetrable hedges on both sides of the road.[10]

A Margaret Ching in the 1990s was also travelling to Gretna with her fiancé when she saw an old woman in Victorian clothes in the middle of the road. It suddenly grew colder, and they thought they had driven straight through her.[11]

At Selsey, Sussex, at 11.30 p.m. one night in either October or November 2001, two teenagers first saw a flash of light and then heard a bang, which seemed to come from a nearby car park. As they approached a grinding noise seem to become more prominent. Later the two youths heard the legends of Civil War ghosts in the area.

At Avebury, Wiltshire, on Silbury Hill, an area well known for 'crop circles' in earlier years, drivers stopped on 6 July 2009 to watch three 'forensic officers' (dressed in light-coloured official-looking uniforms) approach the formations, seeming to check them out. When they saw people watching them, however, they ran off at virtually superhuman speeds.

The Black Prince pub on the Darenth interchange off the A2 is named after the 'Black Prince' who sometimes stayed at Hall Place, Bexley. Since the prince died in battle, his ghost is periodically seen in black armour with the visor closed, often at times of national crisis as a kind of warning omen (such as when Britain was about to be invaded in 1940).[12]

The A4010 from High Wycombe to Aylesbury, Buckinghamshire, is haunted by a farmer murdered in 1828. Occasionally a road ghost is accompanied by a dog, like the man wearing a mac, with his Doberman seen near Stanmore in 1985.[13] A figure in a black cloak and hood floated across the Old Chatham Road in 1965, and again in 2001, before vanishing.[14]

Also, at Millbrook in Bedfordshire, along Station Road, there have long been rumours of a phantom highwayman called 'Galloping Dick'.[15] In desolate country between Preston and Blackburn, Lancashire, especially in or near the village of Samlesbury on the A59, with its legends of witch trials, there are legends of ghostly goblins and cats.

One case is interesting because of the sheer variety of entities seen in the year 2000, including a phantom engine that passes through private property at Stroud, Gloucester. A film crew heard disembodied banging, then a steam train charged through the house. The area is also haunted by a 'white lady' in the adjacent park. Other entities have been seen – Roman soldiers, monks, two American servicemen in World War II uniforms, a phantom coach, a headless horse and a somersaulting dwarf![16]

On the A34 between Atherstone and Preston-on-Stour a ghost of a man – invariably at midnight – disappears straight through a wall.[17] On the A12 between Essex and Norfolk, a phantom man on a bike has been frequently sighted. A young couple were sitting in a car on the Icknield Way in Hertfordshire in 1961 and saw and heard ghostly legionnaires, although local ghost investigators were uncertain whether these were Roman soldiers or other types, or whether they were ghostly soldiers at all.[18]

On the A4146 at Edlesborough, Buckinghamshire, a phantom monk in a black habit is seen near the parish church of St Mary the Virgin. It vanished when the driver stopped and shone a torch.[19]

Motorists in Grimsby who have been on the A18 at night often see a horse and rider galloping towards their vehicle, whom they assumed to be real, and fearing they have killed them both. Getting out, as usual, they come across nothing. This is said to be the phantom of a teenager called George Nelson, who was thrown from his horse in January 1885, breaking his neck. A memorial stone exists not far from where his body was found.[20]

A stretch of road in Somerset near Charmouth was the site of many road deaths in the late 1960s, and was subject to an exorcism.[21] A woman on a white horse gallops across the Tidworth Road that leads to Hungerford, Berkshire, causing motorists to brake sharply. Then, inevitably, the woman and her horse fade away. This is the A338, which has two alternating visions: the white horse rider during the day, and a phantom coach pulled by four horses at night.[22]

Travellers along the byroads near the A59 near Bashall Eaves, Lancashire, can see the aftermath of a mysterious, motiveless gunshot murder that took place in March 1934. The ghost of the victim can be seen as a squat figure with a gaping wound showing through a tattered coat. He is often seen passing through a hedge, bent double, apparently searching for the weapon or assailant that had killed him.[23]

The ghost of a monk and a woman in a grey cloak, with shallow grey pits for eyes, can be seen on the A695, in the north of England, heading towards Tynemouth Priory from Newcastle on lonely nights. The woman, at an undisclosed date in history, sought to confess a murder to a priest who refused to see her. She, and then the monk, gripped by their own versions of remorse – committed suicide, and their apparitions are never far apart from each other.[24]

On the A3400 a farmer on horseback lost his life when he hit an overhanging branch while racing between Atherstone-on-Stour, Warwickshire, and Alderminster.[25] Noel O'Brien, 55, recently lent his Ford Focus to his daughter, Caoimhe, aged 23, who was killed when she crashed it into a wall at a dangerous blackspot near Burndennett Bridge, County Tyrone. Shortly after, Noel and his wife, Marie, found their garage window had been, on several occasions, opened during the night. They concluded that Caoimhe's spirit was sending Noel and Marie a message.[26]

At Bury St Edmunds, Suffolk, near Eastgate Street, from the 1870s onwards a ghost has often been seen, thought to be a soldier from the Crimean war who was shot by the father of a girl he tried to elope with.[27]

Sightings on the A75 in Dumfriesshire go back 50 years. Travellers see groups of dejected, bedraggled people pulling handcarts and carrying bundles, along with the usual collection of horsemen and carriages. They are convinced they have run some of them down, but find nothing.

- At Little Milton, Oxfordshire, on the A329 off Roffield Lane, a motorist saw the same cyclist vanish in front of him in the years 2005 and 2006. He stopped to check in both cases, but found nothing.

- On the A442, between Telford and Bridgnorth, Shropshire, a passenger and driver, at 8 p.m. on the night of 4 March 2009, saw a 'black' human shape in a long coat on the roadside. It appeared to be about to step into the road, but disappeared before doing so. At Ludlow in September 1971 one Evelyn Sheppard, presumably a pedestrian, saw a well-dressed man walking quickly down the street, who vanished before her eyes.

- At Great Haywood, Staffordshire, on the Rugeley Road in 1949, a phantom man was seen on an old-style bike.

- At Eccleshall, on the appropriately named 'Ghost Mile Road', there was, at an unknown date, a ghostly apparition from the Tudor era. There were also reports of vanishing jaywalkers and ancient coaches.

- At Stoke on Trent, on the A34 from Manchester, two people in a car encountered, one evening in September 1993, a white-haired man by the roadside. He saw them and stared at them, vanished, but was seen again around another bend.

- A hooded man was once seen, in the 20th century, in Hungerford, Berkshire.

- At Tamworth, in March 1972, a driver attempted to offer a lift to a tall man in uniform who was standing on the verge. But he was not real, as his image 'shimmied, fragmented and pixelated as if he was a reflection on water'.

- At Blundeston, Suffolk, on the Foxton Road, on 20 September 2009 in the late evening, two people in a car saw a small monk glide across the road, wearing some kind of Hessian garment, and with a slight glow.

- At Reydon, Suffolk, on the Wangford Road, a driver saw a figure in a rough brown cloak at 1.30 a.m. on 23 January 2010. It had a featureless face, and was 'glowing white'.

- At Hatton, on the A4177, in the month of September in either 1982 or 1983, a driver and passenger saw a ghostly figure on the roadside. There was later speculation that it was an historical figure, like a Cavalier.

- At Quemerford, Wiltshire, on a road near a church, at 1 a.m. on a date in December 2013, a shadowy figure in 17th-century clothes was seen striding across the road before vanishing. At nearby Ramsbury, two 'headless men' were seen carrying a coffin. No date was given. And at Southwick, on the A361 Frome Road, a tall figure was seen in 1993. It was later suggested this was the ghost of someone killed in an accident the year before.

- At Lichfield in Staffordshire, on the M6, Sue Cowley and her husband stopped to let animals cross the motorway, but saw some 'shadow' Roman ghosts, about twenty of them, but could see them only from the waist up.

- Enfield has a phantom stagecoach, last seen in the 1960s, that would rise out of the ground, travel in the direction of Brimsdown, a suburb, with a man leaning out of the window, and women passengers inside with large hats.[28]

- A young cyclist in 1961 reported that he saw two bright lights rushing towards him, with two figures between the lights and a third behind them, and possibly four horses pulling a black coach, coasting 6 feet off the ground. The apparition passed right through him. One theory is that the coach and its passengers came to grief on a winter's night in the Essex marshes in the 18th century.

- A Mr Mike Owens recalled other stagecoach hauntings that were related to him in 1968 while visiting a farm not far from Loch Ness. The owner, a retired RAF officer, told how he was driving through the Midlands in a Bugatti just prior to the War when a stagecoach, 'complete with horses and driver and in full, living colour', simply materialised in front of him. He skidded into a ditch but not without causing some damage to himself and his vehicle. Scouring local records he discovered that the road he was on was a major north–south stage route through the Midlands of the 19th century.[29]

- At Kirby, Nottinghamshire, at a place called 'The Dumbles', a man walking his dog in the summer of 1984 saw a (ghostly?) grey coach, driven by two men and pulled by two horses.

- At Farley, Staffordshire, a white horse and headless horseman in armour was seen. No date was given in the archives.

- At Buxhall, Suffolk, in the Rattlesden Road area, a silhouette with a long cloak and lantern was seen. No year was given, but it was a frosty night in February.

- On the A272 at Chobham, in Surrey, at 11.30 p.m. in November 1994, a horse and buggy, driven or accompanied by a cloaked man in a top hat, forced cars coming in the opposite direction to perform emergency stops. Halted drivers conversed with each other about the vision, which promptly disappeared.

- The ghost of a 'highwayman' on his horse was heard in Marlborough, Wiltshire, on an unknown date. Assessing the way the hooves fell, it was said the invisible horse was following a road that no longer existed. At Purton another ghostly horseman – mostly heard but occasionally seen – travelled along local roads.

## Ghostly Assortments on the Roads

Many paranormal websites refer to an 'Old Nick', a stereotypical old man, usually a deceased local, often seen lurking in a pub or country lane; indeed, in Sussex most ghosts of all ages seem to be in pubs. In all counties there are sightings of phantom monks, many of which are faceless or headless.

Norfolk has many spooky sightings on various road and rail bridges. Weston-super-Mare, Somerset, seems to have an abundance of ghosts relating to puzzling car accidents that have taken place along a certain mile of coastal road. Many of them raise suspicions of paranormal activity.

In Nottinghamshire there seem to many phantom airmen and ghost trains. The same goes for Suffolk, where a number of World War II pilots and sundry phantom aircraft are seen near disused airfields. Lincolnshire has its fair share of rail and airfield ghosts. Unusual or uncanny-looking hounds (often known as 'shugs' or 'shucks' – see Chapter 18) are said to be the ghosts of local or well-known people. In Suffolk there are many accounts of 'anomalous big cats' (abbreviated in the occult and Ufo literature to 'ABCs' – see Chapter 17), as well as more than the usual number of shucks, many of them with red (sometimes illuminated) eyes. Unnatural-looking animals, even reptiles, are often seen in parts of Lancashire. On the Devon paranormal website it is claimed that the county has more cryptozoological sightings than other regions, including lake and sea creatures (in Exeter on 25 May 2000 a 'giant bat' was seen).

Halsall Moss in West Lancashire is flat, fertile farmland, and is known as a haunted area. It has sharp bends, lacks lighting and has mists. Drivers often have a pronounced awareness of their surroundings, and heightened senses of sound, light and smell. Other cases of haunted roads in West Lancashire are on the Internet.

Police computer records show that there had been a high number of collisions or accidents on the Moss, which seemed to be on the high side given that the road runs through open country.[30] Rob Gandy, a business academic who has had a long interest in road ghost experiences in that area, reported several events, including ghostly hitchhikers, along Gregory Lane between Southport and Ormskirk, many of which hit a local newspaper. Gandy appealed in the paper for similar experiencers to come forward with their stories. A group of friends were passengers in a car around the year 2000, in the autumn or winter. The time was about 10 p.m. They all miraculously survived a veering crash into a ditch in the Halsall Moss area. On getting out, and facing a long walk to get help, they were struck by the appearance of a fire mysteriously burning on the edge of the deserted road.[31]

A lorry driver was travelling north at night along the A12 some time in the 1970s. He was on a narrow stretch of road outside Blythburgh in Suffolk, when he collided, or so he thought, with a pony and cart in which man was riding and which was accompanied by a woman walking beside the pony. He stopped and walked back to the scene of the supposed accident, fearing the worst. He found nothing. Later he discovered that the folk of Blythburgh had often encountered the cart, and the man and woman, and that they were ghosts dating back to the 19th century. There was no real information about any tragic accident, although the entire scene was repeated each time with the same cart, and the animal itself must have been a ghost.[32]

The dangerous recklessness of these phantom road ghosts is remarkable. They dash across the path of oncoming traffic. At Annan, in Dumfries and Galloway, Scotland, in April 1962, two brothers saw a motley collection of entities in front of their car – animals, an old man and a woman resembling a witch. A white van headed towards them, but promptly vanished. Also at Annan, a woman driver in March 2004 at 9.30 p.m. had to do an emergency stop to avoid colliding with what could only have been described, in the dark, as an old-fashioned stagecoach. She soon realised, via the light of her headlights, that something paranormal had happened because the stagecoach was not real – it had fuzzy outlines 'like you would see on an old black and white TV'. Further she believed it was some sort of omen that created a premonition in her partner, who unaccountably phoned to ask if she was okay.

# Chapter 6

## The Reality of Spooky Cars

It is not surprising that cars seem to be not quite connected with physical reality in Britain's haunted landscape. This is a feature of road hauntings that will continue to crop up throughout this book. Some cars appear before the eyes of other motorists, but result in peculiar disappearances – of both cars and people. Time often becomes distorted, with drivers arriving at their destinations either later or earlier than they should.

And cars move unaccountably. Take the following example. Two friends on a visit to the Kyle of Lochalsh saw an empty car in front of them instantly move a few yards sideways, without actually seeing the car physically move.[1] A mother was driving with her young son in Bracknell, Berkshire, one night. They both saw a car ahead of them, driving sedately at about 30 mph, without any lights on, and, from what they could both see, nobody driving. But in an instant the car was no longer in front of them but parked on the other side of the road. 'The car,' wrote the son in a letter to the *Fortean Times,* to describe the incident, 'did not slow down or pull over – it was as if it had never even been moving. It was almost as if we had missed a few seconds in time.'[2]

Near a crossroads on the Ramsgate to Canterbury route a motor collision occurred in 1922, resulting in the death of two women. So rare were road accidents in those days it made national headline news. But what caused a sensation was testimony at the inquest that both cars were perfectly visible to one another on the half-empty road at the time of the head-on crash, hinting that something spooky – or at least inexplicable – had happened. There was no sign of any mechanical trouble on either car.[3]

In fact the 1920s and 1930s was a rather odd time to drive a car in London. Many motorists complained of being forced off the road by a spectral red bus which loomed out of nowhere before vanishing. A phantom number 7 double-decker came to the attention of the press in 1934 when a motorist driving at 1.15 a.m. along Cambridge Gardens, Notting Hill Gate, west London, suddenly swerved for no apparent reason, and was killed when he smashed into a wall. But at the inquest it was alleged that the phantom bus appeared out of nowhere at that precise spot, as it would often do in the early hours. It would be racing towards other cars, with no driver, and with no lights on. Many drivers swerved out of the way, but when they looked back the bus had vanished. A transport official at the inquest also said that the bus would draw up to the local bus depot in the very early hours of the morning before suddenly disappearing.[4] Other reports say the same bus instead had its headlights full on, as were the internal lights on the top and lower deck, but there was no sign of crew or passengers.[5]

A phantom lorry is sometimes seen at night on the A428 running towards Rugby, Warwickshire. It is large and fast, and travels on the wrong side of the road, and fails to pull over to let oncoming traffic pass. Car drivers, fearfully struggling to brake or take evasive action, believe they are destined for a head-on crash. Instead they see the lorry pass right through them, or 'envelop' them, fading as it does so. A similar event happened at Ryton-on-Dunsmore, Warwickshire, on the A45. And a phantom coach is seen along Leicester Road.[6]

Another spectral lorry is seen on the M7 in Scotland towards Heriot, with the difference between the physical layers of time and present virtually running parallel, with the lorry sometimes on the road and sometimes ploughing across adjacent pathways and streams. This presents a different sort of danger, because the media have reported accidents as a result of motorists following it off the road.[7]

Sometimes it is reported that ghostly vehicles suddenly become solid and cause collisions resulting in deaths. A phantom lorry that appeared to back out of a non-existent opening was mentioned at an inquest in 1930 into the death of a motorcyclist on the A75 between Hyde and Mottram-in-Longdendale, Greater Manchester. There had been other reports of this phantom lorry, although in each case the police could find no such opening or lorry track. The district coroner in the same year in Hyde, Cheshire, declared that a 'phantom lorry' was responsible for a long list of recent road accidents in the area.[8]

Similar weird time and space warps seem to plague the Japanese, and sometimes involve strange obscuring gases or dense fogs. On 4 March 1964, a leading Japanese newspaper reported the disappearance of a car in a cloud of smoke on a highway in full view of three Fuji Bank officials who were travelling behind. When interviewed, the witnesses said they could see an elderly man in the back seat reading a newspaper.[9]

In another alarming case of a likely head-on crash, a young driver in the 1960s, travelling along a deserted narrow road in Cornwall, saw an open-topped car heading obliviously straight for him. He pulled over just in time. As the car zoomed past, he noticed it seemed to be full of young male students wearing dated clothing from the

1940s. Three of them were recklessly standing and singing, with long scarves and coats streaming in the wind. Then the car and its occupants suddenly disappeared.[10]

Loch Ashie, on the B851 in northern Scotland, has had a ghostly reputation. A Major C. J. Shaw was driving in the area, and once slowed down at a corner when he saw an approaching car. He flashed his lights to indicate the other car could pass him as he pulled over, only to find the road empty.[11] Paul Heinowski, in the winter of 1973–74 was being driven at night by his father near the loch. They stopped, and Paul went up the driveway of a house to ask for directions. He saw headlights approaching the road in front of the house which he could see through a gap in a surrounding hedge around the house. He knocked on the door only to hear the car pass *behind* the house instead of along the road in front of it. His father saw nothing.[12]

In 1979 a father driving his family on a day trip to the Essex countryside came to a T-junction in a village which was blocked by a large American 1950s vintage car, but which was in a peculiar 'hideous psychedelic purplish colour'. Not only that, but the owners of the car, oblivious to other cars or their incongruous street surroundings, looked as if they were part of a time warp. The man, looking middle aged, had a black brilliantined hairdo in the teddy boy style, and was dressed in a similarly psychedelic yellow suit, and his wife or partner was also done up with an outdated beehive hairdo. Both were standing outside their car, in the road, eating a picnic lunch. On the roof of the car was the largest spread ever – numerous plates of exotic-looking food and a bottle of champagne in a cooler. 'These guys were just eating their dinner in the middle of the road without a care in the world,' said the father. The entire episode was like something out of a TV comedy with a bad script.

When the father leaned out of the window of his car to ask them what they were doing, the guy responded by saying his car had broken down, and oddly said that he had 'called in the army'. The family backed their car up into another road, turned and passed the same intersection barely two minutes later. But the American car, with its picnic platters on the roof, and its two bizarrely dressed owners, had completely disappeared, which would have been impossible in the short time available.[13]

In a startlingly similar incident, at Gower, in West Glamorgan, a middle-aged couple were discovered listening to 1950s and 1960s music on a radio or record player while squatting on the deserted beach at Whiteford Bay. The date was 17 September 2005. Neither the man nor the woman was dressed in casual attire, but could have been the same strange couple seen 26 years earlier in Essex. The man had a teddy boy suit on, and his hair was done in a Brylcreme style, while his female partner had the same beehive hairdo. And, as in the earlier case, they vanished within minutes.[14]

Two teenagers, one evening of a hot June in 1982, were fishing in a local pond in a rather remote area of wasteland which bordered on a disused railway line in Derbyshire. But the boys had not known that a young motorcyclist had been killed on an ungated level crossing – while playing 'dare' with others (a competition to see who could get to the other side before the train came) – not far from where they were situated. The motorcyclist was killed when he tragically lost his dare. It was later that his ghost returned to career towards the two young fishermen. They ran away fast, but could hear the resulting disaster as the ghost rider crashed down into a ditch some 15 feet deep. When the police and ambulance came there was nothing to be found. But the eerie noises of a roaring motorbike, being ridden flat out, screams, shouts and crashing noises could be heard for years afterwards. Indeed, it is reported that the lad's speeding ghost can be seen every year on the anniversary of his death, and in 'startling detail'.[15]

On a summer's evening in the late 1990s, Gina Culling was driving with her partner on the M62 from Manchester Airport to Hull. Just past Junction 34 she could see a single headlight in her rear-view mirror, and thought it was a motorbike. It seemed to gain speed before suddenly disappearing. But then the single light – the assumed motorbike – reappeared behind her about 10 minutes later, while she was still in the inside lane and wanting to move out and overtake a van. 'Hurry up, hurry up,' she muttered. Then the light disappeared again. Both she and her partner were spooked by this. Even if the bike's light had cut out, due to an electrical fault, they would still have seen the outline of the bike reflected in her rear lights and other car lights. They saw nothing.[16]

Some witnesses said they had seen a car swerve off the road at Burpham, near Guildford, on the night of 11 December 2002, and crash into undergrowth off the A3. Its headlights could be clearly seen glimmering through the foliage. No one seemed to identify the crashing car as a Vauxhall Astra, which was the car the police eventually found roughly where motorists said the incident had happened. But the Astra had been hidden there for some months, with a decomposed body in the driving seat. This turned out to be one Christopher Chandler, who was wanted for robbery, and who was reported missing by his brother in July of that year. Perhaps, it was surmised, the motorists who saw the car disappearing off the road some months later were actually witnesses to some kind of time warp, with a ghostly repeat of the incident that had happened that summer.[17]

Aaron V. Adosa was a passenger in his grandfather's car one early autumn evening in 1999 when, descending a steep hill in Cwmbran in South Wales, they saw a car approaching the single-tracked humped bridge in the distance. The grandfather paused before driving onto the bridge, pulling over to let the other car cross first. But it seemed to vanish. Resuming their journey they could see no exit route on the approach roads for the other car, with steep banks and fenced off buildings. About two weeks later, with his grandmother at the wheel, the same vanishing act happened in the opposite direction, with a car with its headlights on seemingly about to cross over the bridge but disappearing instead. Aaron wrote to the *Fortean Times*: 'Had there once been a car crash here, and were we seeing a sort of action replay?'[18]

Frances, a 54-year-old from Lowestoft, was driving along a narrow side road with parked cars crammed along either side, when she sensed she was about to be struck by an oncoming car with a 'huge white bonnet'. It was impossible to swerve, and she was hit side-on. When she turned to look the car was not white, or even partly white, but was small and black.[19]

A nurse and her mother were travelling back to Liverpool in the early hours of the morning in the summer of 2005. Suddenly a white van drew near, driven by a man of about forty. He drove parallel to their car and seemed to overtake, and then vanished. The nurse said the van, although approaching so near, was totally silent – she could hear nothing. Yet within two minutes the same vehicle appeared again, with the same driver, before vanishing completely. 'There were no turn-offs from the road, and the area is quite flat, so there was no way that the van could have simply turned off the road without us seeing it.'[20]

A woman was driving to Newton Stewart, 40 miles south-west of Dumfries, on a Friday morning in September 2007. There was a straight road which led to an 'invisible dip' which was often a hazard to unsuspecting motorists. Unusually, the road was empty at that time. Soon she saw a black car heading her way, just behind the dip, and made to shortly pull over to let it pass. But the approaching car didn't reappear, and there was no turn-off or exit road anywhere for it to have gone into.[21]

Mr M. Hodgson was on the M1 in a 50 mph zone, and was travelling in the centre lane. But the lorry behind him was 'tailgating' him. It kept flashing its lights, then pulled erratically over to the inside lane and hit the side of his car. But there was a strange addendum. He wrote that the police could take no action because the 'lorry was untraceable'. Was this because, Mr Hodgson asked in a letter to the *Daily Mail* describing the event, it had simply vanished?[22]

In Australia, a James Ess approached an odd-looking truck or van that was packed to overflowing with what looked like decorating or builders' materials. He saw exactly the same unusual van with the driver and the same painters' gear about ten minutes later, and six miles down the road. 'There are no roads or tracks in the area that would allow the driver to double-back to a point ahead of where we'd originally passed!'

About two weeks later Ess had a similar disturbing experience. He was waiting for the lights to change in the suburbs of Melbourne when he noticed a couple of women in a large black 4 x 4 facing him across an intersection. The women were having an animated conversation, with one banging the steering wheel for emphasis. The women were visibly distinct from each other – a brunette and blonde. About five minutes later, at another set of traffic lights, at another intersection, he saw the very same car with the same occupants, carrying on with their animated conversation. Again there was no way they could have reached that point in the road, certainly not in stop-start traffic.[23]

A group of young teenagers in West Yorkshire, who normally hung around together, knew that one of the regulars, Darren, was out on his motorbike that day. One of the teenagers, Neil, had to go home briefly to get something, and the others waited perched on the front garden wall. Neil came to the front-room window and waved to them, but behind him they could see Darren's head rise up, turn towards them and give a big grin. Surprised, they queried Neil about seeing Darren, who was supposed to be out on his motorbike. Neil was equally surprised, saying there was no one else with him in the room. Thinking this was an ominous portent, the friends were relieved when Darren turned up unharmed.[24]

In the 2000s James Williams, in his thirties, was heading back to London with his Aunt Hazel, who was at the wheel of her car, after a night out with his family in Chichester, West Sussex. They were heading along an unknown road – after taking a wrong turn – when they saw in their rear-view mirror the headlights of a white van driven furiously fast and gaining on them. James yelled to his aunt: 'He's going to ram us off the road, pull over!' Hazel veered to the left of the road, and the van sped past, narrowly avoiding a collision with the front of Hazel's car. They resumed their journey, following the red tail lights of the van, which suddenly vanished. Then there was evidence of police activity, with warning signs and cones on the road ahead – an accident scene. Hazel brought to the car to a halt, and realised that the van had not stopped, or had not been stopped, at the police site. It seemed it had vanished for good, and there was no turn-off it could have taken. As they sat in their car trying to make sense of it all, Hazel rang a member of the family to tell them of the accident hold-up, and that they would be late home. 'Yes, there was a terrible accident on that road today,' the relative told her. 'A car and a white van were involved in a crash, and the van driver was killed.' Both James and his aunt then realised with horror that they had witnessed an eerie re-enactment of the driver's last tragic journey.[25]

George Dobbs, trudging through the snow on a country road near a cemetery at Market Harborough, Leicestershire, on a winter's night in the wartime Britain of 1940, saw the dimmed headlights of a car approaching him. The car's lights seemed to pick out a cyclist also heading his way, but the cyclist seemed to have no head! The approaching car then ploughed right into the headless cyclist. George ran through the snowbound ruts to the spot where he had seen the hapless man, expecting to find the result of a terrible accident. But there was nothing to be found – no cyclist, and no cycle, nor any signs of an accident. George fled to a nearby pub at Kingsthorpe, to tell his astonishing story. There was a stunned silence until one Sid Green, who was for years the local gravedigger, leaned across the bar and said: 'That sounds just like the chap I buried 25 years ago. He was knocked off his bike in deep snow outside the cemetery gates.' He paused and added: 'His head was torn off in the crash.'[26]

A prominent civic leader in Peterborough, a retired army officer, was killed in his large black Chrysler at a notorious unmanned level crossing in 1948. Because of this and other poltergeist haunting legends attached to this crossing, including clanging gates that had supposedly been locked, several signalmen refused to work there. Six German prisoners of war held at a military camp near Peterborough were also killed in 1948 at the same crossing while being transported in a lorry in dense fog. In a BBC interview in the early 1970s, a signalman said that a large black car waiting to cross – said to be the dead colonel's black Chrysler – had suddenly vanished. He said that other signalmen had heard the phantom car approach but it could not be seen.[27]

# Chapter 7

## Phantom Cars across Britain

One of the most extraordinary aspects of our haunted highways is the literal Vanishing Car. Drivers report to police that they see a car rushing or swerving towards them, only for it to vanish from their view. Startled, they assume that the vehicle they saw moments earlier had crashed into a roadside verge or ditch, or was involved in some dreadful mishap or road accident which they couldn't quite observe, perhaps because their own car had turned into a bend or reached the brow of a hill, or because they were simply concentrating on negotiating the road ahead. But very mysterious things *do* happen on our roads. Sometimes motorists see a vehicle tailgating them menacingly, only for it to suddenly disappear. People, often pedestrians, see the same vehicle twice – it goes by in front of them once, and then it seems to do the same thing just an instant later.

The occultic literature on road mysteries, as well as the numerous reports that can be found in the British county paranormal databases, are puzzling and disturbing. Drivers themselves are often in a state of shock: they cannot believe that they might have witnessed a paranormal incident. Cars and lorries are, after all, large, solid and very heavy objects – how can they not be solid or real, or be ghostlike? In the Epilogue I try to come to terms with this question, and try to give some speculative answers.

In the meantime let us annotate the amazing events that motorists say they have witnessed or experienced. Take, firstly, four examples of what can happen to drivers on the roads. The first is the experience of two women who screamed in fear as a lorry, in the wrong lane, was barrelling towards them. One of them saw the lorry disappear right in front of their car without hitting them. The other had closed her eyes before this happened, and opened them to see in the rear-view mirror the lorry disappearing into the distance, but in the correct lane it should have been in. Both ladies felt that their guardian angels had saved them that day.[1]

The second involves a Roberta Abbott, who was driving out of Northampton on the A428, which she estimated was in the mid 1960s. She saw a silver car in her rear-view mirror about to overtake her. It vanished. A year or two later, driving this time in Hampshire, she had a similar experience with a vanishing red car that was glimpsed in her mirrors. In both cases there were no turnings the cars could have taken.[2]

The third concerns tailgating episodes. In the 20th century, on the eastbound A4028 at Coventry in the West Midlands, a phantom HGV would be seen tailgating at speed in a line of traffic. But it would occasionally vanish, allowing the vehicle behind to attempt to close the gap. But often the lorry would re-emerge, causing the following driver – already puzzled – to brake in alarm. But the lorry would then plough into the vehicle it was tailing, causing damage, only to vanish again.[3] Another case concerns a kind of reverse tailgating. At Effingham, Surrey, on the A246 at 3 o'clock in the morning of a day in May 2015, a motorcyclist saw red tail lights ahead. Strangely they seemed to be linked to his own speed gradient, because whether he geared up and increased his momentum ready to overtake, or whether he fell back, the lights remained exactly the same distance away. And whereas some road users, seeing a vehicle vanish, merely assume that an accident might have happened, in this case the motorcyclist saw the lights of the car ahead veer off the road, and heard an actual crash. The alarmed biker drew to a halt and dismounted, but could find nothing.

The fourth concerns the 'time warp' phenomenon – the same car reappears moments later. Bobby Zodiac, in November 2014, was waiting for a bus in Stratford-upon-Avon when he glimpsed, through the pages of a newspaper he was reading, the lower part of the wheels and bodywork of a classic red car, which he momentarily thought must have been an MGB Roadster, a car which he had in fact seen in the local area and had actually overtaken on the road several times. But when he looked up, he could see no classic red car, only a 'dark-grey modern thing'. But the real red Roadster, with its distinctive roaring engine, actually appeared moments later. 'So how,' he wrote to Fortean Times magazine, 'did I see it go past about five minutes earlier?'[4] In one peculiar case, listed in the paranormal database for Dorset, a van driver named Adrian Brown, at Wareham in 1991, saw a doppelganger of himself in the same van coming in the opposite direction.

- A Dr Allan McDonald referred to a ghostly Austin car speeding along a road in the Isle of Skye in 1941. He pulled over the let the car pass, but saw no more of it.[5]

- A naval officer and his wife, the Kirkwoods, were being driven across moorland in Scotland in late 1945, when they could see headlights behind a small S-bend. Their driver pulled over into a passing place. They waited patiently, then pulled out only to find the road empty.[6]

- In 1995 a brown car, which looked to be a 1960s model, passed a car driver, but reappeared in front of him at several stoplights.[7]

- In Milton, Cambridgeshire, a crossroads is said to be haunted by a car that bumps vehicles, but leaves no marks or damage.

- At Knutsford in Cheshire, on the M6, a glowing white lorry was seen charging towards a driver from the opposite direction. He pulled over, felt the lorry go past, but it vanished from his rear-view mirror.

- At Helstone, Cornwall, on the road from St Teath, a phantom grey van was seen in daylight in the year 2001, before it vanished.

- At Modbury, Devon, a ghostly black car was seen on local roads in the mid 20th century.

- At Cuerdley, Cheshire, on the Widnes Road in the early 2000s at about 3 a.m., a driver saw a pair of headlights approaching from behind. It looked as if it was about to overtake, but promptly vanished. Thinking the car had crashed, the pursued driver pulled up, turned his car around to look, but found nothing.

- On a B road through Bayham in Kent, not far from Tunbridge Wells, heading for Sussex, an old black limousine is often seen parked by the side of the road in the near distance, and is noticeable because of its old-fashioned oddness. Yet some motorists have said that as they approach it disappears.[8]

- A Dr Martin Moar, on Skye, in the Hebrides in Scotland, early in the 1970s, once had to pull over sharply. The other car promptly vanished, but the closeness of the two vehicles in a particularly narrow lane, in broad daylight, was indeed a startling event.[9]

- At Eyam, in Derbyshire, between Eyam and the Chapel-en-le-Rith bypass on 1 June 2013, just after midnight, a driver was tailgated along country roads by a dark, older, sports car. It overtook the driver's car when it reached the A6 but vanished a short distance ahead. There were no turn-offs.

- In Moreton-in-Marsh, Gloucestershire, in the late 20th century, a rider on his ancient motorbike was seen at Fosse Way.

- At Castleton, Derbyshire, in 2006, around the post office, the Co-op and the Natwest bank, people parking their cars experienced electrical problems – alarms, engines not turning, door locks faulty. Activity at the bases at Radnor or RAF Fylingdales was blamed, but the base commanders denied this.

- At Coresley, Derbyshire, at the Codley Hall roundabout, a motorcyclist spotted a white 1970s car heading in the opposite direction while turning on the roundabout. It was the winter of 2011, late at night. The rider turned his head to get a better look, but the car had vanished.

- At Holme Moss, West Yorkshire, in 1999, along the A6024, motorist Andrew Sylvester saw an old-fashioned car in mint condition vanish behind him.

- At Hyde in 1930, on the A56 between Hyde, Mottram and Longdendale, north of Glossop in the north of England, a phantom vehicle was blamed for accidents and deaths.

- At Coverdale, Yorkshire, along local roads at an undisclosed date, motorists were aware of an intense beam of light careening towards them, assumed to be an out-of-control motorbike. It vanished.

- Along the A4 in Berkshire, west of Hungerford, drivers often say they see a phantom car crossing the road on a rise before vanishing.

- There is a long-running problem of vanishing motorbikes and sidecars from the 1930s onwards, both in Nottingham and the wider county. In earlier years a phantom AA patrolman was said to ride along the A52, although the AA denied that any of their recovery men were riding the A52 at that time. At Orston, along the A52, a car without lights headed straight towards a driver and his passenger at 9 p.m. on 23 January 2014, before vanishing at the last moment.

- At Seaford, Sussex, along the coastline, in October 1976, a couple watched a car lose control and hit a 3-foot-high sea wall, but pass straight through it and disappear on the other side.

- At Edwinstowe, Nottinghamshire, between the town and Ollerton, from the 1960s onwards, a ghostly cyclist would appear in front of moving cars, and pass through them.

- A woman on a phone-in to a legal expert on LBC in the late evening of 11 August 2014, said she was knocked down by a car that seemed 'to come out of nowhere' on a clear road and in good weather conditions.

- In Louth, Lincolnshire, circa 2004, a driver saw a vanishing Victorian cyclist at the roundabout at London Road.

- In 1960 a motorist driving from Plymouth to Chagford in Devon was inexplicably found dead *beneath* the wreckage of his overturned car. No other car was involved, and the police could find no mechanical fault with the car.[10]

- On the A4146 at Ellesborough, Buckinghamshire, probably in 1961, a phantom black Morris saloon was seen by Mr Stanley Prescott of Dunstable, Bedfordshire, and his wife. It came straight at him, and he feared for their lives, but it then vanished.

- A Devon driver in 1967, who had some knowledge of old cars, saw what he described as a 1920 Daimler Landaulette, with the driver's attire hinting that he was a chauffeur.[11] The car soon unnaturally disappeared from sight.

- At Gosport, Hampshire, along Percy Road, in the summer of 2006, a motorist reported that his car unaccountably became immobilised, and the starter ignition persistently failed to work. The paranormal county database included this incident on the understanding that the car was in perfect working order.

- At North Baddesley, Hampshire, along Rownhams Lane, a phantom 'invisible' cyclist pursued others in November 2010.

- Car lights appeared and disappeared regularly at Penhill Beacon, Yorkshire, in the late 1990s.[12]

- In Buckinghamshire, on the linking road between Haddenham and other villages, on 28 August 2008 at 7.45 a.m., a driver saw a slow-moving silver Vauxhall in front of him. It indicated left but turned right. The driver of the Vauxhall turned to look at the witness, and promptly vanished.

- At Hatton, Warwickshire, in the early hours of 27 October 2007, a light-coloured car seemed to be heading towards a bridge a driver was approaching. The driver held back to let it pass, but it vanished. There were, as usual in such cases, no turn-offs.

- At Clyst St Mary, Devon, on the road to Clyst St George, a fast car turned off in front of a driver on 22 March 1997. But the turning point the car disappeared into was in fact blocked. As he passed, the driver could see no trace of the car.

- At Thetford in Norfolk on the A11, a driver stopped at traffic lights. He then saw a classic open-topped vehicle from the 1930s had drawn up behind him, with the driver wearing goggles and a hat. When the lights changed and the witness drove off, he looked back and saw that the 1930s car had vanished.

- At Thetford's Snare Hill, in 2010, a driver saw headlights some 100 yards ahead of him, which disappeared. As usual there was nowhere the car could have turned off.

- On local roads at the town of Fossebridge in Gloucestershire in August 1997, three men in a car were followed by an ageing motorbike. It vanished as soon as it got close.

- At Worlington, Suffolk, in the November of a year in the 2000s, a driver saw a motorbike in his rear-view mirror. It vanished.

- In Berkhamsted, Hertfordshire, in November 1976 at 11 p.m., a driver saw a vanishing Honda 50cc-type motorbike which passed the local golf club grounds. He stopped to check for an accident, but found nothing.

- At some time in 1998, at the high street roundabout at Ware, Hertfordshire, a woman driver had to brake frantically to avoid hitting an old-fashioned car, driven by a 'determined' young man.

- In Rugeley, Staffordshire, at some time in 2006, daylight was fading as a driver was traversing the Hednesford Road. He suddenly he saw a Ford Capri in his rear-view mirror. He took a corner, and the Capri just vanished.

- On the A4 along the Hilly Road at Corsham, Wiltshire, in the 20th century, a woman drove past an 'American style' car coming towards her. But she was alarmed to note the car had no driver.

- At Sligachan, Skye, along the A850 to Portree, a driver pulled over to let a speeding 'meandering' car overtake him. It vanished.

- In Horton, Suffolk, along the A1088, a crashing motorbike was seen at some time in 1989, but the bike and rider vanished.

- Some time in 1995, at night, on the A324 towards Pirbright, Surrey, a witness – with some knowledge of early-20th-century-vehicles – was amazed to recognise a 1920s Dennis T-type old bus of the Aldershot and District bus company. It passed him in the opposite direction. But it didn't seem solid – more like a hologram – and made no sound. The driver's headlights did not reflect off it as it passed.

- At Milford, Surrey, at the A3 junction, at 8 p.m. on 6 November 2010, an off duty policeman was forced to swerve to avoid an oncoming motorbike. He could see the bike's single headlight as it zoomed past, yet the cop could see no disappearing bike in his rear-view mirror.

- At Ryton-on-Dunsmore, Warwickshire, on the A45, a notorious lorry often drove the wrong way in the 1980s, causing accidents. In every case it simply vanished.

- At Bath, Somerset, near the Shockerwick Bridge, an unidentified reoccurring vehicle would appear and disappear at midnight. A blue Morris additionally would appear, forcing collisions among other vehicles.

- At Odstock, Wiltshire, on 24 June 2017, in a lane near a church, a driver and passenger heard an invisible horse trotting alongside their car.

- At Swindon, in the Hannington suburb, in the 20th century, a phantom car sometimes crosses through what appear to be barbed wire fences on both sides of the road.

- At Loch Cluanie, on the A87 in Aberdeenshire, at dates prior to the 1940s, a car used to gain speed to tailgate the one in front, before vanishing.

- At Edinburgh, on the A7, in the mid 20th century and early 21st century, a phantom lorry would cause accidents. In 2010 there was talk of a vanishing orange Austin.

- At Pillaton, Cornwall, in 1978, four people in a car travelling towards the Weary Friar pub encountered a dated, classical, car lumbering towards them. Two of the passengers leaned out of the window to shout a warning to the oncoming vehicle, assuming it had come from a classic car show, but it suddenly vanished.

- At Eyam, Derbyshire, in the mid 20th century, on the road between Eyam and Stoney Middleton, a squeaky phantom pushbike could be heard, and, judging by its increasing tone, assumed to be travelling at an improbable speed. Pedestrians would turn to look, but see nothing.

- In the 1970s the Tarmac report on haunted roads quoted resident Jackie who lived on Drews Lane, Birmingham, West Midlands. She said she used to hear and see cars roll over while being driven. 'There were a couple in a week sometimes, nothing to explain it.'

- In his book *Haunted Land*, Paul Devereux describes how he was driving on the M6 near Birmingham one morning in 1980. He pulled out to let a mini pick-up truck enter the motorway from a slip road. But as he passed it he noticed that the driver's cab seemed to be empty.[13]

- A father and adult son heading for Stocksbridge bypass, near Sheffield and long known to be haunted, went round a bend and saw what looked like a shipping container – then it vanished.[14]

- Visitors to Denbigh Castle in Wales once heard ghostly voices calling for help. Marie Morgan, 43, visiting with her sister Melissa, heard them while climbing steps to a tower. Then their car wouldn't start, apparently a common experience of others who had heard the voices.[15]

## Strange Time Warps on the Road

In October 1981 a group was touring through Salen Forest on the Isle of Mull, in the Hebrides, when a mist descended and attached itself to their car. There was a sense of heavy pressure as if they had entered a vortex.[16] In the same month Alan Cave was travelling from Bath to Stroud, Gloucestershire (an area that had a track record for Ufo sightings). His digital watch, which he knew to be accurate, showed 8 a.m., when an announcer on his car radio said it was 11 a.m. At the time he was travelling under an orange object or substance that looked a bit like a cloud. Then he watched his speedo turn backwards 300 miles![17]

In another case of lost time, a John B. Collins of Poole, Dorset, wrote that in March 2010 he was returning home after visiting friends in the neighbourhood. He left at 11.25 p.m., but the journey home took much longer than it should have. He was familiar with the road layout and villages in the area, and he shortly approached the roundabout that should have led straight back home. He took the correct turn-off. But his car started to develop peculiar problems, and the car he had seen behind him had suddenly disappeared. He then found himself driving along an unfamiliar dark lane with no houses or street lights. This mysterious lane was unusually long, and it took him at least 30 minutes before he could find his way back to the correct turn-off.[18]

## Spooky Dolls on Car Rides

One strange road ghosts phenomenon concerns *dolls* and cars. Jason, living in Scotland, found a doll during a 2004 ghost hunt in an abandoned psychiatric hospital. The doll soon began wandering about his house at night; he found it in different places in the morning and believed, after investigation, that the spirit of a girl patient called Sophia was attached to the doll.

Jason had the doll exorcised by having a somewhat reluctant priest order the spirit to leave the doll, which wasn't really successful.

Realising this, Jason attended a paranormal a conference near Derby and exhibited the doll and other haunted toys, after which he put them in the boot of his car to take back. But this particular doll seemed to have gone missing from the car. Believing he had left it at the hotel near the conference centre, Jason asked his friend, Nick Donaldson, then 32, who lived in Derby, to go back to the hotel. Nick did so, found the doll, took her home, but had the same spooky experiences as Jason, such as the doll ending up on the floor having been placed on a bookcase the night before. He visited a friend who also, like Jason, had some interest in haunting phenomena, then took the doll on another ride in his car, but she promptly vanished only to turn up again at the hotel. Nick, yet again, took the doll to another ghost hunt event to see what else the mediums could learn about her. But on the journey, Nick's girlfriend became frightened when she thought she could hear a high-pitched voice shouting in the boot.

Strange events continued in Nick's home, with the doll regularly escaping from the glass cabinet where he later kept her. He could actually hear the glass doors creeping open during the night, and found the doll again in the centre of the floor. Even when he took the doll to a friend's home, it frightened the pet dog, and Nick and his friend could hear a tiny giggling voice.[19]

In response to a surge in interest in haunted household objects and furniture – including haunted dolls – Neil Packer, 58, of Hinckley, Leicestershire, set up a haunted antiques trading website, and travels to antique shops and boot fairs. Neil once felt drawn to a toy clown that he was told contained a spirit called Bob. He kept the clown in his garage, but Bob's spirit kept wandering off around the house and playing tricks on him and his wife.[20]

In a similar story, Eddie and Mandy Fellows ran a paranormal investigation team, and also acquired haunted dolls. In September

2017 they planned to take two dolls, a boy called Damien and a girl called Maxine, by car to a paranormal event in Wallasey, Merseyside, but by mistake left Maxine behind. When they finally got home at 3 a.m. they found Maxine was 'sitting on the grass in the front garden'. Mandy assumed that Maxine had missed her boyfriend Damien and had gone outside to look for him![21]

# Chapter 8

## Premonitions and Omens

There are numerous cases of uncanny but apparent coincidences concerning cars and roads involving unscheduled stops and delays that have saved car drivers and their families from serious accidents. But are they all coincidences? Is there some unknown supernatural force at work?

Coincidences are known scientifically as synchronous events – two events coinciding inexplicably with each other, an exact or simultaneous harmony with another similar event. Scientists adopted synchronicity as a fundamental constant that could be explained mathematically or with calculus.

Marie-Louise von Franz, a 19th-century Jungian psychologist, believed that synchronicity occurs in nature without any scientifically known cause.

An ordinary *premonition* – which could well have been, in retrospect, simply a coincidence – might be as follows: a Mrs Goodsell recalled how, when she was 18, she was walking to a railway station, but had an uneasy sensation about something that made her stop walking and waste time looking at a 'boring shop window'. Resuming her journey on foot, she heard an almighty car crash as three cars ploughed into a brick wall next to the pavement along which she would have had to walk.[1]

There are warnings galore where drivers are saved from an inevitable car accident, and which often involve traffic light infringements, like drivers shooting through red lights. Paul's car radio once began to crackle badly, so he pulled over to tune it in, but the crucial few moments' delay this caused before he was able to return to the road saved his life. With his car gaining momentum, he could see ahead a car recklessly zoom across a red traffic light as he approached the green and braked to a halt. Just a few moments – no more than a minute – saved him from crossing the junction and meeting the other driver in a dreadful collision.[2]

Laura-May was in her early thirties when she and her small son, Kieran, were killed in a car accident on the M8 in Scotland, probably in the 2000s. Laura-May's sister, Amanda, also in the car, was in a coma for several weeks. Laura-May's mother, Marie, when told of the site of the accident by police, recalled she had premonitions about the highway at roughly where the accident occurred, near Harthill, North Lanarkshire. And this was several months before it happened. Further, she had the 'overwhelming urge' to take a photo of the family group, in the local park, of her two adult daughters and grandson. It was the last one she would ever take of them. Afterwards she had ghostly visitations from Laura-May and Kieran, and the surviving daughter, Amanda, began to experience poltergeist activity.[3]

Wendy Briant had seen a TV programme called *6ixth Sense*, presented by the medium Colin Fry. He was coming to Guildford, not far from where she lived, to present one of his shows, which she attended. She told *Fate and Fortune* magazine that Colin came towards her and was aware that *speed* was a characteristic of the

Briant family. Wendy would often go with her husband, Tim, on motorbike trips, but he had died in September 2011 because of possible speeding. Colin also said that Tim had passed on a spiritual message saying that he was 'well and strong', and was telling Wendy, via Colin, to look after his young son. Wendy then started to go to a spiritualist meeting that hosted visiting mediums. She made friends with the leader of the group, Tina, who surprisingly showed her a picture of Tim in the background of a family photo. Wendy wondered whether Tim's spirit, knowing of the existence of the photo, had led his mother to the group.[4]

## Worrying Premonition Cases

- Samantha was driving behind an open-topped utility vehicle which was carrying furniture. In her head she had a warning to move over in case something fell off the back. Sure enough, after she changed lanes, a table did fall off the back, smashing into pieces on the road.[5]

- Jo Pearce, 33, from Bristol, visited a spiritualist church in March 1982 and learned that someone Jo knew was going to have a motorbike accident. She told her brother Alec, just 20, who owned a motor scooter, to be careful. Then on 12 May she woke with a pain in her neck, and that same day her sister turned up to speak of Alec's death in a road accident. Alec had been an Elvis devotee, and at later psychic circle meetings Jo says she actually saw apparitions of Alec and other celebrities such as Elvis, Laurel and Hardy, John Wayne and Benny Hill! Shortly after, Jo gave up her job to become a medium full time, when Alec and Elvis often popped up at meetings![6]

- Bob Curry tells how as a teenage soldier on leave in the UK in 1970 he visited a pub with fellow soldiers, who were all due to travel back to their unit the following day. Some of them left the pub in a car to continue onwards to a Chinese restaurant, while the remainder returned to their barracks by other transport. The following day Bob was told that the other car had been involved in a dreadful crash with an articulated lorry, and three of his friends had been killed. "'I can't believe it," I cried, my legs buckling underneath me. That's when it hit me. I was about to get in that car, too … until something stopped me.'[7]

- Tarot cards once indicated to Layla Wells, 36, of London, that she was going to be badly hurt in a car a crash. Pushing it to the back of her mind, and only half believing in Tarot predictions, she was nevertheless involved in a car crash while she was out with her husband and 5-year-old daughter. A woman driver had simply smashed into their car. The family survived with minor cuts and bruises – so the 'badly hurt' part of the prediction didn't come true. But sicknesses and anxiety symptoms later seemed to plague Layla, and she was referred to therapy. She realised that the Tarot prediction was referring to the adverse effect the crash would have on her mental health.[8]

- Sarah Fok-Seange, 34, had a premonition in December 2004 that Lee, a friend of her boyfriend, Marc, would die in road accident in his early twenties. The sensation was particularly prominent at a party held in December 2004. Three years later, when the premonition returned, she phoned Marc to ask about Lee, who she feared for, and Marc reassured her that nothing was wrong. But within minutes Marc had rung back to tell her that Lee had just died in the very car crash Sarah had envisioned – the only one to die in a car of five passengers. The strangeness of the event was reinforced when Sarah and Marc visited the scene of the accident the following evening, when she actually saw Lee's ghost among the party of friends that had gathered there to commiserate and celebrate his young life. He came over to Sarah and spoke telepathically to her. Realising she had a psychic gift, Sarah later became a holistic therapist and a 'Reiki Master Practioner'.[9]

- The 1970s rock star Marc Bolan, just 29, died in a car crash in the early hours of 16 September 1977. His girlfriend, Gloria Jones, also a singer, was driving along a road in Barnes, south-west London, and suddenly careered off the road, striking a metal post, then a tree. Gloria survived. But there has long been a rumour that Bolan suspected he would die young, and even suggested he would die in a car crash like James Dean or Eddie Cochran. During a visit with his group, T Rex, to France in February 1977, he visited the Louvre museum in Paris, and spent hours staring at a painting by artist Rene Magritte. The title of the painting was *The Sixteenth of September*, the date of his death.[10]

## The Warning Voices

Some car drivers think they actually *hear* warning voices, often urgently exclaim. Bethany, in late December 2010, was driving along an unnamed motorway when she claims she heard a voice, either in reality or inside her head, telling her to slow down. A plastic bag then flew into her windscreen. She braked hard and saved herself from a serious road accident 'just as a car ploughed into traffic metres ahead of me'. Theresa Cheung says in her book *An Angel Spoke to Me* that the warning voice while driving seems to be a frequent way that spiritual beings speak to people. She says in Bethany's case that she was distracted by thoughts of buying Christmas presents and party ideas while she was driving, when 'our minds are more open to psychic communications'.[11]

Ross was on the motorway with his two young children asleep in the back seat. It was getting late, but he distinctly heard his little daughter say 'Get over, Daddy.' He looked back, but she was still asleep. He thought he must have imagined it, but decided to move over into the slow lane anyway, and did so just in time to avoid the dangerous turbulence of a lunatic driver that shot past him at 90 mph.[12]

Suzi Swanston, 45, in 2011 had been out in her car, and was about to drive further to a shopping precinct in Salford. But the ghost of her deceased grandma spoke to her in the car, telling her instead to 'go home'. 'No, Nana, I really need to go to the shops,' she replied. While driving she turned on the car radio to hear of riots, looting and battles with the police in the shopping precinct in Salford. 'With a shudder I turned the car round and headed for home.'[13]

Michelle Gordon, 34, from Gloucester, was driving with friends to the Fairy Fayre at Glastonbury when she heard a voice in her head telling her to 'go home'. She had been looking forward to this event for weeks, and dismissed the warning voice. In fact nothing had gone wrong, the girls had a great day at the Fairy Fayre, and they had explored the town and the Tor. This meant it was dark by the time they set off for home. Michelle had forgotten about the warning voice, but ten minutes into the return journey the car in front stopped suddenly. She was doing 45 mph and could not stop quickly enough to avoid crashing into it. The car behind couldn't stop either, and slammed into the back of her. Fortunately no one was hurt, apart from Michelle who suffered whiplash injuries. But her car was a write-off. Thinking back, Michelle was annoyed with herself for not taking such warning voices seriously. There had been other near misses involving cars and roads. She was already a novelist, and meditated regularly, but after the Glastonbury event decided to take the esoteric and psychic side of life more seriously, and wrote a book on meditation. She wrote in *Chat It's Fate* magazine, 'I've still no idea who the voice actually belongs to; Is it a spirit guide? My intuition? I don't know, but I trust its advice. It's never told me to do anything bad …'[14]

In 1993 Wendy McCallum, 47, from Camberley in Surrey, was driving a group of friends to Southampton. She made to overtake a car on a bypass, when a woman's voice in her head, 'so real, so urgent', shouted a warning. Everyone in the car got into a crouching position after Wendy's screeched instructions. A serious accident did in fact occur when Wendy's car hit a crash barrier and another vehicle. The passengers managed to get out of the car before it exploded. Wendy was the worst injured and taken to hospital, and her friend Steve, one of the survivors, visited her. He was aware that Wendy had had a psychic experience in the car that could have saved his life. But two months later Steve himself died in another car crash. The psychic messages from Steve from the afterlife, and other strange visitations at night from hooded figures, made Wendy visit a medium who suggested she also become one. 'No thanks,' she said. 'I vowed then and there to have nothing more to do with spirit – even if that meant shutting Steve out …'[15]

Bob and Marie were on a trip to the Lake District, during a summer in the 2000s, when Bob received a psychic message about the impending death of his father, who had been taken ill. Bob drove home as fast as he could, but his father had passed away before he and his wife arrived. A few months later Marie had a 'message' in her head telling her to go at once to the hairdresser's. She drove quickly there and discovered that Bob's mother had had a heart attack whilst getting her hair done. Marie and her friend at the hairdresser's accompanied her in the ambulance to the hospital. The mother-in-law made a full recovery, and Marie assumed this was partly due to the reassurance and affection she had given to her while in the ambulance. But later Marie had a message that said 'Get off the motorway!' while she was driving a caravan to Wales with Bob, with the family in the back seat. When they got to the caravan site they were shocked to learn that there had been a major pile-up on the motorway. Marie liked to think that the warning came from her late father-in-law's ghost. Bob's dad was clearly looking down from beyond the grave.[16]

One day in 1989 Brian Miller was on the M4, and a sudden 'weird thought' popped into his head about a bomb being on the motorway. As so often in these cases the internal voice is thought to be an actual voice, and Brian looked round into his empty car, somewhat irrationally, to see if a friend had sneaked in to play a trick on him. But back at home, during his evening meal, he heard a TV announcer mention that the M4 had been closed after a suspected bomb had been found, but which had turned out to be a false alarm.[17]

Car accidents seemed to plague Tracy's life and relationships. Her mother had died in a car crash when Tracy was just a toddler, and somehow she became psychic. In adulthood she was aware of her mother's warning presence from the afterlife. She sensed that her boyfriend, Steve, might have a road accident after he had driven her home one evening. Tracy later married Steve and had two children.

Still psychically aware of accidents, she was fearful about her son Matt who, as a teenager, drove a moped. One morning she had a frightening phone call filled with blood-curdling moans, but little else. She feared that this was Matt who was severely injured, but no number showed up on the call logger, which was odd in itself. Frantically she dialled Matt's mobile and found to her relief that he was okay. But she warned him to put the moped in the garage for a check-up. She drove Matt to college the following day in her car, and nearly collided with an ambulance with its sirens blaring. It was 8.40 a.m., the same time as the mystery caller the day before. She speculated that if Matt was driving his moped at that time he might have been killed.[18]

## Select Examples of Similar 'Warnings'

- The world-famous singer Tito Gobbi was once driving too fast along a precipitous mountain road. He suddenly heard his dead brother's warning voice 'so distinctly that he seemed to be sitting beside me, say "Stop instantly."' Gobbi did so, but was within minutes of losing his life on a hairpin bend.[19]

- Amanda Jane Ward of Worcestershire was told by her 12-year-old son not to buy a little two-door hatchback. He said he had 'bad feelings' about it. Sure enough, after Amanda took possession of it, there were endless mechanical failures. Then, when out driving with her young children, a phantom voice in her head called out 'Stop, stop, stop', so she slammed on the brakes just in time to avoid a serious accident as a car swerved towards her, but the car behind collided with the rear of the car. 'Our car was written off and I must say I was glad to see the back of it.'[20]

- A woman who was due to give a radio interview, and was pressed for time, heard her dead mother's voice telling her to do a right turn at vital road junction, and take the slightly longer route to the studio. As a result she missed her time slot for the interview and made to return home in a disgruntled mood. However, as she approached the junction where she might earlier have turned left instead of right, she noticed that a major accident had happened, as cars and lorries had smashed into each other. She realised that, if she had taken the original route, she might well have been killed.[21]

- Peter Child, as a 21-year-old in September 1961, went to a motor race event in Monza, Italy, while on holiday with his friend Roger. They parked on a raised embankment to get a good view, when Peter heard an inner voice telling him to 'move up nearer the bend'. He heard it twice, decided to obey, and urged his puzzled and reluctant friend to move the car. Shortly after, a racing car driven by Wolfgang von Trips, a well-known German competitor, span out of control and crashed into the embankment, killing himself and fifteen spectators. Many were in the place that Peter and Roger had earlier vacated.[22]

## Dreaming about Disaster

There are many cases of warnings that come in the form of a dream, which can also be accompanied by daytime premonitions. A mother of a 17-year-old, whom she had allowed to take over the wheel of her car while she took a doze, had a dream-like vision of a speeding red car coming round the bend. Suddenly alerted, she felt the need to warn her son, who slowed down. Sure enough, the red car came roaring round the bend, and the couple avoided a serious accident.[23]

At Rainham, Essex, a teenager in 2005 dreamed that he had borrowed his mother's yellow car only to crash it into a ditch. A few years later he did borrow his mother's car, and the crash happened exactly as in his dream.[24]

Dreams and premonitions were reported by Christine's family, who lived in Tadworth, Surrey. Christine first had a premonition that her granddaughter, Chelsie, 13, would be hit by a vehicle while crossing the road. She rushed to tell her daughter, Jess, who said she had the same sense of foreboding. Both grandmother and mother warned Chelsie to take extra care when out.

But the event came true on 15 May 2014, when a phone call told Christine that Chelsie had been knocked down at a crossroads near her school by a hit-and-run driver, although she was not severely injured. There were no arrests, even though another parent had filmed the accident on a dashboard camera. The film revealed that the car had an unusual laurel leaf on its side panel. The two women – the grandmother and mother – had a *feeling* that the make and colour of the car had been wrongly identified to the police. Witnesses described the vehicle as a black Mitsubishi 4 x 4, and the dashboard camera footage, which showed the vehicle to be green, had been handed to the police. But the blurred footage could not determine the exact make of the vehicle.

Then grandma Christine had another premonition that the car was a green Ford truck. The mother of Chelsie, Jess, then rang Christine about a month later to say she *dreamed* that the same 4 x 4 was parked outside her house, which actually happened the following evening. The dream came true – a green Ford Ranger was right outside. It had the leaf design and the same driver at the wheel. So it was indeed a Ford Ranger, and not a black Mitsubishi, said Jess.

Christine herself in the meantime had a further premonition four weeks later, out in the open, that made her turn back, and sure enough when she was still some distance away from her home she saw the very same model of green Ford Ranger that had preoccupied the mother and daughter's thoughts. She rushed back to Jess's house, and both came running back with a camera and took shots of the car. Jess managed to get its registration number. They then contacted the police with the photos, and the driver was arrested.[25]

Carla had a dream about her former boyfriend, Ian, driving off a cliff with herself in the passenger seat. In her dream she sensed that he was suicidally depressed. She wondered whether this was a premonition about Ian's imminent death. It probably was. There were more nights of bad dreams about Ian's mental and physical health. Then, during a waking state, a phone number appeared in her mind. She managed to remember it, and fatefully dialled it. It was Ian's number. They had a reconciliation and later got engaged, although he was still mentally unwell and confessed he once wanted to take his life in his brother's car. One day she was in his new car when it skidded on black ice. They both survived a serious accident, but the car – 'his pride and joy', Carla said – was written off. Ian's depression increased, and in December 2009 he took his own life by way of an overdose. Cars in his truncated and sad life had finally destroyed him, and nearly destroyed his girlfriend.[26]

Some days before he took delivery of a new car, David had a bad nightmare. He was driving towards Hinckley at night, and accelerated along a straight stretch, just past a bend where a notorious medieval gallows stood. He said his dream felt real, with warm night air blowing in through the windows. He decided, after all, not to buy the car, and later heard that the new owner of it had indeed died at that very spot.[27]

Victor Roberts agreed to buy an old 1966 model blue Hillman from his friend. He had a dream that he was driving along in it on a warm summer's day, and actually smelt cut grass. He was even singing along with the car radio. Then, in his dream, he was involved in fearsome car accident: 'There was a flash of some obstruction in my path.' He knew he was severely injured, foaming flecks of blood, and aware that his leg had been severed at the thigh. And the car he was driving had been a blue Hillman. Shocked and cautioned, Victor didn't after all buy the car. His friend then traded it in part exchange to local motor company. A month later the two men heard that the purchaser of the car, actually one of the mechanics at the garage, had died a month later 'in exactly the circumstances as I had dreamed; the Hillman left the road and collided with a lamp post'.[28]

David's mother had a dream about a tyre blow-out while she and the family were travelling along the motorway. Two days later David was in the family car in the back seat with his sister and mother, with Dad driving. Sure enough, there was a loud bang as one tyre exploded, and the car span out of control. Mother instinctively shoved David closer to his sister, suspecting that their side of the car would somehow be damaged, without knowing why, but it had something to do with her precognitive dream. The careering vehicle then crashed into a metal fence and seriously damaged the side of the car David and his sister were just seconds earlier sitting in, so his mother's intuitive action – and her dream – had saved David from serious harm.[29]

Robert was twenty in 1992, and was involved in a road accident in which the girl in his car died from her injuries. In a court case he was accused of walking away from the scene of the disaster. He was depressed with guilt for some years afterwards, which led to repeated dream premonitions about car accidents, often involving members of his family at traffic lights, which he thought were nightmare throwbacks to his depression and guilt. But the accidents in these dreams were genuinely precognitive – they did happen to members of his family.[30]

A combination of warning premonitions and dreams occurred to Sue in July 2013. She first dreamed about a plane crashing just yards from her car while she was driving, 'with shards of metal skimming my face'. She thought it was a premonition-like warning. She had the premonition when she drove off in the morning, and dug out her RAC card and mobile just in case she needed them in an emergency. Then, just forty minutes from her destination in Chepstow, on the Welsh border, a ball of smoke billowed from her car bonnet. She stopped on the hard shoulder, and ran for her life as the car exploded in a fireball, with the shards of glass duly happening.[31]

Sue had another distressing dream that she would be involved in a horrific motor accident, and that she was dying, but that her own late mother was saying to her that the time was not right for Sue to pass over. The dream sadly came true, as Sue did have such an accident just a day later. She was so severely injured that she was in a coma and on a life-support machine. There were urgings that the life support be switched off. By this time daughter Kay had arrived at the hospital, and sat with her mother, tears rolling down her cheek. Against all the odds Sue survived and began to make a slow recovery. But she remembered little about the accident or the hospital, only that her own mother was in constant spiritual attendance, telling her that, as in the dream, it was not right for her to join her family in the spirit world.[32]

# Chapter 9

## 'Saved by Angels'

Theresa Cheung wrote that over the years, reading about people's experiences, she is convinced that sometimes angels do save lives while in the guise of other people. So often these life-saving interventions are attributed – literally – to a 'guardian angel' rescuing them at the last moment from certain death or serious injury.

The looming truck out of nowhere is a perennial threat to innocent motorists. Some people swear that they miraculously avoided serious car accidents because their spirit guides were watching over them. As Glennyce S. Eckersley also put it, writing in 1996:

> In recent years there has been an enormous upsurge of interest in angels and angelic activity. This has been fuelled by the experiences of thousands of people who have felt an angelic presence in their lives, seen visions and experienced life-changing encounters.[1]

She asks whether premonitions or 'guidance' were involved in these often-cited miraculous life-saving events.[2]

In Neil Annerley's case the 'angel' was his spirit guide called Red Buffalo. Many of Neil's tragic experiences, including being beaten up, involved cars. As a teenager he was returning to an army base in Germany in October 1965 after two weeks' leave in his home town of Liverpool. He had seen Red Buffalo in his room from the age of 4 onwards, and always in full Native American regalia. On this particular day he said that a small voice from Red Buffalo told him to pull into a service station. As he did so he heard screeching brakes and an alarmingly loud motorway road crash just yards distant. It later emerged that thirteen people had died in this tragedy, from which Neil had been spared.

Later, when on an army exercise, another vehicle crash happened just feet away from him when he had bent over to retrieve a screwdriver that had fallen out of his pocket – which he attributed to the artfulness of Red Buffalo. Neil had moved his head out of danger, and was again saved. His life was also saved from the consequences of later car crashes. In March 1967 he had loaned his car to his mate Bernie, which was virtually written off in an accident. This delayed Neil's return to England for spell of leave via the car ferry service at Zeebrugge, from which the ill-fated *Herald of Free Enterprise* departed. The ferry overturned in the sea, a disaster that took the lives of 193 passengers. Neil said that Red Buffalo had saved his life yet again, since he had made Bernie crash the car so that Neil would have to get a later ferry. Neil was also rescued by a mysterious stranger from being drowned when his canoe capsized, and he miraculously survived a helicopter jump exercise that went wrong, and avoided a petrol tanker explosion at a German service station when he dozed off at the wheel and missed his turning. He said that he felt Red Buffalo's reassuring presence in his car at the time.

However, Neil wasn't so lucky one night in Chesterfield, when he was attacked as he was getting into his car, and was violently beaten up. When he felt his life ebbing away in the ambulance, he began to have an end-of-life experience, but Red Buffalo appeared to tell him to 'go back – this isn't your time'. 'Over the years,' wrote Neil, 'I should have died eight times. Six times Red Buffalo helped me. And twice when I did die, he sent me back.' So impressed was Neil with these miracles that he decided to become a full-time medium.[3]

Karen was unfortunately in a bad relationship with her partner, and one night after a stormy row, decided to flee the marital home and take her young son, Jake, with her. She drove off into the night. She intended to go back to her old home town and her relatives, but thought better of it – it was also a very long journey. She didn't have much money with her, and knew her son was getting tired and hungry, and it was far too cold to keep Jake out all night sleeping in the car.

It was now getting late and she spotted a young woman walking alone, pulled up beside her, and asked if she knew of any low-cost guest houses who could put her up for the night. The woman surprisingly said that her brother owned a small guest house, which was just around the next corner. Karen proceeded to the address, took Jake from the car, and explained the situation to the small dark-haired woman who answered the door. 'And what did this lady look like?' asked the landlady. 'She was quite slight, but with fair curly hair and a wonderful smile,' replied Karen. 'Ah', replied the landlady. 'I think I know who you mean.'

The following morning she and Jake went downstairs to the dining room for breakfast. A man turned to face Karen as she entered the room. He said he understood that the woman Karen met the previous night was his sister, Chris. He paused and added that Chris 'is no longer with us. She was killed about six years ago. She took up with this chap who was no good, and he ended up murdering her.' The shocked Karen then realised that the young lady who had given her rooming directions was in some ways her alter ego – someone who was in a similar position to herself. Chris's ghost had chosen her allotted task, in the world of spirit, to help any other poor woman who had suffered as she did.[4]

Children can recall being pushed out of the way of speeding cars, but with no idea how it could have happened.[5] Julie and Roger, and Julie's family, were on a caravan holiday in Devon. Jonathan, just three, began to run jerkily through a hedge at the end of the caravan park, and they knew there was a main road behind it. Julie was frantic as she heard a car travelling fast along the road.

The odd aspect of this story is the peculiar slowing down of time, as seen in earlier cases. Any tragedy involving little Jonathan should have taken place in minutes or seconds. In fact the car sped on past the gap where Jonathan had lurched through, thus convincing Julie and Roger that their child must have been killed. They never heard a screech of brakes. But the driver was already holding Jonathan when Julie got there. He had stopped, picked up the child, and handed him over, saying merely, 'He's fine.' But Julie pointed out that 'We didn't see him pick him up, even though Jonathan had only been there a millisecond.' With relief she passed Jonathan to husband Roger, and turned to thank the man. But he and his car were nowhere to be seen, although 'looking up and down the lane you could see for quite some distance'. Other members of the family had witnessed the incident too, but no one was able to describe the man or what he was wearing. It was as if he had never existed.[6]

Angela took her fourth driving test in 2001 at the age of 42, and passed. She was pleased because she had always disappointed her dad at so many failings. This time he said, 'Didn't you do well!' But Dad was not so pleased with the second-hand Peugeot she had bought, because he sensed something bad about the car. To allay his feelings and to reassure Angela, he pulled out a blackened 1912 penny from his pocket that he kept for luck and flipped it into the air. 'There, that will bring you luck,' he said, tucking the coin back in his pocket and patting it.

But bad luck seemed to plague Angela's car as time passed. A collision at a roundabout left her with whiplash injuries, and she sold the car. Then her father passed away in 2011. Angela bought another second-hand car, this time a Citroen Picasso. Rummaging about inside, she was astounded to find Dad's old penny in a pocket in the back of the driver's seat. It is just possible the previous owner had possessed a 1912 penny, but in the 21st century they had become valuable collectors' items, and not likely to be lost so easily. But she recognised the unusual dark markings on it that could not possibly have occurred normally. She even heard her father's familiar whispering voice, saying, 'Didn't you do well!' The next morning, pressing the key fob to open the car door, she actually saw her dad sitting at the driving wheel. Later, paranormal events would happen to the car, especially when she was thinking of her dad, with the windscreen wipers suddenly becoming active, or the radio changing stations.[7]

Ian Varrow, 48, told how on his motorbike he had a strange experience when he was younger, and had collided with a red car that had pulled out of a junction just ahead of him. He blacked out momentarily. 'The next thing I knew, I was standing on the other side of the car looking back at my mangled motorbike. How did I get here? I wondered.' He seemed to have been teleported, he said. He had definitely been injured, and was taken to hospital, but had no memories of the actual collision. Later, on an Internet chatroom, he got talking to a man who was a 'Wiccan', who told Ian that a spirit had pulled him away from danger.[8]

Kerin Webb, 55, from Bournemouth, wrote to *Chat It's Fate* magazine to tell of how, as a young cyclist in 1983, he was saved from certain death by what he could only believe was his guardian angel. He suddenly felt invisible hands grab him by the collar, lift him from his saddle and fling him into the air. As he rolled in the middle of the road, cars narrowly avoided running over him. Clambering to safety he noticed that his bike was a complete wreck. A motorist who stopped said that he saw a load of scaffolding had come loose, and had swung into Kerin and his bike. 'But I'd felt nothing,' wrote Kerin, 'and like my bike, I should have been crushed. Instead, miraculously, I was unscathed. It was as if I had been pulled out of the lorry's path, then placed back down seconds later.' After one or two other miraculous escapes from disaster Kerin, who said he was already of a spiritual disposition, decided to become a full-time psychic medium.[9]

Pam's father died in hospital not long after she had driven some sixty miles to visit him. She started on the return journey in a distressed mood, saying to herself that the police would understand if she went through traffic lights or round a roundabout the wrong way. Gripping the steering wheel, partly in distraught anger, she stared tearfully at the black road ahead of her as it endlessly rolled on. But surprisingly she never saw another car – not one – on the entire sixty-mile journey. 'When I arrived home and Roy saw the state I was in, he asked me how on earth I had driven home. I said that I had not driven home, I had been brought home!'[10]

Billy Roberts, now in his early seventies, reports that he was a sickly child, in and out of hospital. He then said, in an article in *Fate and Fortune* magazine, that he and a friend, when they were children, saw an expanding beam of light in Billy's front room, which turned into a 'beautiful glowing figure' with wavy shoulder-length hair, which Billy took to be an apparition of the Virgin Mary. He rushed to tell his mum and his aunt, who saw the vision too. Surprisingly, his mother actually believed the Virgin Mary had appeared in order to cure Billy permanently, and got him to touch the vision. It then vanished, but a streak of rose-coloured powder remained where she, or it, had stood. 'It glistened and smelt of freesias.' His mum told him to scoop the glittery powder into a pill bottle because it must have curative and magical powers. Billy often kept the bottle in his car. One day, when he was twenty-seven, he gave his friends a lift home from a nightclub in Liverpool. But his car skidded on a patch of black ice and hit a lamp post. He was hurled through the windscreen, but oddly only suffered concussion, while his friends in the back were severely injured. He believed the magical powder had saved his life.[11]

## Angels That Save Lives

In the 2000s Radley had an incredibly lucky break. Running late for an appointment, he thought he could just beat the traffic lights that had turned amber. He noted a blue van waiting for the light to turn green on the other side. All of a sudden Radley's accelerator failed – his car was slowing down rather than speeding up. Chills ran down his spine as he saw the blue van hurtle past, and he knew he had just avoided a head-on collision. 'It's still a source of great amazement to me that an unknown force saved my life that day'.[12]

About ten o'clock one evening, as nurse Shirley was driving towards the hospital to start her night shift, a car pulled out in front of her and forced her into an adjacent narrow country lane. She saw a large vehicle, a 'people carrier', heading straight for her, and thought the end was nigh. Her fear made her let go of the steering wheel, and she closed her eyes. But she found, miraculously, that her car had passed between two vehicles, one on the left and one on the right. This itself, given the small dimensions of the lane, was actually physically impossible. She said later that she 'knew' an angel had taken control of her car, 'saving not just my life but the lives of the people in the other two cars'. In the meantime the people carrier had disappeared.[13]

Jenny's amazing experience was rather similar to both Radley's and Shirley's. Her brakes failed on a fast-moving busy road junction: she prayed, and begged for a miracle. She blacked out with terror, but her car missed a collision with other vehicles, as well as a lamp post, and ended up in someone's front garden. But the miracle was granted: 'Someone drove my car that day like a Formula One driver and it wasn't me.'[14]

A driving instructor, David Smith, 56, having once given lessons to a woman who said she was 'psychic', and seemed to confirm this by mentioning hitherto unknown things about himself and his family, said she seemed to pass on her psychic abilities to him. While out on his instructing duties he heard a 'spirit voice' warning of a dangerous junction ahead, which could have been fatal if it was not for his quick reactions to get the car and his learner out of danger. He mentioned several other spooky events in his book *The Psychic Driving Instructor*. He said he was sure angelic intervention helped him out of dangerous motoring escapades and near misses, instructing him to speed up or slow down at crucial dangerous moments. On one occasion the traffic lights turned green, and as his student started to surge across the junction, some schoolgirls stepped out in front of them, forcing David to hit the dual foot pedal control to bring the car to a screeching halt. This was extremely fortunate for everyone, as a car that had jumped the red lights from another angle would have hit them side-on.[15]

Theresa Cheung, who wrote about many similar life-saving accounts, told her own road story. When she was a child her mother drove her to a hospital to visit a friend who had suffered a stroke. It was bad midwinter weather, with fog increasing. Then either there was a fault in the car's steering, or her mother had had some kind of spasm, because their car lurched into the fast lane. Intentionally or not, they overtook a car but nearly collided with it side-on. Then a period of road rage occurred, as the angry driver tried to cut in front of them. But when Theresa looked out of the car window she could see ahead two people frantically pushing a stalled car into the side of the road. She concluded later that if they had stayed in the slow lane – and with visibility so bad – they could have slammed into it.[16] Again Theresa, like the others, said that an angel had taken over the wheel that day.

Derek Acorah, a well-known TV spirit medium, who has commented and written on angelic interventions and premonitions in people's lives, describes his own uncanny experience. He and his wife, Gwen, were stationary at a set of traffic lights when his engine stalled. It seemed impossible to restart it. Eventually a garage was called and the car recovered. But an investigation found a major structural fault not connected with the engine. This rather shocked Derek, because the car had stalled only a short distance from where he was about to start a high-speed journey on the M6. The couple could both have been killed or seriously injured. 'As soon as I heard the mechanic's report,' he wrote in his book, 'I knew that spiritual intervention had taken place ...'[17]

## More Incredible Lucky Breaks

These life-saving delays and interventions come in surprising ways. Kim was driving herself and two colleagues home at 9 p.m., after an unusually long spell at their office based in the west of England. Then, moving off the motorway onto a narrow side road, Kim felt a high-pitched ringing in one ear, which made her halt the car. The ringing stopped, so she thankfully continued the journey. But shortly a car hurtled past them on the wrong side of the road. If Kim had not stopped there would have been nowhere for her car to go to avoid having a head-on collision at the time the other car was heading for her. She said: 'Without that ringing in my ear I wouldn't be alive today and neither would Tim or Lisa. There was a guardian angel with us that day.'[18]

- Ginny Short, 51, on her way back from a horse show with her horse in the back of a truck, was in serious danger when a car pulled straight into her path. 'Miraculously,' she wrote, 'although me, my sister and my daughter were all flung from our seats and back again, the lorry passed through a gap – safely past the car.' She said it was an angelic intervention that saved her. Strange time lapses seemed to prevent the collision from occurring. Everything went into slow motion, and there was an ominous silence. The horse didn't move, and there was no noise from the back of the lorry. 'The next minute we were straight and on our way home without a scratch, or without a bang from our precious cargo.'[19]

- In January 2010 Olivia hit a patch of black ice on a side road, and her brakes seemed to fail just as she was about to turn right to avoid heading into a main road that had been sign-posted. She braced herself, eyes shut, for an inevitable collision, which, as in other cases, never happened. She said every nerve in her body was throbbing, and bolts of light seemed to be shooting through her. When she opened her eyes she was amazed to see that her car had halted, undamaged, just inches from the warning road sign.[20]

- Abbie Griffiths, 21, believed the spirit of her great-grandmother was looking after her, a notion instilled in her by her grandmother. Abbie had long believed this must be so since she miraculously survived unscathed after falling out of her family's car onto a busy highway at the age of 4. She also survived nearly choking to death after putting a twopenny piece into her mouth at the age of 6. Her grandma took her in her arms and rushed to get help from a Co-op store, but the coin miraculously shot out of her mouth with 'supernatural force'.[21]

- Robin was waiting at traffic lights, but sensed he had to take his time and move off slower than usual when the lights changed. Cars behind him began to hoot angrily. He was edging gradually past the lights when a car sped towards him at 80 mph from his right side. Robin was able to stop without causing a serious pile-up which would have happened if he was driving faster, and which would have harmed not only him but the other drivers behind.[22]

- A woman motorist recounts how in 1968 approaching a T-junction, with lights turning green, a voice urged her to look left, and she just avoided being struck by a speeding car. She put it down to a guardian angel.[23]

- Paula, now 63, said that when she was a kid her little sister told her she could see angels surrounded by a golden light. Paula, jealous about this, unkindly teased her. But one morning on the way to school her sister fell into the path of a car on the road. Paula managed to pull out her out of the way just in time – 'and as I did I saw an angel shielding her from harm. I was really nice to her after that'.[24]

- At Devauden, Gwent, Wales, at some date in the 20th century, a woman driver heard the 'stop' warning in her head, and avoided a serious accident with a car driving on the wrong side of the road.

- A Barry Wilson, 48, living in Wigan, was about to visit his family for Christmas in Berkshire. But he found, just when he was about to leave, that he had lost his car keys. A search among the sofa cushions revealed nothing. A married couple, David and Andrea, who were staying with Barry at the time, surprisingly also lost their car keys. David believed that he and Barry and Andrea were protected by a spirit guide. David – who was 'psychic' – found the car keys just three days later in Barry's house – in a drawer. He said that the spirit guide had deliberately hidden the keys to prevent Barry from having a possible car accident on his trip to Berkshire.[25]

- Amanda had baked an attractive-looking cake for a friend's birthday party, piled high with strawberries and cream, and tried to open her car door with one hand while balancing the cake in the other. But she dropped it, and it splattered both inside the car and onto the road. She went indoors to get a cloth and a dustpan, and heard a loud crunching sound. Another driver had taken a bend too quickly, and smashed directly into Amanda's car. She realised she could have been killed or severely maimed if she had actually got into her car and started to drive off.[26]

- Kirsty's headlights suddenly went out. Then she heard a lot of noise and saw sparking from the engine, and sensed danger.

She was about to pull over, stop and leap out of the car, when a large white bus hit her. She thought the end had come. She blacked out momentarily and had some kind of spiritual experience, with what sounded like angel wings hovering over her as the bus ran into her. She awoke moments later to hear the bus driver shouting at her to get out of the car. 'I think he too was shaken up by what had happened because he thought he had killed me.'[27]

- Donna's new boyfriend, Michael, was driving her to a party to be held in Bristol. But they got lost in the suburbs, and Michael started to drive faster to make up for lost time, but collided with a large van, parked irresponsibly on a sharp bend. Donna experienced the slow motion often inherent in similar danger scenarios, as she heard Michael yelling, and the splintering of metal. But she also saw a bright light surrounding her, and a shining angelic figure was gazing at her through the car window. She suffered a broken leg and Michael had only whiplash injuries. Yet, amazingly, both car and van were complete write-offs. Members of the ambulance crew were utterly surprised at this.[28]

- Strange angelic sensations on haunted roads can have unusual origins. Mark reported that one frosty morning his car went into a skid on the thin ice, hit the kerb with a thud, and halted. What surprised him was that hardly any damage had occurred, and Mark didn't have a scratch on him. Yet he was stunned to note that an entire column of cars coming in the opposite direction had also halted, because the lead car had noted what had happened to him and his car. He surmised that his skidding car could easily have collided with an oncoming vehicle with fatal consequences. He said: 'I've never felt so frightened in all my life. How on earth did all those cars stop on time? ... I really feel that my guardian angel looked after me that morning ...'[29]

- Judith's husband was driving them both to work early one morning. But their car accidentally hit a concrete barrier on the highway, which spun it into the opposite flow of rush-hour traffic. Incredibly, the oncoming cars parted, slowed and separated, calmly going either side of their stalled vehicle. They both got out, limped to the side of the road and waited for help. A motorcycle rider stopped and called the police who in turn rushed them to hospital for a check-up. The police were surprised that such a turn-around in the middle of traffic hadn't caused a fatal accident. Later Judith's husband said that a little voice spoke to him when the car started spinning around. 'Let go of the wheel, everything is going to be fine.' This he did, and everything was.[30]

- In November 1998 Mandy had to start early on her car trip, around 6 a.m., but because she had to go to bed late only hours before, working to get a pageant ready, chronic tiredness overcame her and she fell asleep at the wheel. She was jolted awake by stones hitting her windscreen that were thrown up by the tyres. The car span out of control. Her brakes had failed and she hit a large reflector pole, causing her to skid across the road. But it was the blowing out of the front tyres that actually caused the car to grind to a halt. Even so the car was a wreck. Again the police, rushing to the scene, were amazed that she had survived.[31]

- Wendy McCallum, 48, from Camberley, Surrey, as we saw in Chapter 8, had a warning in her head but survived a serious road accident. At another time she was heading back home with her young daughter from a holiday near Chichester, when she suddenly had a vision of four cars 'all hurtling along nose to tail', and seemingly coming towards her. There was a warning of imminent danger from her guardian angel, Emily. She slammed on the brakes and skidded to a halt just short of a T-junction, which she didn't know existed as it was situated dangerously behind a blind bend. It was then, seconds later, that she saw the four cars in her vision actually shooting past on the main road. Wendy – by suddenly halting – just avoided being a victim of a massive pile-up, and would probably have lost her life.[32]

- A lady who had attended an angel workshop told her husband about its benefits. He was sceptical, but did accept the little angel figurine she bought as a keepsake for the car. Later, when reversing out of a car park, another car ran into the back of his and he heard a 'huge bang'. Fearing the worst, he expected a lot of damage. But his car barely had a scratch – all the damage was to the other car. Then he noticed that the little angel ornament had cracked in two.[33]

- Motorist Alice felt compelled to pull over, halt her car journey, and check her briefcase for some sheet music she thought she had left behind. Continuing her journey, she arrived at a sharp curve in the road and noticed that a car that had just passed her moments before had been wrecked in a serious accident. Without Alice's halting of her own car earlier, she could herself have been involved.[34]

- A Sandra Heaney, 42, was driving on a virtually empty A66 near Appleby, Cumbria, heading towards Newcastle. A huge lorry loomed towards her, and smashed into her car side-on. In fact so serious was the impact that the two vehicles got entangled, and there was the sound of grinding metal and smashed glass. Sandra was dragged helplessly along the motorway, until her car broke free. It span into the oncoming lane and straight through a hedge bordering the road. She was injured and stunned, but managed to restart her car and continue driving. But the surprising emptiness of the motorway – the evil lorry and its driver were nowhere to be seen – at that point made her wonder if she was in the afterlife already. Some time later she visited her brother and told him about her miraculous escape, and he said 'You were so lucky ... someone was watching over you.' At that moment both Sandra and her brother glimpsed a black shadow behind her. But rather than being freaked out, Sandra felt at peace. 'I knew that shadow was my guardian angel – the one that saved me in the crash.'[35]

- In Holly's case it may have been sheer irritated impatience that saved her. She was stuck behind a convoy of vehicles, which included a large articulated lorry. She turned off at an exit, but found herself on an A road, which added time to her journey. She had to drive about three miles before finding signs back to the motorway. As she approached a slip road, however, she was caught in a tailback, and as the queue of traffic progressed slowly she could see blue lights flashing ahead. She was suddenly aware that there had been an accident, involving the very same articulated lorry that caused her to turn off the motorway in frustration, an act that no doubt saved her life.[36]

- Christine was standing by the family car, waiting for her husband to emerge from a high street shop. When he did so their little daughter started to run towards him, but Christine could see that she was in danger of being run over when another car suddenly approached, with the driver looking for a place to park. Before she had a chance to shriek a warning, the child seemed to bounce off an invisible wall, inches away from where the car would have hit her. Christine attributed this to an angelic intervention.[37]

- Kylie was delayed with her work as a child minder, and she and her partner were late driving to a party scheduled for that evening. But they saw a serious car crash on the way in which, had they not been late, they could have been involved. 'I am also a believer,' she said later, 'that things happen for a reason.'[38]

- Pedestrians have uncanny road experiences, too. Natasha was about to cross an apparently empty main road when she felt someone yanking her backwards, as if to save her from danger. She turned and found no one there. This happened twice. But then she heard a screeching sound, and a young driver, who she said later was drunk, speeding down the road. Here, as so often, the rescuing angels seem to be able to delay the time an inevitable accident is about to happen, because the driver 'seemed to have come out of nowhere'. But Natasha's delayed crossing of the road by some unseen force probably saved her life.[39]

- Martin was walking his two young sons home from school. They proceeded to cross a main road when his younger son, who Martin thought was holding his right hand, seemed to pull him back from the road as a car flew past. Yet the odd thing was that Martin, seconds later, noticed that both his sons were on his left-hand side. Some invisible hand not only saved Martin's and the boys' lives, but had been holding his hand for some while beforehand.[40]

- Sarah Morgan-Paul, 47, had ordered online a cheeky fluorescent green fancy dress outfit, which her partner, Stephanie, said had been delivered and placed on the kitchen table. They then took their dog for its usual morning walk, but Sarah felt an inner voice telling her to go back home as quickly as possible, a demand somehow connected with the new dress. She and her friend decided to go back to have a sneaky look at the dress when a car careered past them and crashed through a garden fence they were destined to pass. It could easily have killed the pair of them had they not retraced their steps at that moment.[41]

## Angel Helpers – 'Out of Nowhere'

The expression 'he came out of nowhere' is used time and again by victims of road disasters. Author Doreen Virtue says that 'angel meetings also involve pivotal meetings with helpful strangers, who either intervene or deliver an important message ... and then vanish without a trace'.[42] Jacky Newcomb wrote about this strange rescuing phenomenon. 'A stranger who appears out of nowhere to help you change your tyre, a stranger who warns you from driving home in a particular way. Often these "people" help you and then disappear as if they were never there.'[43]

Glennyce Eckersley, a writer on spiritualism and angelic interventions into people's lives, asked whether premonitions or 'guidance' was involved in these often-cited miraculous life-saving events. In fact her research suggested to her that the angelic experience was more common in the US where there have been many 'dramatic rescue' scenarios on US highways. In Britain there is more of a 'gentler type of encounter'.[44]

Nevertheless, the miraculous timing of such angelic interventions is amazing, as is the sudden appearance of the angels, even equipped as they are to do what is necessary to help, as if they had foreknowledge of the specifics of the trauma. For instance, 21-year-old Kelly had a very old Ford Fiesta with a faulty radiator. While she was in traffic it seemed to overheat, and she pulled into a car park to try to fix it. She took off the cap and was hit in the face by a spurt of boiling water. 'A man came out of nowhere and chucked cold water over me, which I was later told saved my face from scarring.' Not only that but the man accompanied Kelly to the hospital, and actually went into the cubicle where she was to be treated. 'Everything will be all right now,' he said, and promptly disappeared before either she or the nurse could thank him.[45]

Here is another example of an angel fully equipped for its predestined rescue mission. Linda's mother was driving her and her small child to see Linda's son, Jake, performing in his school play. They decided to stop off to buy a meal from a local takeaway. Unfortunately, Grandma shut the car door and left the keys in the ignition, with Linda's baby still sleeping on the back seat. Neither of them had a spare key nor were they members of an auto club. They were both in despair, because Jake would be disappointed not to see his mum and grandma in the audience, and they were worried about little Lucy, about to wake up any minute. Linda mumbled a plea for help. Out of the blue a white car pulled up, and young attractive blonde woman got out. Linda thought it strange that the woman was wearing a pale-yellow T-shirt on such a cold day. The woman asked what was wrong, and Linda explained the awkward situation to her. 'Without another word,' said Linda, 'the woman opened her car door and pulled out a metal tool. In one easy movement she inserted the tool into the car door and popped open the lock. 'Oh bless you, bless you,' was all I could think of saying. The woman smiled and said, 'Bless you too, Linda.'

Theresa Cheung asks whether this was just another Good Samaritan story with a heavy dose of good fortune, with a clued-up woman arriving with just the right tools (normally used only by police or auto club mechanics). But it spoke again of angelic intervention, as Linda had quietly asked for help. But, more importantly, the woman was a total stranger. How did she know Linda's name?[46]

But Linda's description of the blonde woman in a T-shirt was unusual. Most ghostly intervention is illustrated by the way no one is able to describe the helping persons, or what accent they had, or what clothes they were wearing, thus reinforcing the grey, colourless characteristics of a phantom – just ghosts pretending to be real people. Recall the case of little Jonathan, who was picked up by the motorist and handed over to his parents. No members of the family could remember what the motorist looked like. Nor do the survivors have any luck in getting information from their helpers, or have any knowledge of what district they might have come from – whether local or far away. This is surprisingly confirmed by arriving medics and police officers, who are, in most cases, obliged to write up an account of the accident and include names and addresses of victims and witnesses. In many cases they never report the existence of the helping angel.

## 'Out of Nowhere' – More Amazing Examples

- Some time in the mid 1990s Jane's car hit a van that suddenly reversed into the road. She and the van driver were severely injured, with whiplash injuries causing her windpipe to be blocked. Choking and unable to move, Jane just waited in her car to be rescued by a passing motorist, but the road was virtually deserted. Then a man with 'sparkling green eyes' arrived out of nowhere, literally, and lifted her head to enable to her breathe properly. He then held her in that position until the ambulance arrived fifteen minutes later. Jane eventually made a full recovery, although the van driver was in hospital for many weeks. But Jane was never able to trace her rescuer, and paramedics didn't see him leave, and his presence at the scene of the accident was not written up in her medical report. To all intents and purposes he didn't exist.[47]

- Joyce from Edinburgh had her life saved by a short, bald, plump male angel. He might even have been a potential groper! She was about to step into a busy main road when he put his hand across her stomach. 'I was so surprised at his action, I literally stopped my foot, leaving it hanging in mid air, to look firstly at his hand and then at him.' Just then a speeding car passed right in front of her, almost touching the kerb, just where her foot would have been. The plump man promptly disappeared.[48]

- Some motorists even appeal to their guardian angel for help with car and engine difficulties, which often happens simply by calling out in despair. Pauline was alarmed at a screeching engine noise, and she needed a stress-free journey that day. As soon as she asked the angels for help the noise stopped.[49]

- Jennifer Thomas recalls how her car failed to start on a morning when she had an important appointment. The battery seemed completely flat, and her husband rushed to a nearby garage for help, leaving her in the car. Jennifer realised that even if the mechanic had arrived and fitted a new battery, valuable time would have been lost. She 'connected' with her guardian angel, and sure enough when she turned the ignition key the engine sprang into life![50]

- A British family touring Ireland began to experience problems with their car, and it finally juddered to halt. The father, Colin, opened the bonnet and stared at the engine, but had no idea how to fix it. It looked as if the family were stranded. Hoping for help from a passing motorist, they were on a high vantage point and could see nothing but deserted lanes stretching endlessly. But, again emerging uncannily from nowhere, two smiling men got out of a bright red car. Within five minutes they had Colin's car working again. Then, without another word, the men got back into their own vehicle and drove away. Yet as Colin looked back only fifteen seconds later, he was astonished to see no sign of the red car anywhere. The vehicle's disappearance was literally impossible because Colin could see the road ahead for miles as it wound around the mountain. His wife Sarah said that perhaps the men were angels in everyday dress.[51]

- Kim Watkinson, 58, somehow felt the need for the first time to ask her niece Amy, who made jewellery and bracelets out of different types of crystal – said to have protective powers – to visit her one day and let her have one. 'I've always been interested in the power of crystals but, even for me, this seemed completely out of character.' A few weeks later Kim had to drop her husband, Noel, 51, off at work one Saturday morning in February 2016. She remembered to put Amy's home-made obsidian bracelet on. On the journey back home, while travelling on a quiet country road, a piece of grit got into her eye, she hit a grass verge and the car rolled over. She was trapped in the wreckage, and could smell petrol. She found her mobile and dialled 999. She was now panicking, fearing the rescue services would not arrive before her car blew up. Suddenly the panic subsided and a calm, comforting presence consumed her. Moments later a truck driver came racing over, and he pulled her free through the broken car door. When she was taken to hospital the medical staff and police could not understand how she survived the accident. She later pondered on why she thought she needed the protection of the bracelet. Then she realised that the accident had happened on the 15th anniversary of her father's death. He had been unable to prevent the accident, so had done everything in his power to protect her 'by first inspiring me to get the bracelet, and later being in the car to keep me calm'.[52]

- Shona was driving through Cornwall, with her husband in the passenger seat, when she saw a 'large animal' in the road. She hit it at 70 mph, and lost control of the car, which overturned into a ditch. She cried out for help and saw a 'white burst of light, and my life flashed right in front of my eyes'. She could see blood but felt no pain at all. Her shocked husband, like her, was trapped in the vehicle. Then an invisible energy pushed her forward, and she climbed out of the wreckage, but her husband could not manage to follow her. Two men then appeared out of nowhere and dragged Shona's husband to safety, and did first aid to stop Shona's bleeding. She needed only a few stitches in the hospital. She believed the light energy was divine intervention, and the two men were angels![53]

- Aliesha relates that on 14 January 2004 she wanted to beat the traffic lights. But a blue van hit her Mini side-on. She said it seemed to happen in slow motion, and she knew that she was injured. She blacked out for a few seconds. Then an odd thing happened. A woman with green hair had climbed into her car on the passenger side. She felt the woman wiping blood away from her head, telling Aliesha not to worry because an ambulance was on its way. Within minutes both the police and the medics arrived. Aliesha turned to thank the lady with green hair. But she had vanished.[54]

- Anne Hassett, a young woman in the early 1970s, who had already survived two near-fatal car accidents while driving with friends, was again in danger years later when her car blew a tyre while on the M5, and the vehicle slewed across the hard shoulder and flipped onto its roof. She was trapped by her seat belt while her friends screamed for her to get out because petrol was leaking. Then, out of the blue, a 'man in a brown jumper' pulled her free and cradled her until the ambulance arrived. But the other friends saw no one. Anne believed she had been saved by a male angel, and became a medium, giving psychic readings.[55]

- Sheila was driving with three friends, one in the front seat and two in the back. They were all chatting and laughing when suddenly a car cut in front of them and caused Sheila's car to somersault. The two front passengers were saved by their seat belts. 'I was certain,' she later said, 'that my friends in the back would be injured or dead – without seat belts on there was no way they could have survived – but when I looked round they were absolutely fine.' Sheila attributed this miraculous event to the supernatural. 'Sure, my hands were on the wheel, but I wasn't steering. Someone else was, someone else took over. I believe that someone was my guardian angel.'[56]

- A head-on crash killed several occupants in a car, with just one surviving. At that precise moment a man appeared out of nowhere, waving his arms and signalling to approaching cars that an accident had happened. Many cars stopped, and the man suddenly disappeared. He turned out to be one of the individuals who had actually died in the crash just seconds earlier. His immediately appearing ghost seemed to be projecting an image of himself to warn others.[57]

Finally, take the following case of a road phantom who actually seemed to promise free fuel for a stranded motorist. Stephen got lost while driving through a remote part of Scotland in the early 1980s. It was getting dark, snow was falling, and he knew he would shortly run out of fuel. He stopped alongside a parked car and asked the driver for help. The other man peered into Stephen's fuel tank and said, surprisingly, that he reckoned Stephen still had ten miles of petrol left, which would take him to the next filling station. 'Just follow me,' said the man, starting up his car. But when they came to a steep hill Stephen thought he would use up the remaining fuel too early – if there was any, with the petrol gauge showing virtually zero.

By now, however, the other car and its helpful driver had simply vanished into thin air, and there were no tracks in the snow to show that his car had ever been on the hill that they were labouring up a few minutes earlier. Stephen managed to fill up at a petrol station looming in the distance, but realised that his petrol gauge was accurate and he did actually run out of fuel completely about the time he met the other man. He couldn't have driven another mile, let alone ten.

Later, Stephen realised with some alarm that he couldn't recall anything about the man, his clothing, his hair colour, his voice, or the make of his car. It was as if the event had only happened in some kind of vague dream.[58]

# Chapter 10

## The Vanishing Hitchhiker Legends

Over the years, legends about hitchhikers who vanish from the back seats of cars have grown. A number of variants have been spawned since the 1930s. In most cases a young woman is picked up in rainy weather, or she is carrying a load, and says she lives just a short way away. Usually a desultory conversation takes place, then silence until the destination is reached. When the driver looks round the girl has vanished. According to the legend the driver goes to the address the girl has given him. He meets the parents or guardian who startle the driver by saying that their daughter or tenant had died some years earlier, often at the same spot where he had picked her up. They then often add that the driver is not the first to pick her up at that spot.

Variations on this theme are plentiful: the girl leaves a purse, or some item of clothing. Or sometimes the seat leaves an impression of someone who has sat there, and is warm to the touch, or if she is wet, the seat is damp. When the driver arrives at the girl's house he will be shown a picture of her wearing the same dress, or the relatives will produce a photo album and point her out.

In fact the vanishing hitchhiker is *the* classic automobile ghost legend. After the Great Depression it spawned a number of subtypes with oddly interlocking details, with different types of situational circumstances which various researchers try to spell out, and which can be adapted according to ghostly local legends. It became part of urban folklore, but had nuances of local detail.

Hitchhiking legends are to be found the world over, depending on the nature of local roads and varying conditions. But there are few hitchhiker legends coming out of Russia, or from parts of South America or China (surprisingly quite a few hitchhiking legends are to be found in Japan), perhaps because they do occur but escape the attention of English-speaking researchers.

One theory is that the legends relate to the vampiristic and anti-heroine characteristics common to European demon-lovers, and these were perhaps added to US folklore in the 1930s. The car and the hitchhiker had only 'general elements' of ancient European and American tales of wagons, carts and horse transport, all with their own versions of vanishing hitchhikers.[1] In other words the phenomenon is often culturally reinterpreted. They are hybrids – uneasy blends – of fact and fiction.[2]

It is interesting to note the 'Death Car' legend, where a used car is on sale at a cheap price because someone had earlier died in it, giving rise to later spooky incidents.[3] Decanus Fragaria, 51, relates such a spooky 'Death Car' experience in *Fate and Fortune* magazine. He saw a car advert for a red Toyota Corolla in someone's window. The woman who was selling it said it belonged to her dad, Ernest, who had recently passed away, and she wanted to sell it to someone 'who looked after it as carefully as he did'. Decanus bought the car, but within just a few days, as he was driving home one night, he sensed the presence of the previous deceased owner – an elderly man sitting next to him in the passenger seat, wearing a tweed jacket, with thinning grey hair and wire-rimmed glasses. Having some empathy with spiritual or psychic issues, Decanus knew the ghostly man – Ernest – would not cause him any harm, and 'just carried on driving … there seemed something sad about Ernest clinging on to the car that had meant so much to him'. After a while, however, Decanus suggested to the old man that it was 'time for him to move on', and soon after, Ernest vanished.[4]

Mary bought a second-hand yellow Mini from a garage, but things spookily started to go wrong. She was momentarily trapped inside when the door locks went down, only to disengage themselves moments later. The headlights dimmed and brightened by themselves, and there were other engine and light failures. The garage could find nothing wrong with the electrics. Then, on a country road near Birmingham, the car ground to a halt, and Mary saw a shadowy male silhouette on the back seat. Screaming, she spun round, but the figure had vanished. Then the car came back to life. Using a Ouija board when she got home, she learned that someone had been killed in the Mini and presumably the car had been rebuilt, so the ghostly image in the back seat had been the dead owner.[5]

However, the negativity about the Death Car has been constantly updated since the 1930s, where other horrors or peculiarities – including dead animals having been found in the vehicle – have devalued the car's saleable value. The basic plot of the hitchhiker story – 'something rather odd about that car' – becomes more important than the incidental details of dates and places, because the storyline can always be altered.[6]

The reason that the hitchhiker legends predominate more in the US could be because of the larger degree of ownership of cars in the 20th century, which had a significant effect on social customs and mores. The auto had allowed youngsters to separate themselves from their family and even from the company of peers.

The ghost, often but not exclusively, is an attractive young woman in white or light-coloured clothing (even in winter), giving rise to the hitchhiker expression 'Women in White' (see Chapter 13). The driver would sometimes give the girl his coat, and she is always taken – at least at the time she is picked up – for a real person. Nevertheless, in many cases she is not real, because she would (sometimes traditionally in the folklore legends) reappear on the anniversary of her demise (a road accident or a murder, or some other death-dealing tragedy). Another familiar scenario often emerges: a woman has just come from a party or dance hall, and appears in a bloodied dress, and is suspected of being the likely victim of a road accident. She waits passively at the roadside or walks along it late at night.[7]

In many cases she approaches her future testimonial witnesses, often flagging down male rather than female drivers, and becomes so legendary that some male motorists hope that this will happen to them; to be flagged down by a young woman in a nightgown or flimsy dress. Although lone male drivers are more likely to be out at night, it is at the same time surprising that female hitchhikers would also be about. Poor weather conditions and rainfall are a necessary ingredient in the legends, encouraging drivers to give females a lift. And this also enables the credibility of a story that can be checked with weather records.

Indeed, many of these female phantoms will get into a male driver's car, either through opening the door herself, or just suddenly emerging in the back seat. The only singular difference seems to be the girl's hair colour – more often blonde but occasionally dark, but seldom with tints in between. Indeed, the reference to ghostly paleness, or to long fair hair, or to the absence of skin tone or clothing colour – the 'Woman in White' syndrome – is curious. If a topcoat is worn it is invariably tinted light grey or fawn – it is seldom of a dark colour.

## Beginning Hitchhiker Legends

A vanishing hitchhiker in the traditional mould, fulfilling the convention, occurred in Horsham, Sussex, at a junction along the A24. The girl gave the driver her phone number. She vanished, and when the driver rang the number the usual explanation was given – she died in an accident years earlier near where he picked her up.[8] Some variations of this story say she was picked up outside a Horsham café. The most important legend – about which I shall devote considerable attention in the next chapter – relates to the famous 1965 north Kent story about a dead bride-to-be, and whose ghost apparently seeks a ride back to her home town, which is usually regarded as Maidstone.

In the early 1970s an unnamed motorcyclist picked up a girl who said she lived in Gillingham. When he arrived at her road he felt the girl slip off his motorbike, but when he stopped he could find no trace of her.[9] At Rayleigh, Essex, a woman was killed some time in the late 1950s in a motorbike crash on the A127, where her ghost often stands. She flags down cars, telling drivers that she is looking for her boyfriend (also killed in the crash), and asks to be taken to the Blinking Owl Café, where she and her boyfriend were headed. This is a similar case to that of the young woman who asks drivers to search the road for her boyfriend who came off his bike – and who vanishes on the road while the hapless driver goes on a fruitless search, although this woman vanishes from the car.

A phantom female hitchhiker is said to have plagued the Queensway Tunnel under the Mersey. The legend dates back to the

1960s, when a young woman riding pillion on a motorbike fell off and later died from her injuries. But this could not actually be verified by the tunnel authorities and the police. Nevertheless, there were other rumours of accidents in the tunnel, and there were two episodes in the 1980s that were personally experienced by two tunnel police officers. A woman hitchhiker was thumbing a lift dangerously near the portal entrance to the tunnel on a narrow hard shoulder where pedestrians are forbidden to walk, and where it would have been virtually impossible for any driver to stop. Yet the same woman had been sighted by several other motorists at exactly the same illogical spot. In both cases the police individually or together returned via the adjacent Wallasey Tunnel to apprehend the woman, but she had vanished.[10]

Blackwall Tunnel between Greenwich and Tower Hamlets had a typical hitchhiker vanishing story, and it is repeated several times. The victims are always on a motorbike. The hitchhiker can be either female or male, and can be at either the north or south entrance to the tunnel. But as they always ask to be taken to Leigh-on-Sea, Essex, it is more likely that they will be hitching at the north entrance. Then they vanish.[11]

A young motorcyclist named Harold Weaver Smith, while travelling along the A6 in Greater Manchester around the year 1990, thought that a young woman, holding a motorcycle helmet had thumbed a lift. He stopped further on, looked back and tooted his horn to attract her attention, but she had vanished. Some years later he read a ghost story in a book about another motorcyclist, riding the same model of motorbike, and also in the Manchester area, who had given a young woman a lift on the pillion, but she had vanished by the time the biker had reached her house. At the house the elderly parents came up with the familiar legend – the hitchhiker's description matched that of their daughter who had died in a motorbike accident years earlier.[12]

## Hitchhiking Ghosts

The male hitchhiker is potentially more menacing and, as we shall see, more frightening and ghostlike. There are several cases where the haunting characteristics loom large. Strange people, uninvited, suddenly appear in the passenger seat of a driver's car – or in the back seat.

Mrs Jean Clarke's experience goes back to the immediate post-war years. The hitchhiker in this case, and his subsequent behaviour, clearly showed him to be ghostly. Jean was driving a shooting brake on the Suffolk–Essex border in 1950 when a strange man suddenly appeared beside her in the passenger seat, dressed in a long fawn coat. The man did not speak and just pointed. Soon he gesticulated that he wanted to end his journey; 'Then,' said Mrs Clarke, 'he just floated through the door. I thought he must have opened it silently while I was watching the road ahead … shortly afterwards I discovered that I was in the village of Borley, though at the time it had no significance to me.' Then she mentioned the well-known haunting of Borley Rectory, and wondered if there might be a connection.[13]

There are other cases of voiceless hitchhikers, just pointing to the distance. Roy Fulton, aged 26 in October 1979, was driving his van through flat, open countryside to Stanbridge, Bedfordshire, on his way home to Dunstable. At a halt at a junction, a young man wearing dark trousers, jumper and a white shirt walked to Roy's van and silently opened the passenger door and let himself in. When Roy asked him where he was going, the silent man, sitting beside him in the front passenger seat, merely pointed ahead. He did later, however, grunt the word 'Totternoe' – a village beyond Stanbridge. As Roy approached Totternoe, he offered the man a cigarette, but he had vanished. There was no way he could have exited the car without Roy knowing, and he was travelling at 45 mph. Still, as so often, there was surprising evidence that this *was* a real person he had picked up. After he left the vehicle Roy found the passenger seat to be warm.[14] Indeed, Roy later said there was nothing unreal about the man – he was very solid – but he did look unnaturally pale and had a rather long face, topped off with a crop of short, dark curly hair. Indeed the stranger's reality was confirmed by the interior light coming on when he opened the van door. The Dunstable police found nothing unusual at the spot, but according to the *Dunstable Gazette* of 18 October 1979 a young man had been run down and killed by a drunk driver 'years ago'. His body was found at the exact spot that Roy picked up the hitchhiker.

In Nunney, Somerset, in 1977, a phantom road ghost – or a ghostly hitchhiker – gained adverse publicity which virtually jeopardised some street anniversary celebrations. The male figure that was in the middle of the road at the time was thought to be the victim of a fatal fright he received when he himself gave a lift to a hitchhiker – either male or female – who dematerialised from his car. The figure in the road caused other drivers, having heard of the legend, to swerve and crash. Thus the ghost became a road hazard in the conventional sense, and a posse of local investigators became active to 'trap' it.[15]

Tim had travelled from Suffolk on his way to Liverpool when he stopped to fill up at the Watford Gap service station. He returned to his car and found a stranger standing by the passenger door, who asked for a lift to Birkenhead. Tim reluctantly agreed. They chatted desultorily on the trip, and soon they neared Liverpool. Tim told his passenger he would drop him off at Woodside. 'As chance would have it,' he later recalled, 'I pulled up outside a police station. He got out, shook me by the hand and I drove away. As I looked in the mirror, he disappeared from view.'[16]

In the early hours at some date in the year 1996, a taxi driver – Raymond Breakspear – picked up what he thought was another customer. But the man disappeared from the back seat of the cab within minutes, or even seconds. Raymond had heard no sign of the door being opened, and neither had the interior light come on.[17]

A young policeman was driving his own car near Llanrhos, which is close to Llandudno in Wales. The year was probably 1960, and it was night-time and raining. When he reached a bend in the road near the local church he saw a hooded figure dressed in what he thought was a duffel coat, and pulled up to offer a lift, but the figure suddenly vanished. After he retired from the police, he wrote a letter about his experience to a retired police officers' journal. He received a letter from an officer whose father, in the 1930s, had seen a hooded figure at that same spot. It was surmised that perhaps it was the ghost of one of the local monks who had carried large stones to supply the masons building the Llanrhos church.[18]

Irene Allen-Block and her husband, Brian, were driving to Bristol Airport from their home in Wales on 14 February 2018. Their satellite navigation seemed to play up at about 4 a.m., and they stopped to ask an elderly pedestrian for directions. He explained that he liked to go for (very) early morning walks, and said he could show them the way, and got into their car without an invitation. He got out of the vehicle when they reached the airport. When Brian pulled a ticket out of the car park machine, he looked round, but the elderly man had disappeared, but it was unclear where he could have gone to in just a second or two. Perhaps he was a morphing apparition, because

Irene's and Brian's description of him and his clothing differed quite substantially.[19]

## The 'Man in the Mac'

The unknown 'Man in the Mac' is a common occurrence, and it is rather unnerving to know that the same kind of figure, wearing the same kind of apparel and being of the same age, reoccurs on Lancashire roads. Further, he is never picked up as a hitchhiker, but appears in the same garb in motorists' back seats. Is it always the same ghost? There is, in fact, a difference between the hitchhiker who thumbs a lift and halts a car, and the ghostly back-seat passenger who appears out of nowhere, but often the two phenomena are mixed up in the paranormal road literature.

The 'Long Mac' character resurfaces regularly. At Taunton, on the A38 in the year 1970, a potential hitchhiker in a long grey coat stands by the roadside. A similar character in Shropshire, if he is not offered a lift, throws himself under the vehicle, according to the county database. The 1970 event was a re-enactment by a ghost because several times the self-same man, doing the same suicidal gesture, vanished. Further proof of this ghostly event occurred again in 2016. It was described as the same man, right down to the long grey coat.

But the Man in the Mac can be truly frightening. A Mrs H described how, driving along Narrow Lane near a junction in Halsall, West Lancashire, on a winter's night in the 1990s, she had halted her car at a junction. She bent forward to see if the road was clear, and could see, out of the corner of her eye, the misty figure of a large elderly man in a grey gabardine coat with a scarf, tied like a cravat, in the back seat. She said later she was not frightened, but her immediate reaction was one of 'I've got a ghost in the back of my car. If I can get back home quickly then I can show my husband!' But of course, as usual, the man had vanished long before she got home.[20]

Similarly, Mrs B of Southport was driving alone along the main A570 trunk road from Ormskirk in a late evening in October 2004. She had the feeling there was someone in the car with her, before seeing, with a shock just minutes later, a man sitting in the passenger seat next to her as she approached the Leeds–Liverpool canal. She described him as wearing a woollen winter coat and a hat. Her attention was momentarily distracted, and when she turned back he had gone. She was not frightened, but the following day mused on the strangeness of the event.[21]

In February or March 1965, 'Bill' was driving along Gregory Lane towards Ormskirk when he saw in his rear-view mirror the figure of a large elderly man in the back seat of his Mini. Bill noticed his flat cap, mac and grey scarf, tied – as usual – in a cravat style. Frightened, he pulled up the car, and got a large metal tool from the boot. But the old man had vanished. Bill became scared and drove off at speed, knowing that the event was not caused by the poor light conditions or an hallucination. Some years, later Bill met a man at a social event who had virtually the same experience at the same place.

Rob Gandy, mentioned earlier, who had described this event in the 1990 winter edition of the *Fortean Times*, went back in 2014 to find out if any repetitions had occurred. The local paper in Ormskirk helped out by appealing for new witnesses of similar events, without giving any descriptive clues about the old Man in the Mac experiences of fifty years earlier, but misleadingly referred to them as phantom hitchhiker stories – i.e. people who had been 'picked up'. Trying to check these stories out without giving information away, Gandy also did not refer specifically to the strange 'Old Man of Halsall Moss', who would stand in the road and cause other disturbing and unnatural events to occur (see Chapter 11).

A woman from west Lancashire, in late 1998, thought she had picked up a Roman ghost. It was a dark, misty early evening, and she was heading towards Aughton. She soon had the impression that a man had got into her car, and was sitting directly behind her. She was too scared to look in the rear-view mirror, or turn round and look at him. She kept saying the Lord's Prayer and hoped for protection against evil. The feeling of terror gradually lessened as she continued driving. A sense of relief overwhelmed her when she slowed down at a crossroads near a well-known pub, and the man seemed to exit the car without actually opening the door. She managed to get a glimpse of him heading for the pub, and saw that he was probably in his late forties, but strangely wearing a leather skirt or apron. So he could not have been the legendary Man in the Mac. She said later she was amused about the incident, but added that 'the hitchhiker was not of this century, he had belonged to another time … perhaps the mist had activated an old memory of someone getting into my car at another time … the explanation I felt most comfortable with was that I had picked up a presence of a man from centuries before – even a Roman, as he had that leather apron on – who wanted to get to that hostelry. I understand that the Moss [in that haunted part of Lancashire] was used after many battles of different sorts, to throw bodies into it.'[22]

Unconnected and simultaneous occultic events once happened to Samantha and Philip, from Portrush, N. Ireland. They were returning by car from a visit to a friend. Dozy and reclining in her seat, Sam felt fingers running through her hair, and noted with alarm that Philip's hands were still on the steering wheel. Philip then admitted that a short while earlier he had seen a 'tall, black shadowy figure' by the side of the road, and it was not the first time while driving he had seen such apparitions, which seemed to be forebodings about future car crashes. Indeed one had happened to Philip earlier. The shadowy roadside figure occurred again just two days after Samantha's unnerving experience, and sure enough the two of them in the car had a serious accident with the car turning over. Philip believed that the shadowy figure with its warnings was the ghost of his caring granddad.[23]

Cab drivers and owners are victims of hitchhikers in another sense. Sometimes the owners of cabs or commercial vehicles wilfully neglect to tell their drivers of any strange events, the obvious reason being the likelihood of putting off the driver who would be naturally fearful of hauntings. A driver of a newspaper delivery vehicle for a newsagents in the 1970s in Birmingham, during the dead of night, suddenly saw a face in his rear-view mirror of a man in the back of the Transit van, one of several supplied by the depot. When he looked round there was no one there. This happened two nights running. He asked his foreman whether there was anything odd about the particular vehicle he was driving. The foreman said that it had been stolen one night, and had been found abandoned in Manchester a couple of days later. This led the driver to suspect that some kind of psychic imprint had been left in the van.[24]

- Derek Halliwell, a taxi driver in Kendal, Lancashire, in July 1974 saw, in his rear-view mirror, an unknown elderly woman in his back seat. Startled, he pulled over, but she had vanished. He resumed his journey only for the woman to reappear. Scared, he drove on until she vanished again, presumably for good. Another passenger told him that the woman was the ghost of someone who had been killed in in the rear seat of that same cab two years earlier, but the cab proprietors never passed this information on to Derek himself.[25]

- Alan, at about 3 a.m. on a Sunday in June or July in the late 1990s, was driving his taxi on Gregory Lane towards Birkdale, when an elderly man with a cap suddenly appeared in front of his vehicle. He disappeared.[26]

- At Titchfield, Hampshire, on the A27, at various times during the 20th century, a phantom monk appeared in the back seat of cars, and vanished once seen by the driver.

- At Leighton Buzzard, in the 20th century, a van driver picked up a young male hitchhiker, who vanished after a few moments.

- At Brandon, in Suffolk, on the A 1065 towards Lakenheath, at 6 a.m. one day in 2011, a woman driver saw a young teenage lad in her back seat, who, of course, promptly vanished. A male driver saw the same spooky event in February 2014.

- In Wybunbury, Cheshire, on the A51, a driver picked up a hitchhiker in motorbike leathers. It was on 20 October 1996. The young man soon vanished, but the driver was startled to note that the seat belt was still in place, and the car door was locked.

- At Calverton, Nottinghamshire, at George Lane and at George Hill, in the 20th century, a hitchhiker materialised in a back seat at both these locations. On the George Lane occasion it was an old lady, and on the Hill a black-hooded figure was seen in the rear-view mirror.

- One evening in 1973 a Mrs Taylor was driving on New Road, Taunton, Somerset, when she encountered a middle-aged man in a long grey overcoat standing in the middle of the road, seemingly searching for something. She swerved, but when she got out of her car to admonish him, he vanished.[27] This might have been the same figure seen again in the Taunton area, as well as on the A38.

- At Colchester, Essex, on the Mersea Road, in a hitchhiking case, a woman driver happened to momentarily glimpse a teenage youth in her rear-view mirror. When she turned her head the vision vanished, only for her to see the youth again in the mirror when she returned to face the road. And at Pebmarsh, not far away, a recurring vision occurs – on 'stormy nights' – of the ghost of a monk which dashes across the road.

- At 10 p.m. on 29 July 2006, at Poynters Lane, North Shoebury, Essex, a woman driver swerved to avoid a man in a striped polo-style top who simply stepped out of a nearby hedge before disappearing. According to the Essex archives he was a 'well-known phantom'.

- At an abandoned air base at Lakenheath, Suffolk, in the spring of 1951, a phantom hitchhiker was an RAF pilot. He was clearly a Second World War ghost. As soon as he was picked up he vanished. At Felixtowe, Suffolk, at a crossroads, a driver saw a WW2 pilot in his back seat. When he reached a certain point the pilot vanished. No date is given for this.

- At the gatehouse of St. Osyth priory, a figure of unknown gender appeared in the back of a young man's car, then disappeared.

- One rainy night in Staffordshire, around 1990, a motorist saw a beleaguered motorcyclist standing on a motorway slip road, holding an apparently empty petrol can. He pulled up and agreed to give the motorcyclist a lift to the Keele service station to fill up his can. Shortly after, the driver returned to the motorway, with the motorcyclist sitting next to him. He turned to speak to him, but he had vanished.[28]

- At Cinderford, Gloucestershire, in 2010, a driver offered a lift to a person at half past midnight who was waiting at a bus stop after the last bus had gone. He vanished, as did the other person standing at the same place whom another driver saw on 12 February 2012 at 7 p.m.

- At Ormskirk in 1965 an old man wearing a cap suddenly appeared in someone's back seat. Again he vanished. The Lancashire database says a similar back-seat apparition also happened in the town in 1970.

- At Saffron Walden in Essex, in November 1983, the ghost of a USAF pilot killed in 1943, on returning to Britain from a sortie, appeared in the back seat of a woman's car as she drove past the crash site.

- At Clyst St Mary, Devon, in 2002, some witnesses reported a soldier who appeared unannounced in passenger seats on the neighbouring route to Clyst St George.

- At Greenfield, in Clwyd, Wales, in 1961, a driver saw an old man in his 'passenger seat', presumably the seat next to him. The old man had a cap and walking stick. The report says the driver was so frightened, he got out of his car and literally ran off. After some while he forced himself to return to his car, to find the man 'gone'.

- At Rugeley, Staffordshire, on the A460 between Rugeley and Hednesford, on several occasions in the 1980s and in 2001, a phantom nun with a 'disturbing face' appeared in car rear seats. But she was never visible in the rear-view mirror, only when the driver turned round, presumably after seeing a movement out of the corner of his eye.

- A driver said a girl had flagged him down in wet weather outside a cemetery in Waterlooville, Hampshire. During the journey the girl said very little. He arrived at the address he had been given to let her out, but she had vanished, leaving behind a wet imprint on the seat.[29]

- At Tangham, Suffolk, in the late 19th and early 20th centuries, a woman in white suddenly appeared in a horse and cart driven by a male driver – an early hitchhiker story. She vanished as soon as the horse and cart reached nearby woods.

- At Scunthorpe, Lincolnshire, on a lay-by near Keadby Bridge, a taxi driver picked up a young girl, who asked to be dropped off near a football ground. The year was 2001. Like all the others, she vanished.

- In November 1974, cab driver Mr Brian Mohan caught sight of a mature lady in his back seat while he was driving along the A6 to Stockport, Greater Manchester. She had long hair, and was wearing a black coat, white blouse and a black bow. When he pulled aside the glass partition she had already vanished. He stopped the car, checked it over and looked up and down the street, but could not see her anywhere. The cab remained in the firm's yard for months afterwards, as none of the drivers were prepared to take it out.[30]

## Hitchhikers – Real or Not?

The notion that the disappearing car-rider is a modern version of a ghost is the inevitable, if reluctant, position to take. Further, a question arises as to whether the hitchhiker is a ghost to begin with, or then disappears to become a ghost. Or is he or she a phantasm or a hologram, or *a potential* ghost?

Drivers might be forgiven for thinking that they had picked up a normal female, especially one that was waiting outside a pub. In addition, all hitchhiking cases can't automatically be *untrue.* Most of the hitchhiker stories do have their own internal consistency because others have the same experience in the same area, and police feel the need to go to investigate. But without the paranormal explanation, and without a definite or credible destination, the hitchhiker story is dangled in the air. It becomes an incomplete phenomenon, either because the girl is already dead (which naturally poses enormous explanatory problems), or the occupant of the house the driver is directed to denies any knowledge of her – at least of her still being alive. Is there any connection between the ghostly antics seen on the roads, and those seen in other historical circumstance? Are they all part of the same syndrome? Is the vanishing hitchhiker, a subject which Brunvand tried to tackle in his excellent book of that title, in other words, part of the haunting of British (and American) roads? A valid reason for road hauntings is the tragic loss of life on them – invariably untimely and violent – which outstrips all other forms of transport deaths involving planes, trains and ships. Between 1951 and 2006 there were 309,144 deaths on British roads. There were 3,400 deaths in 2000, declining to 1,700 in 2013.[31]

But there are puzzling divergences in the hitchhiker legends: the paranormal aspect is not always understood or believed in. Some hitchhiker accounts dwell on the ghostly aspects, and other researchers refer to the degree of police involvement, and other verifiable features in the road travelled, and how plausible would be the experiences of drivers. Indeed it could be asked – in view of the predominance of women hitchhikers – whether sexual connotations play a sublime, unconscious, but on the whole a duplicitous role. Some male drivers must think they are being double-crossed by their female hitchhiker. Indeed the one impression that gives credence to the ghost theory – that the hitchhikers are not real people – is that the young women show no apprehension about being picked up by male drivers. They have no fear or expectation of carnal experiences. Indeed, some researchers into this phenomenon, and its ghostly connotations and parallels, ask whether even a conversation with the girl – now assumed to be a ghost – happens.[32]

Michael Goss attempts throughout, in his book *The Evidence for Phantom Hitchhikers*,[33] to evaluate the credibility of the hitchhiker stories before putting them into various factual or legendary categories, and then examining the legends themselves as part of folklore or hearsay, or long-lost true events that have been borrowed after they have themselves acquired an occultic character. Goss thus dismisses most paranormal explanations as being part of a secular folklore, and more likely adhering to a folklore motif.[34]

# Chapter 11

## The Phantom Jaywalker

The 'jaywalker' is someone who clumsily or blindly steps out into a busy traffic-clogged road. This is a common feature in road accidents involving pedestrians around the world. Many, of course, get killed in the process. So it would not be surprising, if you believe in ghosts, that a spiritual copy of the unfortunate jaywalker will sometimes appear in the same road, often on the same calendar date that they died, to be run over again by another motorist.

The Phantom Jaywalker legend is the haunted highways story that has evolved into the modern anxiety of being involved in a road accident. The hitchhiking legend is often confused with, or is dependent on, the phantom woman who can either step into the road – as if trying to stop a car for the purpose of a ride – or instead seems to deliberately get knocked down.

Strange silhouetted figures have been seen in streets or lanes; shadow men and with fluttering cloaks, densely black, but with no features on the face. They were either extremely tall or very short, and non-human in appearance. Unrecognisable figures walk down the street or dodge through traffic, only to disappear suddenly. Michael Goss says that the spectral jaywalker and phantom hitchhiker are two syndromes that are different, while Sean Tudor says they are more similar, and are aspects of the same phenomenon.[1] The repeated feature is the driver knocking a person down only to find – when he gets out of his car – no body, no blood or anything else. There is no dent in the car, inevitably, because the person is a phantom.

In many cases the 'Woman in White' – so called because of the predominance of female apparitions on the road, often blonde, and because of the pale clothing they tend to wear – is the victim of murder, road accident, suicide or other tragedy. Nevertheless, it cannot be said for sure that most of the jaywalkers, male and female, reported in the various paranormal databases, are actual ghosts. They often appear to drivers to be real, solid people who dangerously cross over a busy highway in front of them, or are seen at the edge of it ready to do so. They would be the cause of anxiety about running over someone. A close reading of the narrative from the archives – and too often there is insufficient information about the event – could give some clue as to whether the jaywalker is a 'phantom' in the accepted sense These apparitions often appear (in both senses) to be real flesh-and-blood people stepping out to collide bizarrely with the bonnets of motorists' cars, only to vanish virtually immediately. But the belief that the unfortunate driver has experienced a ghostly encounter comes from police reports of their regularity on the same stretches of road.

One reason for police involvement in many hitchhiker cases is the concern about road safety, even extending to warnings that local people should not spread road ghost rumours on pain of punitive fines.[2] There are virtually identical stories in France and Spain, also with road hazard warnings which car drivers try to ignore.

According to Bob Sturgeon, who used to run a roadside snack van at Carrutherstown close to Kinmount Straight, Dumfries and Galloway in Scotland, many traumatised lorry drivers had told him about jaywalking ghosts. They had seen groups of bedraggled people, pulling handcarts and carrying bundles, trudging along, which were possible hauntings from centuries earlier.[3] In other cases the colliding vehicle experiences nothing, and simply 'passes through' whatever person or persons the hapless driver has struck, as in the case of the three male figures in Victorian clothing walking across the road at Whittlesford, Cambridgeshire, on 4 January 2005. The vehicle went straight through them. There was a similar typical case at Acle, on the A47 in Merseyside, on 30 March 2009, where the jaywalker walked in front of a car, and turned to look at the driver while the car passed through him. The area was traditionally known to be haunted by a horse and cart.

At some date in 1981, at Carmarthen, Dyfed, Wales, on the A40 between the town and Llangathen, a lorry driver saw a parked pick-up truck and three men standing about it. Then, bizarrely, one of the men pushed another into the path of his lorry, but the driver felt no bump. Alarmed, he was about to stop, when he noticed in his side view mirrors that not only the man he thought he had collided with, but also the other two men, and even the truck, had all vanished.

A cyclist pulled out in front of Phillip Baum's car on 9 August 2001, on the A12 between Ipswich and Lowestoft at about 10 p.m., and he felt an impact. Mr Baum stopped, got out and checked all around the car and underneath, and there was no sign of the cyclist or his pushbike. He ran back to ask other stopped motorists if they saw anything: they didn't.[4]

At Warrington, Cheshire, on the A50, on the road leading to Knutsford, a driver passed a man trying to flag him down. It was May 1955, and the man had the typical 1950s dark clothing and slicked back grey hair. The driver halted some yards further down the road, wondering whether to pick the man up, but to his surprise found him barely 6 feet behind his car. It was impossible, he thought, for the figure to have reached that spot in so short a time.

At 10.30 p.m. one evening in October 1956, Mr Frederick Moss was driving with friends, all in their sixties, away from Marlborough, Wiltshire, when his headlights lit up a thin elderly man standing in the middle of the road near a memorial stone, and wearing a long brown mac. The figure ignored Mr Moss's car horn, so, thinking that something was wrong, or the man was ill, Mr Moss stopped a couple of yards distant. For a moment all four occupants stared, surprised and uneasy. Mr Moss then opened the car door – and inevitably the figure disappeared. It turned out that in 1879 a 14-year-old boy had tragically died in when he was crushed beneath the wheels of an overturned heavily laden cart on a quiet Wiltshire road between Marlborough and Hungerford. A tiny memorial plaque exists, and is said to mark the spot where Henry Pounds Watts, the boy's father, had died in 1907.[5]

In 1960 on the A12 between Great Yarmouth, Norfolk, and Lowestoft, Suffolk, a lorry careered off the road and killed the driver when it smashed into trees. The coroner recorded an open verdict. The same thing happened to another car driver some twenty years later, who miraculously survived. Within a year a cyclist also swerved into the path of a car at the same spot. Shadowy figures have also been seen – the spectre of an old man standing in the slow lane – but cars just pass through the phantom. Former policeman Frank Colby, also of Lowestoft, claims to have seen a hunchbacked figure with long straggly hair on the A121. He just walks along the carriageway and disappears. It was probably, said local people, the ghost of a William Balls, a postman who was found dead during the winter of 1899.[6]

There are two notable cases of ghosts having been run down outside the Witton cemetery in Moor Lane in Birmingham. A plumber was travelling along the lane in the early hours of one day in 1966 when he had the sense of having a collision with someone. There was no trace of the person. He reported the incident to Queens Road police station, and the story was given local media publicity.[7] In 1995, a driver was also convinced he had run over a figure outside Witton cemetery. He also felt and heard the collision with his car's bonnet. But the victim vanished without a trace, and a futile police search ensued.[8]

In most jaywalker cases the entity simply vanishes from the centre or the side of the road. Curious jaywalking events happened in Hertfordshire, dating to before the Second World War. In the spring of 1935 a motorist at South Mimms saw a figure on the roadside flagging down travellers before vanishing.

In the post-war years at Batsford on the Lower Luton Road, a driver swerved to avoid an older man standing in the road. The driver later reckoned it was either March or May 2014. It was probably May because he reappeared then to two other witnesses, both of whom said his head was bandaged, and he held an old rifle. On the same road in 2011, in the early hours of the morning, a driver passed an older couple who vanished from his rear-view mirror.

A Bob Vandepeer claimed in a local newspaper that he witnessed, at Detling Hill on the A249, a man in a flat cap run out from a gate on the left, directly into the path of the car the witness was in, which was driven by a colleague. The year was probably 1972. The victim was struck 'head-on'. Both men jumped out, but there was no body or any evidence of an accident, only what looked like a handprint on the bonnet of their car. 'There was no way he could have crawled off. He would have been lying in the road seriously injured,' said Bob.[9]

On the A229, around the usual time of 2 a.m. (when most jaywalkers seem to appear), on Saturday 26 June 1999, a Bob Prowse was passing through the village of Hartley near the junction of the B2085 (where there had been at least one fatal accident) when he picked out a figure – just for a split instant – of a tall, blond-haired man on the road ahead, standing strangely erect and motionless. Doing 60 mph he screeched his car to a stop. He was convinced that at that speed he had run the man over. He paused, stunned, and eventually – slowly and cautiously – reversed his car to the spot. But he found nothing.[10]

It was a wet and unpleasant night when young Sophie Glessing was driving across the desolate marshes between Rye and Hankham, Sussex, where she lived, late at night on 9 November 1976. She turned off the coastal road onto an unclassified lane, now beginning to flood, but as she reached the crest of a hill her headlights lit up a well-known local character, a Mr Hawkley, trudging along towards his cottage at the top of the rise. He was known to have become rather eccentric since his wife had died a few years earlier. But Sophie was astonished to see him, on this bleak and wet night, wearing only green and pink pyjamas, a camel dressing gown and slippers. But he was by now only about twenty yards from his home, so Sophie didn't bother to stop and give him a lift. Accordingly, she waved cheerily and motored on her way. It would have been pointless anyway, because Mr Hawkley was actually a ghost. The following morning, when Sophie commented to her neighbour on Mr Hawkley taking such a strange nocturnal ramble, she learned that he had died three weeks earlier.[11]

# The Man Who Would Not Die

In many haunted highway stories the strange repeated occurrence of a man signalling or waving a torch at motorists is often reported. For example, in 1978 at Holcombe, Devon, on the A374, along the Teignmouth Road, a middle-aged man dressed in a grey coat used a torch to wave down motorists. In some reports it is assumed he was run over, but no body was found. In fact the 'The Man with the Torch' is a rather common ghostly scenario on British roads, and indeed is the counterpart to the 'Man in the Mac', as we shall see. He is mentioned in several paranormal databases and other sources; for instance, the same torch-waving event happened to a driver at Wellington, Somerset on the A38 and near to a hotel in the 1970s.

But the most extraordinary example of the torch-waving jaywalker was reported in *The Western Morning News* in August 1970, and has been acknowledged in other occultic sources. The A38, before the M5 was built, already had a dreadful haunted reputation in post-war Britain, especially the ten-mile stretch centred on Wellington in Somerset. *The Western Morning News* in August 1970 reported how a Mrs K. Swithenbank was driving late one evening from the village of Oake to Taunton when she saw a figure in the middle of the road immediately after she had rounded a bend. He appeared to be a late-middle-aged man in a long grey mackintosh, and was pointing a torch to the ground. But there was no time to brake, and she thought she had inevitably run over him. However, as so often, when she looked around, the road was completely clear in both directions.

But this was a 'black spot' for this particular apparition – he had been experienced before, the same figure with the torch – by two other motorists going around that bend near the Hetherton Grange Hotel. Other drivers and a motorcyclist said they saw a similar phantom only a few miles further away to the west – at a place called White Ball.

A lorry driver, a Mr Harold Unsworth, reading the local press reports, decided to reveal that he had been flagged down by a similar mackintosh-clad phantom while driving his lorry back from his depot at Cullompton at 3 a.m. some twelve years earlier. But he had kept quiet about it for fear of ridicule. The weather was foul, he said, and the man was hatless and soaking wet, revealing curling grey hair down to his collar. So Unsworth decided to give him a lift. The man asked to be dropped off at the old Beam Bridge at Holcombe. This figure, real or not, was an unusual rider in that he was talkative, but Mr Unsworth felt – from the man's conversation about gruesome accidents at the bridge – that his passenger was a bit too creepy for his liking. But days later, again travelling along the A38, Mr Unsworth saw the very same man again, in similar weather conditions, standing at the same spot. Once more Mr Unsworth gave him a lift in his lorry, and again dropped him off at the bridge. To be walking about in the early hours of the morning, in inclement weather and hitching a ride to the same spot, seemed to Mr Unsworth unusual, and when he saw him again just a week or so later he began to think it was incredible – the rain, the mackintosh, the torch and the conversation were the same each time. Perhaps the man was just mentally disturbed, and for a while the occurrences – at that particular location that Mr Unsworth passed frequently – stopped.

But in November 1978, just a couple of months later, like in a film loop, the man in the mackintosh bizarrely appeared again at the same place. Mr Unsworth again gave him a lift for a short journey. But three miles further on he could see, through the murk and the streaming rain, a torch being waved frantically to flag him down. When his headlights shone fully on the figure he noted, with growing alarm, that it was the same weirdo he had given a lift about twenty minutes earlier – he could see the same straggling grey hair and the grey mac. No vehicle had passed in either direction and it would have been impossible for the man to cover the distance –from the place where Mr Unsworth had left him further down the road – on foot at the time.

Then it became clear that the Man in the Mac was a phantom – or at least was about to transition into a phantom. As Mr Unsworth decided to drive on, he swerved to pass the figure. But as he did so, the man leapt in front of his lorry. But there was no impact: Mr Unsworth braked heavily and brought his vehicle to a halt. But the figure did not disappear suddenly – he could be seen still standing in the road, but to the rear of his lorry. Further, his reality was confirmed by the angry shaking of his fist, and his loud swearing. He was real enough – for a moment – or was he? The lorry, after all, had run him over, and he had been run over before by Mrs Swithenbank and others, but he was not dead or injured. But when Mr Unsworth looked back again, the man had vanished. For good this time. He was never seen again on the haunted A38.[12]

Cheryl Spicer was driving with her parents though Warminster, Wiltshire, one rain-sodden night in the mid 1960s. They suddenly saw the shape of a person in a long, shiny black raincoat and a shiny hat. He was flat out on his back with the rain pelting down into his face. They all felt rather guilty later as they drove on without asking if he needed help. About a week later, however, the mother had been speaking to a friend who said that a Ufo book had mentioned the very same phenomenon, in the same area, where the same figure in the same raincoat was seen (or at least it was wearing some kind of skin-tight black tunic which appeared to be glinting as if it was wet).[13]

Strangely, on the A12 near Hopton, Norfolk, the ghost of an old man with grey straggling hair was often seen before and often seen in collision with vehicles. On 2 November 1981, the figure confronted Andrew Cutajar in the middle of the road. But his vehicle seemed to pass right through it, causing Andrew to momentarily lose control in shock. Was this the same man lorry driver Mr Unsworth had picked up at Taunton?[14]

Paul and his mother were on a journey to visit a small community of Benedictine monks in the Leicester area, but they got lost in the environs of the city. Suddenly, driving down one unusually empty street, an uncanny silence descended. They spotted one old man in a grey overcoat, and stopped to ask where they could find the holy community. Paul and his mother had the strange sensation that the old man knew what they were going to ask him, with the gentle nodding of his head even as the first words were spoken. He told Paul that he knew the monks very well because he used to visit them a lot, and he gave road directions. They thanked him profusely, and went on their way. But as they looked back as they drove off, he had vanished into thin air, and the street had begun to get busy again. And the sound had returned.

When they arrived at the Benedictine community they told the monks what had happened and described the old man. Indeed, a man like that had once visited them often, one monk said. But he had died many years earlier of a heart attack.[15]

One night in 1973 a taxi driver on the A5 in Hertfordshire thought that he had literally collided with and actually driven through what he was thought was a cricketer dressed in white flannels. He pulled up and tried to look for the man, but in vain. This was indeed a ghostly apparition, because in 1958, on that very spot, two cricketers had died in a traffic accident.[16]

In Lount, Derbyshire, in a road outside a landfill site in the early 1980s, a driver thought he had killed a male jaywalking teenager. But there was no bump, no body was found and no damage to his car occurred. This aspect is always surprising, because a 'bump' ought to indicate a physical contact with something. The fact that nothing is sensed by some drivers seems as if a ghostly trick has been played on the road user. But the trick is an encompassing one: whether the driver experiences a real collision or not is irrelevant – no body is ever found. The ephemeral and unreal aspect of the ghostly encounter is strangely unaltered.[17]

At Ravenshead, Nottinghamshire, on the snowbound A60 in the winter of 1984–85, a jaywalker vanished in front of a car. Distressed by this, the driver called the police from a phone box, who actually found footprints on the road, but there was no body, indicating how such jaywalkers could at times assume a real solid identity but at other times are – or become – mere ghostly phantoms.[18]

First reported in 1998, shaken motorists claimed that a jaywalking male apparition often appeared along the A15 road at Sleaford, Lincolnshire, holding his hand up as if he wanted to halt the traffic. Another figure was little more than a black silhouette dashing across the road. Witnesses often felt that they had driven into him, but no one was found when they stopped to check. Margaret Green, who used to hold ghost walks through Lincoln, said the fleeting figure may have been the ghost of a young man killed in a speeding road accident. The other apparition may have been the same ghost warning drivers to reduce speed. Some connected this warning ghost with the 'Ruskington Horror', near Corby Grange, linked with a plague burial site.[19]

## 'The Old Man of Halsall Moss'

Rob Gandy refers to what has now become the legendary Halsall Moss area in Lancashire, a haunted area between Southport, Merseyside and Ormskirk, West Lancashire. In an article in *Fortean Times* magazine he referred to the elderly figure that was often seen in the road and then to vanish, who became known as the Old Man of Halsall Moss, so well known and reported on that he was shortened to OMHM.

Gandy highlights several weird but corroborated stories about OMHM. While driving home to Wigan in the early 1970s a man thought he had run over someone and got out to look for him, and inevitably found nothing. He contacted the police. In another case on a September evening in either 2010 or 2011 at about 10 p.m., a Miss W. of Formby was a passenger with friends travelling across Halsall to go to a party in Maghull. More friends followed in another car. When the two cars were in the Moss's open country they saw a man moving across the centre of the road, which the drivers and passengers guessed was New Cut Lane or Gregory's Lane. He appeared to be drunk, Miss W. later said, and was wearing old farmer-type clothing and a hat, of an earlier era. Both cars managed to avoid hitting the man, and both pulled up and turned round to check if the man was okay. This could have taken no more than two minutes. There were open fields on either side of New Cut Lane, with the road offering a clear view for miles. Yet the man had simply vanished. On the return journey on the following morning, at the same spot, they encountered a police investigation checking into the same event – the disappearing OMHM that a driver had reported to them.[20]

In another incident involving New Cut Lane that Rob Gandy cited in his *Fortean Times* article, a guy called John was driving his

E-type Jaguar at around 65 mph at 9.30 p.m. on a dark, wet night late in 1974. As he approached a bend he also saw the 'old farmer' in the middle of the road. Now a strange, frightening thing happened. As John swerved to avoid the figure his Jaguar 'took off' – literally – and flew into an adjacent field. The car ended up 50 feet from the road, facing the wrong way. The police arrived out of nowhere, and John was taken to a local hospital for a check-up. He soon recovered, and was driven at his request the next day to the field where his car landed, and he took photos of it *in situ* (which were reproduced in Rob Gandy's article).[21]

John assumed that people in a nearby farmhouse had alerted the police and ambulance service, but when he made enquiries with them they said they hadn't done so. Further, it was surprising how little damage was done to John's car, flung unaccountably into a field. An assurance assessor said the car 'must have flown like an aeroplane', actually turning in the air to end up facing the wrong way in the field. The E-type Jag was designed without a conventional chassis, and it should have broken up into pieces when it landed. Gandy's article does not say whether John contacted the rescue services to see who had actually reported the facts of this strange incident.[22]

There are often difficulties in determining, as we have seen, whether or not a solid human being has been struck. At East Hanney, Oxfordshire, on an unknown date, but presumed to be in the 20th century, a man in an overcoat and cap ran out in front of cars, 'but vanished on impact', according to the archives, which is an incomplete explanation because it does not reveal whether a bump or colliding sensation was experienced by the driver.

- On the A12, somewhere in Suffolk, a jaywalker was seen one late afternoon of a day in the winter of 1988, and also again in August 2001. Also in the 2000s in a Suffolk town, a driver and his wife travelling at 70 mph saw a cyclist pull out in front of their car. They felt the bump, but as usual there was no body.

- At Gillingham, Dorset, a motorist encountered a ghostly coffin being carried along the road. This particular road had the legend of this happening, and the coffin was said to have fallen from a horse-drawn cart. No date was given.

- At Billingshurst in Sussex, from October 1947 onwards, a tramp sits on a milestone, and then glides in front of traffic before vanishing. There were reports of this happening more often since later road updates occurred.

# Chapter 12

## Dangerous Phantoms across Britain

While most people consider monks to be holy men, and members of various Christian orders and denominations, they have nevertheless been responsible for many frightening and even menacing apparitions on Britain's roads. The number of sightings by motorists of 'monks', in their long cloaks and hoods, is quite extraordinary.

Suffolk seems to have been quite heavily populated by monks. At Thornham Parva in 1975, a cyclist passed two hooded monks in white. They actually greeted him, but he was shocked to find that their hoods were empty. At Wickham Market, near Putsford Wood on the B1078, in the 1980s, a truck driver who stopped for a call of nature near a plaque marking an old hangman's gibbet was tapped on the shoulder by a skeletal form in robes and hood. Later, in 1997, at the same place – near the plaque and gibbet – a couple whose car broke down one night were harassed by a shapeless object that approached their vehicle.

Other ghostly characters, in all kinds of garb, have been encountered many times, and fully documented in the various county paranormal databases.

- At Luton, on the Old Bedford Road, two in a car saw a 'tall black shadow' run through park railings on the road at 3.15 a.m. on 8 March 2012. The driver braked sharply, but the entity disappeared.

- At Newbury, on the roads around the White Swan pub circa 1955, an 'airman', said to be identified by an expert as wearing a World War I uniform from shortly after the RAF came into existence, was seen by two people in a car. He was offered a lift, as they assumed he was an actor or a member of an exhibition troupe. Of course he vanished. The paranormal database for Berkshire said that local people had known about this ghost for some time, but were reluctant to talk about it.

- At Kingsthorpe, Northamptonshire, the ghost of a cyclist who was killed in 1915 often reappears when the weather matches the day he died, and the apparition seemed to start in the winter of 1940. Significantly, the road passes by a cemetery, although the archives do not make clear whether his body was buried there.

- At Ash Magna, Shropshire, in the 1970s, a motorcyclist saw a ghostly hooded monk floating about a foot off the ground.

- In Sussex, at the junction of the A272 and A24, an old jaywalker appeared in front of a motorcyclist in October 1947. The rider felt the impact, retained his balance, halted and returned to the scene. The old man had vanished.

- On the Isle of Skye in the 1950s a driver saw headlights in the distance while travelling on a narrow and isolated road. He pulled over and waited, but nothing came. There was no turning or exit road that the other car could have turned into.

- At Caterham in Surrey on 28 July 1963 a motorist saw eight monks in black cloaks and cowls 'running and leaping around' in a strange manner.

- At Hullavington, Wiltshire, near the Burton House school at 6 a.m. one morning in January 1967, a man in grey was standing in the middle of the road. He raised his arm and vanished.

- At Lamport, in the 1970s, on the road between Market Harborough and Northampton, a lorry driver ran over a figure, presumably a monk, in a brown habit. This haunting was also known to local people, as pedestrians had also seen it carrying a 'bright light'.

- At Woodborough, Nottinghamshire, in 1971 on the road to Allington, an ancient figure, another 'Cavalier' type, was seen with a dog.

- At Cobham, Surrey, on the A3, on 27 November 1965, a musical group in a car all saw a figure in an army greatcoat, with a strange glow and hollow eye sockets.

- At Hindhead, Surrey, on 24 September 1971 a tattered jaywalker emerged, possibly, according to legend, the ghost of a sailor murdered in 1786.

- At Gretna in the county of Dumfries in 1957, a lorry driver, while travelling along the Sark Bridge Road, narrowly missed hitting two middle-aged jaywalkers. He stopped to shout at them. And then – a common feature – they vanished. In this case a 'ghostly' car was also seen in the vicinity.

- At Debenham, Suffolk, on 4 January 1973, a van was in collision with a jaywalker – a cloaked figure who ran off into a verge.

- At Nunney, Wiltshire, heading towards Frant in 1977, there was another case of a 'vanishing hitchhiker' but no details were given.

- At the Eton waterworks a World War II figure was seen. No date was given for this. In the same area a local policeman from an earlier era used to join a watchman for a cup of tea. But the cop's footsteps could still be heard patrolling the area long after he had died.

- At Upton Grey, Hampshire, in June 1993 at 10 a.m., a man saw the ghost of a shepherd with two dogs – a known relative of the witness. He died a few days later.

- At Haddenham, Buckinghamshire, on a road between villages, motorists often experienced omens. A man called Noble Ebden was murdered on the road, and his ghost appeared at the corner to warn of encroaching danger.

- At Longstanton, Cambridgeshire, on an unknown date but assumed to be near where a big cat was seen in 1966, a driver saw a shadowy figure on the roadside with no facial features. He vanished from the rear-view mirror.

- At Capesthorne, Cheshire, in 1999, a monk appeared on the road, but had no feet. The driver stopped, but the vision promptly vanished.

- At Church Lawton, on the Liverpool Road West, a driver saw an entirely grey figure on the pavement – the clothing, the features, the hands. The date was 9 September 2011. The entity vanished when the driver slowed and drew parallel to get a better look.

- At Winsford a cyclist saw a man drifting along the road on 18 November 2010, at twenty minutes past midnight. He wore a long heavy coat and a large trilby. When eye contact was made the entity vanished.

- At Bude, Cornwall, at some time in the 1970s, a group of miners in very dated clothing were seen tramping down Catstock Road. One assumes from the database that this was at night, because another surprising aspect was the fact that the men were carrying lit candles! (This seems unlikely, and could have been a bizarre ghostly joke played on the motorists.)

- At Camelford, Cornwall, in 1984, a grey figure trotted along the road before vanishing.

- At Cremyll, Cornwall, on the B3247 leading to the ferry terminal, a driver saw a shadow of a short man with a cloak but with no legs cross the road. It was 7 p.m. on some date in July 2004.

- At Barrow-in-Furness, Cumbria, at a disused shipyard, a shadowy figure was seen in either 2005 or 2006.

- At Hillsley, Gloucestershire, on no particular date, ghostly monks cross the road between Hillsley and Hawksbury.

- At Chorley Wood, Hertfordshire, at Chenies Hill at 11.30 p.m. on New Year's Eve 2014, a shadowy figure apparently blended itself into a nearby fence after dashing across the road, a vision which was witnessed by a driver looking back at the road in his mirror.

- At Ashton Flamville, Leicestershire, near a churchyard in the 1980s, presumably in daylight, a passenger saw only the moving 'upper torso' of a male figure in the road.

- At Broughton Astley, on the B581, a grey hooded figure walked in front of a car with two occupants. It was 10.30 p.m. on the night of 11 August 2014. The driver braked suddenly and the two of them watched in stunned silence as the figure slowly vanished near a gate.

- On the A11 between Norwich and London, recurring in January and February after 6 a.m., a lone figure with a hat was seen on the road, before vanishing.

- At Acle in Merseyside, along the A47, a figure was seen on the roadside with 'no face'. Other figures, say motorists, mysteriously appear and disappear.

- At Shelfanger, Norfolk, in the 1990s, along Wash Lane, a mother and young daughter in a car saw a 'burning man' in the road.

- At Thetford, Norfolk, on the A11, a ghostly figure appeared on 20 November 2006. It was late evening, and the time estimated at no earlier than 11.30. The ghostly figure appeared on the driver's bonnet, but more oddly, giving rise to concerns about road deaths, the figure was smartly dressed in a light-coloured suit, and was smiling. He, of course, vanished.

- At Tivetshall St Mary, on the road to a well-known local church, a figure in 'old-fashioned clothes' and a trilby appeared at 11 p.m. on the night of 10 June 2016. It was later surmised that this was the ghost of someone killed by a car in the 1950s.

- At nearby Corby a woman driver and her passenger heard a male scream, and wondered whether it was anything to do with the figure they passed at the roadside. The date was 10 April 2011. She turned back to look, and soon events led to the police getting involved, but who found nothing.

- At Wickfen, Cambridgeshire, in August 2016, a driver saw a man and dog on a local road who promptly vanished.

- A Whiteacre Heath, Warwickshire, in January 2010 at 8.45 p.m., a transparent caped figure was seen, although its gender was not known.

- In the Highlands, at Croy Brae Hill – the A719 – an optical illusion occurs: the hill seems to be going up when it is going down.

- In Ayrshire, along Scotland's B708 in April 2015, a hooded figure was seen by the roadside. The driver stopped, the figure vanished.

- At Wrexham, Clywd, early one evening in 1999, a driver and passenger both saw a tall 'dark' hovering figure cross the road. Also at Halkyn, off the A55, a 'ghost' was seen.

- On the A37 to Glastonbury, Somerset, in the summer of 2001, a driver and his wife saw a boy holding a goldfish bowl rush up an embankment at 'superhuman speed'. He then dashed in front of their car, and collided with it. As usual, when the couple stopped, they found nothing.

- At Abbotsbury, Dorset, on the B3157, a jaywalker vanished on 31 August 2014, at 3 a.m. Before doing so, however, it appeared that his legs 'evaporated' before he reached the side of the road.

- At West Hendred, Berkshire, in 1964, two sisters in their car saw a phantom jaywalker. At the same place, in the summer of 2010 at 11.30 p.m, a woman driver also saw a jaywalker.

- At Penteuchaf, Gwynedd, Wales, there is the recurring winter phenomenon of a smart young male jaywalker.

- In Buckinghamshire, on the A421 dual carriageway between Tingewick and Buckingham, two figures, one tall and the other short, were seen dangerously crossing the busy road on the morning of 17 January 2016. They disappeared onto the opposite verge. Again, this could be a literal 'phantom' jaywalker.

- A ghostly jaywalker in distinctive old-fashioned clothing was seen at Chesham, Buckinghamshire, in December 2010, when a van driver saw him run out and then run down the central reservation. Another proof of the paranormal is that the person was moving faster than the van's speed of 50 mph!

- Similarly, at Chesham, at a local place called Rednor Bottom, two motorcyclists saw a strange figure in black leap from a gate into their path, and vanish.

- At High Wycombe, Buckinghamshire, at White Hill, in December 1936, a vanishing jaywalker was seen by a lorry driver. This was a ghost that was apparently known to local police as a result of other rumours or reports.

- Along the M11 in Cambridgeshire, close to Junction 13, a dark figure crossed the highway shortly after midnight on 24 June 2013, strolling as if the road was devoid of traffic.

- At Barrow-in-Furness, Cumbria, along Clive Street, circa 2008 on a dark rainy night, a driver and daughter saw a male jaywalker cross the road diagonally. The driver stopped and the figure disappeared.

- At Hassop, Derbyshire, on a road passing a local pub at no known date, a phantom soldier caused road accidents.

- In Surrey, at Warlingham, on the Farleigh Road in September 2009, a tall jaywalker, looking distinctly ephemeral, was seen. But, inevitably, only for a very short time.

- At Snailwell, Cambridgeshire, a driver travelling on a local road at 5 p.m. in November 2012, passed a 'US airman' walking in the road, who seemed to be 'glowing'.

- Similarly, at Moreland, Cumbria, a man dressed in early-19th-century clothing was walking down the road and was also glowing with a yellow light.

- A Victorian figure, without the glow, was seen at nearby Penrith, Cumbria, at a road in the suburbs of Flusco where another road appears. It was May 2012. The driver was forced to stop by the figure in the road who 'refused to move'. But the figure disappeared 'faster than Usain Bolt'.

- In Telford, Shropshire, around the year 2008, a driver saw a glowing figure crossing the road. Then 'it broke apart as if made from dandelion seeds' (was this a kind of 'pixelisation'?). A woman passenger said the figure looked 'old and evil'. Was it morphing into something else, or changing its form?

- At Boughton Heath, Cheshire, at an unknown date, a jaywalker darted out of a side road in front of cars and vanished.

- At Cheddar, Somerset, on the B3135 between Green Ore and Cheddar, a figure by the roadside was seen by a driver at

7.45 p.m. on 23 October 2003. His engine cut out and his lights dimmed. He had difficulty in starting his car after the figure moved away.

- At Alfreton, Derbyshire, on Christmas Day 2015, a car containing a driver and passenger had to brake sharply when a transparent cloaked figure with a hood jaywalked across the road. It vanished before it could reach the hedges on the other side.

- At Thaxted, Essex, on the road to Saffron Walden, a woman driving into town in the spring of 2010 saw an elderly couple on the road, who promptly vanished.

- At Thorpe-le-Soken, Essex, drivers avoided running over a man known by legend to be a ghost, who promptly disappeared.

- At West Mersea, Essex, around the year 1990, a car passenger saw a white-cloaked figure cross the road, look back and then vanish into a hedge. Some witnesses saw the same thing happen, in exactly the same way, in 2004.

- At Stow, Gloucestershire, in early December 2004, a couple of friends out in a car on a visit saw a Victorian man in a top hat. They avoided him, but the witnesses were surprised to see him in the exact same part of the road on their return journey just a few hours later.

- At Guildford, Hampshire, the occupant of a car watched a white figure cross the road on 13 January 2018. The driver braked, and the figure disappeared.

- At Evesham, Warwickshire, on the A435 between Evesham and Beckett's Farm, a couple saw a hooded black face jump onto their windscreen, but no body was visible. The face moved about before vanishing. The year was 1997.

- In 1994 at Knipton, Leicestershire, on the road from Belvoir Castle, a figure with no legs and a long coat tried to thumb a lift from a startled motorist. He tried not to stop, but it jaywalked and forced the driver to a screeching halt. The entity then vanished.

- At Huddersfield, Yorkshire, on Somerset Road in the early 1980s, a woman driver crashed into a parked car to avoid a young boy jaywalker. The description she later gave to the police matched that of a boy killed in a car accident on that road years before.

- At Ingleton, on the Lancaster Road in 1937, a man in a blue suit had been killed in a road accident. For a week drivers would repeat the accident of hitting him.

- At Seascale, on the road to Whitby on 5 August 2013, a passenger in a car was convinced he saw only a pair of legs dart across the road, while the driver saw nothing.

- At Bobbington, Staffordshire, in the summer of 2009, two people in a car spotted a monk in the road – who promptly disappeared into a nearby field.

- At Ipswich, Suffolk, along the Belvedere Road on 18 December 2012 at 8.50 a.m., a driver saw a figure in a trilby hat and dark-grey clothing – before he inevitably vanished. This figure was also seen by a man walking his dog, who said the jaywalker tipped his hat before disappearing.

- At Great Waldingfield, Suffolk, on the road to Sudbury at some time in 2012, a driver saw three men in large boots and long coats strolling along the side of the road. A legend persists that a US air base once existed in the area, and there were some deaths, and these figures might have been phantom airmen.

- At Ixworth in April 2016, a driver and passenger saw a ghostly man run across the road. And at Lowestoft in the mid 1980s a jaywalker wearing a 'Benny' hat and with an 'unforgettable' face was seen.

- Several alarming jaywalker events have occurred in Surrey from post-war years right up to the present. At Godstone, on the A22 heading north on 27 December 1967, a jaywalker with 'a thin face and moustache' was encountered just after midnight. He was wearing a light-coloured trench coat. The driver braked, causing the entity to vanish.

- At Guildford, Surrey, on 14 January 2018 at 2 a.m., three people in a vehicle saw a figure in white cross the road.

- At Chilworth, between Rices Corner and Percy Corner in 1960, a cyclist saw another cyclist apparently without hands or face, which was just a 'blurry area'.

- At Horley, on the A23 close to the Cambridge Hotel, a disappearing elderly male jaywalker was seen in March 2007 at 9 p.m. He wore a flat cap, tweed jacket and blue trousers, and had an upright military stance and gait.

- At Stoneleigh, on the road to Nescot College on 14 February 2012, a taxi driver saw a 'dark' jaywalker that had no features. The entity leapt 14 feet into the air to clear an embankment.

- At Chichester, on the A259 towards Bognor, a driver and his passenger thought they impacted a jaywalker on some date in 2003. Rumour has it that this was not an uncommon experience on that stretch of road. On 2 February 2014 a driver swerved to avoid a man in black.

- At Ditchling, in December 2004 at 11 p.m., a man with a wide-brimmed hat walked into the road. The driver stopped to offer a lift, but got scared as the figure approached his car but appeared to have no face.

- At Johns Cross, on the A21 near Vinehall School at some time in 1983, a scruffy man disappeared half way across the road.

- At Loxwood, Sussex, in a village road, a figure often stands at the roadside, and sometimes jaywalks.

- At Haseley, Warwickshire, during the late 20th century, there were reports of a ghost crossing the road in front of traffic, near a well-known church.

- At Lighthorne Heath on the B4100 in the year 2000, a motorcyclist saw a tall, thin man in a black robe cross the road. He had a stick and a bundle over his shoulder.

- At Crathes, Aberdeenshire, on an unknown date, a driver on the A93 towards Banchory saw a jaywalking monk.

- At Wootton Bassett, Wiltshire, on 6 April 2014, the occupants of a car saw a jaywalker vanish into a nearby field.

- In Ayrshire, along the B708 during the night of 8 February 2014, a driver saw a 'grey' male jaywalker. He turned on his full beam and the figure immediately disappeared.

- At King of Shotts, a small town in Lanarkshire, early in the 21st century in misty conditions, a woman driver hit a jaywalker with such force that he bounced over the car. Surprisingly he landed on his feet, apparently uninjured. The driver stopped in alarm, but inevitably the man had vanished. There were rumours of hauntings on the Canthill Road where the incident happened.

- On the A15 northbound in Lincolnshire, a male figure in a leather jacket and with black hair suddenly appeared on the roadside on 14 November 2013, and just as suddenly disappeared.

- At Nantycaws, Dyfed, on the A48 in the early hours of a day in 2010, a vanishing jaywalker was seen, and also on another day in January 2016. Both had vanished before being hit.

- On the A34 between Atherstone and Preston-on-Stour, a ghost of a man – invariably at midnight – disappears straight through a wall.

- At Knutsford, Cheshire, along a road known as the Tatton Mile, a driver saw a man standing in the road with his hand out, signalling to stop. Cars swerved, and the figure vanished.

- Garson and Monica Miller were driving towards Annan, Scotland, on the Kinmount Straight, Dumfries, in March 1995, when a figure of a man in what could have been a monk's habit, and carrying a small sack, jumped out at them. They were convinced they had run him over, and contacted the police. Nothing was found.[1]

- Donna Maxwell, 27, was driving with her children in March 1995 to Annan from Eastriggs on the old A75 when a jaywalker jumped out in front of her car. She heard nothing and felt nothing. He vanished, and she contacted the Annan police after driving home.[2]

- As already given in Chapter 11, David Bingham, a 30-year-old Birmingham plumber out on an emergency call, swore he had hit a pedestrian in the early hours of 2 January 1996 as he drove past Birmingham City Cemetery in Moor Lane, Witton. The victim appeared in front of Mr Bingham's vehicle, the victim's horrified eyes staring at him as he was knocked over. But David found no trace of blood, or any injured person, or damage to the car. Badly shaken, he reported the matter to the Queens Road police. A police spokeswoman said other ghost sightings had been made in the area.[3]

- On 14 December 2010 at 4.30 p.m., at Fakenham, Norfolk, on the A148, a driver braked to avoid a cyclist who pulled out and then vanished.

- At Ellesmere, Oxfordshire, a headless woman was seen on several roads, circa 1997.

- At Annan, Dumfries and Galloway, on the A75 to Gretna, some time in the 2000s, a woman driver hit a male jaywalker wearing a red jumper, before he vanished.

- At Robertsbridge, Sussex, on the A21, a phantom cyclist was seen in the year 1977. This was thought to be a ghost of someone who died in the mid 20th century when he was hit by a lorry.

- At Dunstable, Bedfordshire, on the A5 between Markyate and Dunstable, two phantom cricketers who had been killed in an earlier accident were seen in 1958 walking along, and apparently heading for the Packhorse Club.[4]

## Road Ghosts – Suicidal or Spiteful?

The fact that more than one person can see the same ghost, or the same apparition can be seen repeatedly by different people at the same location, raises doubts about the conventional explanation of ghosts. It seems unlikely that it is the percipient's own mind that is responsible for the apparition, a point often addressed to sceptics of ghostly visions who prefer a psychological explanation. F. W. H. Myers, who devoted himself the study of the survival question, defined a ghost as 'a manifestation of persistent personal energy, or an indication of some kind of force being exercised after death in some way'.[5]

It is clear that road ghosts, as hinted at earlier, do indeed play malevolent tricks on motorists. There are plenty of explicit examples in the databases, as we shall see later, of the bizarre maliciousness and madness of a frightening type of jaywalker – gliding, screaming, headless, glowing – whose only purpose is to cause alarm and distress.

But pause for a moment: why would the ghost of a dead road victim want to step into the road to frighten an innocent motorist, or even cause an accident? This, of course, begs the question of whether there might be an element of spite or revenge involved. Road ghosts, alas, too often show signs of malevolent insanity. Indeed, throwing oneself in front of a vehicle, or standing in front of it waiting for it to hit one just to make the car swerve dangerously, is more disturbing than the vanishing hitchhiker itself. It is an action which 'seems to fail as an attempt at meaningful communication … rather it appears to be aimed at inducing horror, for reasons we can only guess at. And it is difficult to understand why the forlorn ghosts of women killed in accidents should suddenly want to dash out in front of moving vehicles – and cause distress to the driver – if the aim of a ghost is to try to communicate with the living.'[6] The dated clothing or the contemporary summery outfit, or the old woman in black, are also enigmas. But the white clothing, as suggested by Sean Tudor, could represent the white of the burial shroud.

A woman taxi driver in her forties quit her job after a frightening apparition on the A15 in the spring of 2003. It was in the early hours of one morning where other incidents had occurred – just after the Ruskington turn-off. The figure came screaming at her with an open mouth, before disappearing under her car. She felt no impact, and when she stopped could find nothing. She contacted the police – already aware of the spooky legends – via her cab radio, who came along, and inevitably found nothing.[7]

The Cannock Chase is twenty-six square miles of woodland and heath south-east of Stafford. A Caroline Parks, at midnight in February 2010, almost crashed her car on a stretch of road between Hednesford and Rugeley when she had to swerve to avoid hitting a figure that materialised virtually in front of her. Through her rear window she could see a translucent figure with bright yellow eyes in a long coat and brimmed hat. It looked, as in so many cases, as if its feet were not actually touching the ground. It disappeared into the surrounding woodland. Her uncle had apparently had a similar experience in the past when out on his bike. The same sort of figure just floated up into the air when approached. In the year 2012 five other sightings of this black, hovering apparition were reported.[8]

On the Oldnall Road, a notorious accident black spot between Halesowen and Stourbridge, Midlands, a member of a paranormal research team called Parasearch had his own experience when his headlights caught a small girl standing in the middle of the road. He swerved onto a grass verge. Looking back he could see nothing. Parasearch then advertised in a local paper for any similar experiences. They learned that in 2008, a Nick Harrison had to swerve to avoid a small boy, dressed in Victorian garb. Other witnesses said their apparitions were either standing in the road or were walking along the side of it, and just vanishing. The Parasearch group also mentioned an event in nearby Foxcote Lane. A Tony Griffiths braked sharply when a figure dressed in Victorian apparel, but with blurred facial features, stepped out of a hedgerow to cross the road, and actually passed through Tony's car in the process.[9]

Arthur Shuttlewood describes a witness telling him about a grey-clad figure with long fair hair and unknown gender that jumped in front his car near Calloway Clump, a hillside copse to the north of the town of Warminster, Wiltshire, on 16 December 1965 at 7.40 p.m. The term 'suicidal maniac' was used, and Shuttleworth relates the similar experiences of other drivers in the same month.[10]

On 4 August 2017, at 1.30 a.m., a driver and passenger were on the bypass at Christchurch, Dorset, heading for Bournemouth. They saw a man in military uniform on the central reservation. When the driver turned round for a second look, the figure had vanished. The car grew cold and there was electrical interference and a 'car stop' event (see Chapter 20). On 13 October 2009 at 7.45 a.m., a woman driver saw a man in a green jacket and dark trousers standing in the motorway, just past a slip road at Junction 24 on the M1, near Castle Donnington, Leicestershire. She realised she could not stop in time, but the person suddenly vanished.[11]

In the summer of 2010 at Northampton, between Spinning Hill and Bailiff Street, two drivers had to brake hard after a tall figure stepped off the kerb. The figure vanished when he reached the other side. At Guisborough, Yorkshire, in 1988, four occupants of a car saw what looked like a monk in a hood in the dead of night.[12]

Steve Everett was travelling to work around 6.30 a.m. on the B1389 in Witham, Essex, in February 2004 when he saw a 'rough-looking man' in a parka jacket at the side of the road with a bicycle. As soon as Steve drew level, the man walked out in front of his car and vanished.[13]

A man driving home to Wigan in the late 1970s thought he had knocked down someone. He got out to look for the victim, found nothing, but reported the incident to the police, which raised some humour among his workmates when they found out.[14]

The madness of road ghosts often becomes blatantly apparent. Michael was giving a friend a lift home to Newton, near West Kirby, Merseyside, on his Honda motorbike. He cannot recall the exact date, but it must have been in 1979, and it was early in the morning. As they were travelling through a hamlet on the B5139, Michael's headlights caught the image of a youngish man with long hair. But the figure seemed to be clutching a round road sign, but strangely with his arms and hands twisted behind his back. His legs also seemed to be bent backwards. Michael slammed on his brakes, and did a U-turn, but there was nothing there.[15] He later discussed the matter with his friend, who pointed out that there was a cemetery beyond the wall bordering the road at the point where they saw the figure. Michael said it was unlikely that someone would go to elaborate lengths to play frightening tricks on motorists in the dead of night. He had pulled up fairly abruptly, and the figure would have been seen trying to run away along the roadside, or attempting to climb back over the cemetery wall.

Sometimes the hapless road user becomes aware that he has interacted with a road ghost – but the *wrong* road ghost. About the year 2007, Peter, about sixty at the time, was travelling by motorbike south on the A5, approaching High Cross in Leicestershire. There is a major old Roman junction there with Watling Street, and a B road, Fosse Way. It was a warm summer night, about 10 p.m. About

200 yards from the junction he saw a man with a bag on his back, standing on the grass on the central reservation which separated the two lanes of traffic. Travelling at 70 mph, Peter was startled to see the man slowly cross the road just seconds before Peter would have crashed into him. He just thought it was a 'near miss', and that both he and the man were very lucky. However, his partner the next day said that he must have seen the High Cross ghost, a story common in the Lutterworth area where she once lived. Rob Gandy, whom we have met earlier – the writer on esoteric matters for the *Fortean Times* – sought out local press references to this ghost story. Indeed, those relating to the open road seemed only to be about Roman soldiers. Gandy noted that Peter said the ghost had colourless clothes, and just appeared to be grey all over – a darker version of the Woman in White. But the dangerous strolling tactics, and the oddness of the scenario on a busy road, led Gandy to believe that Peter did actually see a ghost.[16]

A road ghost was seen on a single track road near Wichcombe, Gloucestershire, in 1956. An RAF officer witnessed a glowing male figure that emerged from the trees on his right and passed through the bonnet of his car, and then continued up the hill.[17] In November 1973 the son of a woman who had been run over was returning the following day after visiting her grave. When he reached the hill his car came 'came over freezing cold' and he felt loud thuds on the back of his driving seat.[18]

In the early hours of the morning of 17 January 1989, Graham Marsden, a 45-year-old businessman, filled up his car at a service station on the M27 near Southampton, Hampshire. He was last seen walking towards the men's room, and then vanished, with his refuelled car left unattended. There was no way he could have walked along the motorway without being seen. The police searched the surrounding woods, but found nothing.[19]

Several cases were mentioned in Andy Gilbert's book, *Credible Witness*, of actual police reports of highway ghosts. Two policemen were on mobile patrol duty in the north Birmingham area on an undisclosed date at the time Austin Maestros were being used by the police as Panda cars. They joined in the pursuit of a stolen car at night by other officers in Austin Rover Montegos. The fleeing car eventually crashed and flipped over. A person ran away from the scene, virtually right in front of the Maestro, which very nearly hit him. In his headlights the patrol driver could recognise the young guy as someone he had once arrested. He pulled up and the two officers joined the other officers in checking the crashed car. He radioed the name of the villain to the police station, and told the other officers who, surprisingly, 'didn't seem interested'. But so severely damaged was the car that it was believed by the officers that nobody could have got out of it. When the fire brigade cut away the crushed metal, they found one body – the same man who had actually been identified and reported to police HQ as fleeing the scene.[20]

A gliding road ghost was seen one night by a patrolling PC in the early 1990s along Abbey Road in the Whitley area, near Coventry. Possibly there used to be an abbey at that location. The phantom was in the middle of the road, looking like a monk in a brown habit, but with no face or feet. It then levitated over the police car and disappeared.[21]

On the A15 in Lincolnshire, a ghostly hotspot is some twelve miles south of Lincoln, and four miles north-west of Sleaford, near a junction with Ruskington. In 1998, a Kevin Whelan phoned into a TV programme called *This Morning* to describe a ghostly encounter in this area. A face suddenly emerged from around the driver's side pillar of the car, and came round onto the windscreen. The distressed face was olive-green; the rest of any attached body was not solid-looking but faintly luminous. The thing held up a fluorescent hand in a halting gesture, before simply sliding away.[22]

Finally:

- In 1966 on the A15 in Lincolnshire, twelve miles north of Lincoln near a junction, Sarah Martin and her boyfriend were heading home to Cranwell, Lincolnshire, when they saw a black silhouette dash out in front of their car. They went through it.[23] In the latter years of the 20th century at Charlesworth, Derbyshire, on the main road running out of the moor, four people in a car saw a semi-transparent Victorian-dressed lady, complete with ruff, jaywalk through a gate.[24] In 1986 at Bryanston, Dorset, near a river and woods, a floating figure crossed the road.[25]

- At Eglwysilan, Mid Glamorgan, on a mountain road at night in November 1987 a motorist saw two figures holding hands. But he noticed, in his headlights as he drew nearer, that they had no legs, or even noses, and were hovering over the road surface. He pulled up abruptly, and stared in disbelief. The figures in turn stopped to stare at the driver and his car. They drifted towards and away from him, and then vanished.

# Chapter 13

## Female Road Ghosts

Young female ghosts seem to predominate in much tragic literature involving forms of transport, a point I mentioned in Chapter 1. Female jaywalkers – young women in light-coloured clothing, often typically wearing the 'pale beige raincoat' – appear in main roads all over Britain. Older female ghosts are more likely to be indoors – Yorkshire has a number of 'grey' or 'white' ladies, often wearing silken dresses that are more likely to be heard rather than seen, in pubs and hotels.

There are European examples of women road ghosts. The Dutch historian Cornelius Kempius (1516–1587) referred to ancient Dutch legends of *witte vrouwen* or *witte juffers* (white ladies) who emerged from caves to surprise travellers abroad at night, or the *weisen Frauen* of Germany, or *dames blanches* in France – all similar characters.

But why should the suicidal 'spectral jaywalker' invariably be a single young woman? In the US the 'Woman in White' is either an apparition or a real person, or is part of the haunted highways syndrome. She is also embedded in the hitchhiker legends. But the ghostly aspect is vouched for by the fact that motorists often see her gliding, rather than walking or running, across the road, and their apparitions are so alarming that they have themselves caused road accidents.

However, as so often, motorists are confused about what they think they have encountered on British roads. Everything about the figure, the person, they see ahead of them looks real: in fact *more* real than indoor ghosts because the entity is affected by the open-air conditions at the time – the same weather conditions that the motorist is experiencing. The actual solid reality, the bodily movements and reactions, and the movement of clothing caught in wind or rain, belies the idea that motorists are seeing ghosts. But at the same time something – a haze or a glow – indicates that it might well be a ghost. For example, a female figure was seen on the B3114 south of Chew Stoke, Somerset, by hairdresser Carol Gillen, who had to slow down as the figure boldly crossed the road, oblivious to any approaching traffic. Again the woman was dressed in an old-fashioned Victorian costume – a silk dress with 'leg of mutton' sleeves. But Carol noted the clothes were 'billowing back with the breeze, and the whiteness of her dress was very bright, as if electric. Her hair was loose, very thick and longish to the top of her shoulders, and blowing off her neck.' But here is another oddity: the girl was wet from recent rain, but had no feet – as if she was partly in and partly out of the real world.[1]

There are reports of colliding apparitions on the A23. Patrick and June Geary, driving just ten miles north of Brighton, saw a girl in a white raincoat walking along the central reservation. It was 8 p.m. on a dark, wet night at the end of November 1976. The feet and hands of the figure seemed to be missing. It stepped into the road, but it seemed to glide over the top of their car and then disappear.[2]

A sense of malevolence is often reported. A teenage girl smashed her car into a lamp post on the carriageway of the A229 below Crossington service station, Kent, on 18 October 1990, but escaped, remarkably, with only cuts and bruises. She closed her eyes in fear during the impact, but could see in her mind's eye a woman with lank black hair, staring at her as her car spun out of control.[3]

Lorry driver Laurie Newman spotted what looked like a girl walking along beside the A4 on the Chippenham to Bath road in the early hours. He slowed down to pass her, but the figure sprang up to the side of his vehicle, clinging onto the side, and leering through the side window. Her head was fleshless – an actual skull![4]

Julia Nash was driving on the B2166 near Chichester, West Sussex, around 8.30 p.m. on a November evening in 1999. An older woman in a black hood and cloak appeared across her bonnet and looked at her 'with dark and amused eyes'. Because of the busy traffic she had no option but to carry on, actually shouting at the thing to get away! She was doing about 40 mph while she went into a bend, and the ghost just dissolved into the hedges at the roadside 'in a kind of jagged way'. There seemed to be no body, just the head and hood, which turned to look at the stream of traffic coming towards it before it disappeared.[5]

But female ghosts are seen in urban areas, on pavements and down alleyways, too. A shadowy woman dressed in dark clothing was seen in a shopping centre in Glasgow in 2016 four times by different people, virtually hovering over the pavement.[6]

The stretch of road between Ravensden and Wilden on the B660 in the Midlands is haunted by a woman wearing a dated long black dress down to her feet. She seems solid and real enough as motorists pass her on the grass verge, but is invariably gliding rather than walking along the surface. Dogs refuse to go anywhere near her. Pedestrians only become alarmed when they begin to perceive her malevolent face as they approach her, and become even more so when she vanishes from sight when about to pass them.

In 1981 a young Christine Walker and two friends, travelling by car to a disco in Carlisle, Cumbria, on a wet February night, saw an old lady trudging along the wide grass verge, lugging a shopping bag on wheels. But there were no houses or roads close by. They momentarily thought of offering her a lift, but the three of them were already squashed into a sports car that normally held only two people. The following Monday at the office the talk turned to the supernatural, and one person mentioned the ghost 'that haunted the Carlisle road, pulling a shopping bag', and always along the same grass verge. Christine was astounded. 'I've actually seen her,' she said, 'just two days ago, in fact!'[7]

Three young men were about to turn into a pub car park at the village of Bolney, West Sussex, at an unknown time and date at the beginning of the 1990s, when they seemed to hit a woman who suddenly appeared, but there was no bump. In fact the event caused a minor collision with a low wall. Again, no person was found, but customers outside the pub actually saw the woman suddenly appear. They also saw her vanish when the car hit her.[8] This apparition was seen before, and was alleged to be the ghost of a woman killed on that stretch of road many years earlier.

At Moreton, Somerset, at Chew Valley Lake on the B3114, passengers saw a 'drifting' lady cross the road on 8 June 1999. She had long wet wavy hair and an old-fashioned dress. The driver stopped, and the database archives simply say that he 'called the police'. It was later revealed that other motorists or pedestrians had seen the same vision, and she was named as one 'Catherine'.[9]

Many of Surrey's roads are reputed to be haunted, and this is sometimes attributed to reckless pre-war hit-and-run driving in the county that was more common in the days before road safety laws were enforced. The Hogs Back and Leatherhead have stories of road hauntings, and there were peculiar legends of female ghosts, some 'sprawled on the road'. At Swan Corner, Leatherhead, at some time in either 1930 or 1931, a tall 'phantom' woman was seen in the road, but promptly vanished. There were reports that she was the ghost of a killed jaywalker. In the 1960s a woman in white with long hair stood at the roadside. A witness in a car stopped to offer her a lift, but she vanished.[10]

Two police officers in the mid 1990s were travelling in their patrol car near a National Trust property called Wightwick Manor near Wolverhampton, and were heading towards a wooden bridge. As they did so they could see on the bridge itself a woman who was slowly gliding – rather than walking – across it. She was dressed in a long white Victorian-style dress, complete with bonnet. As the officers passed under the bridge they looked back. The woman had vanished.

Two other police officers were travelling late at night in the mid 1960s along the A41 towards a village called Chadwick End, Warwickshire. Their headlights picked up some nuns – all dressed in black – walking along the side of the road. They pulled up and got out of the car with the aim of warning the nuns of the danger of walking around in dark clothing at night. But the nuns all suddenly disappeared. The officers radioed this event to control, and shortly another police car on the same road radioed to say they had also seen the nuns, about half a mile further on, and also walking on the wrong side of the road. The same thing happened. The officers got out to warn the nuns, and again they vanished from view.[11]

Bill Hopkins, a school headmaster, saw a young woman step out of a hedge near Llanidloes, Powys, into the path of his vehicle one night in May 1973. The figure was an apparition, looking straight at him through his windscreen with a sorrowful face, and seemed to pass through his car. This was an unusual case, because in his rear-view mirror he could see she was still alive and standing, looking back at him. There were rumours of other similar incidents at that spot, and indeed it happened again in July when a chef, Abderahman Sennar, hit what could have been the same apparition.[12]

- On the A435, near Caughton Court, near Alcester, Warwickshire, some time in the 1990s, a middle-aged woman in a beige raincoat stepped out into the road, then vanished.[13]

- A limping blonde girl in a pale raincoat startled motorists on the A23 north of Brighton, Sussex. In 1964 one driver saw her dash to the central reservation and then vanish. She may have been the ghost of a girl killed in a motorbike accident in the area. But others saw her also in the village of Pyecombe (see below).[14]

- At Barrow Gurney on the A38 south-west of Bristol, several drivers have dangerously swerved to avoid hitting what they thought was as woman in a white coat, who then vanished.[15]

- In the Pembrokeshire villages of Johnston and Steynton, near Haverfordwest, a motorist thought he had knocked down an old lady with white hair and wearing a fawn coat. But yet again there was no one there. A driver on the opposite carriageway thought the same. Shaun Sables, head of a paranormal investigation group, says several motorists have come forward about this, saying they often catch a glimpse of a woman out of the corner of their eye.[16]

- At Thringstone in Leicestershire, on the A512 in the year 1961, near the Grave Priory, a pale female ghost was seen at the roadside.

- At Ayton, Yorkshire, near a major crossroads, two female apparitions were seen at an unknown date, but presumably in recent years. They were 'pale', on horseback, and would 'chase cars'.

- At Pyecombe, Sussex, on the London Road where the A281 meets the A21, a woman in a pale beige raincoat ran across the dual carriageway some time in the latter years of the 20th century. She disappeared half way across, but several motorists claimed they had struck her, and the police were informed. Further down the A281, a ghostly blonde stumbled along the roadside – but vanished if approached.

- At Bedworth, Warwickshire, a woman in the iconic long white dress or nightdress stood at the roadside, waiting for something or someone. Two dates are given for this, one was in 2005, and the other, more specifically, was 28 May 2012, and they were probably the same entity. Some months later, approaching Christmas, a woman dressed in black, with her hands against her face, was seen by a woman driver. At Alcester, in the same county, on the A435, in late 1995, a pale middle-aged woman in yet another pale beige raincoat (the familiar PBR), was sometimes observed pushing a bike. One car swerved and crashed.

- At Llangennith, West Glamorgan, Wales, in the late 20th century at 6.30 a.m., a 'white lady' jaywalker was seen.

- At Arundel, Sussex, on the A27, a woman in a PBR, 'smiling maniacally', and illuminated from below, was seen at 10.30 p.m. on a date in 2011. She was standing by a road sign, and adopted a 'strange posture'. The police were called, and there was a rumour that she had 'escaped', or discharged herself, from a nearby hospital. At Bolney, on the A23 near the Queens Head pub, in the early 1990s, a woman jaywalker in a grey dress was seen, causing a car with three passengers to swerve and crash off the road.

- At Maddington, Wiltshire, a young girl in a 'long white dress' was seen in a village road. At Broad Bundon, in the mid 20th century, two men driving near the Forked Elm pub saw a white figure on the roadside. And, although the figure had long hair, they said they were uncertain as to its gender. But they noted that it was floating about a foot off the ground.

- At Oare, Somerset, a bus driver saw a 'woman in white' cross a road in a village street before vanishing. At Stratton St Margaret, a nun in white was seen, but no date was given.

- At Bucklebury, Berkshire, at Beenham Junction on an unspecified date, a 'white lady' drifted along. At Hurst, on a road between villages, at Easter in 1971, a woman drifted down the road, scantily dressed.

- At Skipton, Yorkshire, along the High Street, a coach and horses was seen at an unknown date, and the name 'Lady Anne Clifford' was mentioned. At nearby Stirton, in August 2009 at 3 a.m., four friends in a car saw an older woman in white on the grass verge, holding a white handbag. Surprised at seeing the woman at such an early hour, they reversed back to check – but she had vanished.

- At Mainsriddle, Dumfries, prior to 1890, a woman in white was seen on local roads.

- At Cwmbran, Monmouthshire, close to the to the 'Leaving Wales' sign in late 2003, a coach driver spotted a woman, in the dead of night, with long hair and a black dress on the hillside. She descended the hill as he drove closer, and jaywalked. The archives report that 'no body was found'.

- At Llanidloes, Powys, on the A470 in the 'Red Bridge' area, a ghost allegedly passed through traffic in May 1973.

- At Buckholt, Gwent, in the 1960s, a pedestrian saw the 'face of a beautiful woman' on the road before it vanished.

- At Broughton, South Glamorgan, a driver hit the ghost of a girl from some time in the 1960s, which vanished. The road already had a haunted reputation.

- At East Lulworth, Dorset, in 1982, a driver twice, on different dates, passed a woman and a crying child, with both being dressed in what the database said was '1860s clothing'. The woman and child, on each occasion, vanished on a second look.

- At Fleet, Hampshire, along the Bagwell Lane, a 'woman in white' phantom occurs, who crosses a field and vanishes into a pond.

## Female Ghosts – the Long History

As other examples of female ghosts and transportation scenarios, culled from historical archives, we can take the luxury Atlantic liner the *Queen Mary* that was in service between Britain and America from 1934 until 1967, and used by many famous politicians and celebrities for years. It was converted into a troop ship during the war, actually ferrying thousands of troops, including 'war brides' on their way from wartime Europe to England, and sundry babies and children, and yet it is haunted by adult female ghosts.

In the early 1900s Marion, daughter of a Midlands railway platelayer, was living in a cottage with him just 200 yards from the main line near Brooke End signal box. The father, a Mr Gorman, wasn't keen on the romantic friendship Marion had with the young new signalman at the box, a Ronald Travis, and she often disappeared for long nights with him at the box. She slipped out one night to see her lover, but stumbled and fell on the tracks and was hit by an oncoming train. In fact the wheels of the train severed her head. This gruesome event so disturbed Travis that he was removed to other duties at another box. But it wasn't until the late 1940s that her headless ghost began to appear, even re-enacting the stumbling on the rail tracks, and the ghost sometimes 'staggered towards the signal box'. She was also seen in a bloodstained white dress.[17]

Female ghosts go back a long time in history. The bizarre life of the adventurous transvestite Lady Ferrers, who in the 17th century – and already elderly – took on the life of a male mounted highwayman herself, robbing coaches and killing solitary wayfarers – often by dropping on them from overhanging branches – came to a fatal end when inevitably one of her potential victims fought back. Her mounted ghost can be seen near Markyate, north of Harpenden on the A5, but again her horse takes to the roads and lanes of her previous existence, passing through hedges and fences, and galloping a foot or so above the present land surface.[18]

Along the A6 running from Whaley Bridge to Stockport is the apparition of the bereaved wife of Sir Piers Legh (1389–1422), a knight who died in a campaign against the French in France in June 1422. The mourner is dressed from head to foot in white. She is presumably gazing mournfully at the ground as she walks.[19]

The B1249 that runs between Beverley and Driffield in the eastern part of Humberside is plagued with the ghost of Lady de Bevere, cruelly murdered by her sadistic husband Droge de Bevere, who was rewarded with the castle at Skipsea by William the Conqueror for services rendered during the battle of Hastings. She is wandering around seeking someone who will help find her body and give it a decent burial.[20]

The legend on the A64 between York and Norton is that of Nance. Nance was seemingly once concerned with disrupting the crimes of Yorkshire highwaymen in the old days. She was a farmer's daughter from Sheriff Hutton, and towards the end of the 18th century became betrothed to a young mailman on the coach route from York to Berwick-on-Tweed. His long absences led to Nance taking up with another man, and running off with him. Shortly after she gave him a child, he deserted her. Months later the coachman was nonplussed to see her exhausted and undernourished figure standing by the side of what is now the A6, and holding a baby in her arms. He drove Nance and the baby to an inn in York, where both died shortly afterwards. But Nance's ghost appeared to the coachman while he was bringing the mail southbound to York just two years later. She grabbed the reins and raced the horses to the same inn in Coney Street, York, where she had died. Then she faded away into nothing, but her patrolling ghost can still be seen along the A64 north of York at Sheriff Hutton. This time she is not frail but lithe and quick, and has over time earned the reputation of guiding motorists out of dangerous patches of mist and fog by running ahead of their vehicles.[21]

The A541, which runs past Plas Teg, Flintshire, Wales, is known as the Ghost Road, after dozens of motorists have said they had 'crashed' into a female apparition known as The Grey Lady. Janine Hopkin was one driver who couldn't avoid a collision with this phantom. As usual when the police arrived they could find no body nor any sign of an accident. The resigned police told Janine that Plas Teg was notorious for this particular roadside ghost. Many believed the Grey Lady is the spirit of the tragic Dorothy, daughter of Plas Teg's original owner, Sir John Trevor. She had apparently died after falling into a well. But oddly, unlike ghosts from road accidents, the Grey Lady appears not at the place where she died, but where her ghost crosses the spot where she would have met her lover.[22]

The ghost of a nun seen in Bures, a town on the Essex–Suffolk border – and connected with legends associated with the notorious Borley Rectory, Suffolk, and the mysterious sound of the hooves of horses – seems to be part of an integrated but disjointed post-death scenario. The nun – appearing on her own – is alleged to have actually spoken to people, presumably in modern English, to say that she was a Catholic from France, and that she was strangled in May 1667, owing to religious friction or other problems. Before she was murdered, she said she fled from the priory with a lover in a coach, which soon became the familiar phantom coach and horses careening along country roads, but in sound only – people could hear the eerie clattering of invisible hooves.[23]

Another woman was hanged in about 1710 as a witch – a 'Mistress Hicks' – at what is now the crossroads of the A448 and A450, where she is sometimes seen by traffic. The crossroads are not far from the grounds of a moated Tudor house owned by the Catholic Archdiocese of Birmingham, near Bromsgrove.[24]

But in the case of phantom women, there does seem the ability to change clothes into more fashionable wear as time passes. Andrew Green in *Ghost Hunting* referred to a ghost of a 19th-century woman seen in the remote corridor of an English mansion originally wearing red shoes, a red gown and black headdress. Later images of the woman changed this into a pink dress and pink shoes and a grey headdress. Later still she had a white gown and grey hair. Later the image was no longer seen, and was replaced with the sound of a woman walking along the corridor and the swish of her dress.[25]

- Another female ghost appears on the A605, near the village of Ringstead, Northamptonshire, and in particular its churchyard. This is said to be Lydia Atley, murdered by a local farmer when he was told she was expecting his child out of wedlock.[26]

- One female headless ghost in a crinoline is to be found in the secluded Essex village of Canewdon, and emerges from a churchyard and floats a couple of feet into the air and then heads rapidly towards the river.[27]

- A ghostly woman on a white horse is said to haunt the streets of Chatham, Kent. The legend is that she was searching for the murderer of her boyfriend, but got killed herself.[28]

## Little Girl Ghosts

Motorists often claim to have seen a little girl in a white nightdress standing at the side of a road in Wigtownshire, south-west Scotland. Kathleen Cronie, 38, from Dumfries, Scotland, runs a paranormal investigation group. In January 2009 the group travelled to Garlieston Straight, a road in Wigtownshire famous for a girl-in-white legend and other ghostly goings-on. Sitting in the car, a team member picked up the image of a man called Albert Johnstone, a farm labourer, who had died in the 1870s, and was apparently the guardian of the little ghostly girl, named Laura. Albert appeared to the team on several subsequent visits. And in March 2013 a team member, John Hill, said he could see some thirty ghosts surrounding their car, all in old-fashioned clothes, almost as if they had made a deputation to report their histories to the now familiar car and its ghost investigators. On a later trip in January 2015, Albert appeared again, heartbroken. 'She's gone,' he groaned. Little Laura, the girl he had looked after, had disappeared.[29]

Mrs Elisabeth Bain was driving through the main street in Mitchell, Cornwall, which had many quaint tourist shops, in the late summer of 1965. She saw a young girl of about nine wearing very dated clothing, skipping out of one of them, almost as if she was a manifestation of a Victorian time warp – actually part of the era that the shops seemed to be located in. The girl was wearing a knee-length dress of heavy navy blue material, a starched white pinafore with pleats, and black boots and dark stockings. Indeed the girl didn't seem to know she was actually in a 20th-century busy traffic-clogged street, and dashed across it straight into the path of a lorry. Mrs Bain braked in horror, but the lorry driver made no attempt to avoid the girl. When the traffic moved on, Mrs Bain looked from side to side and could see no child, certainly not an injured one.

If this was an apparition, then it repeated itself. When Mrs Bain reached Hayle, some thirty miles beyond Mitchell, and probably an hour later, she saw the little girl again, but this time just a reflective image of her head and shoulders in the car's windscreen, as if she had suddenly loomed up from the car's bonnet. The image lasted only a few seconds, and it was then that it dawned on Mrs Bain that the girl only existed as a phantom, in other words she did not really exist.[30]

## Females Who Beckon

Sometimes the woman steps into the road and holds up her hand in a 'halt' gesture. Young 'Ian M', in the autumn of 1976, was being driven home by his father from his workplace at Misterton in Nottinghamshire, to their home in Gringley. It was dark, and in the headlights they could see the figure of a young lady standing on the edge of the roadway. She was smiling and beckoning with her left hand (the beckoning ghost could be the equivalent of the thumb-cocked stance of the hitchhiker). Again, spitefulness is revealed when it or she realised she was not going to be picked up, because the smile turned into an angry scowl, and then she floated backwards through a closed iron farm gate. Then she gained amazing speed, virtually flying across the field until she vanished.[31]

Another example of this halting gesture was reported in early 1983 by a lady calling herself 'Keeley'. She and a companion saw a female ghost on the A46 at Six Hills, Leicestershire, as they passed a well-known hotel at 5.45 a.m. She was in the road with her hands held up as if to ward off a collision. She was very pretty-looking, about twenty-three, with long hair. They screeched to a halt and thought they had struck her, but there was no thump, and there was nothing there when they went to check.[32]

## More Bizarre Women

Victoria Carey of Milton Keynes took her husband and young daughter, Karen, on a ghost hunt in August 2007, to visit an old barn in Buckinghamshire she heard was haunted. Passing though the village of Lillingstone Lovell, she spotted an elderly lady outside a church, rather scruffily dressed and standing next to a car. The woman waved to David, behind the wheel, and to Victoria, but with an odd slow-motion wave, with her head cocked to one side. The family then stopped the car to ask directions to the barn. What the woman then said was even odder; although elderly she said she had just visited her fiancé, and was not feeling too well. She had been sitting in the church, which was about to lock up, hence the reason for her standing outside it. Then she said, 'I have just taken a picture of myself in case I'm the next one to die.' Victoria wondered who else had died. However, the old lady soon recovered her equilibrium, got into her car, and drove off. 'That lady was really spooky, Mummy,' said Karen.

David then continued the journey in the opposite direction, but he noticed that the old lady, in her car, was right behind them! Victoria said, 'She must have been driving super fast to catch us up, how could a sick old lady do that?' As David turned south, the family noticed the old lady had turned north towards Towcester, but on the wrong side of the road! Fearful for the lady's life, David swung the car round to follow her, but there was no sign of her car in any of the roads and villages she would have had to pass through. Victoria then realised that the old lady and the church were just half a mile from the haunted barn – she put two and two together.[33]

A Mr Bryant was particularly interested in church architecture, and turned off the main A38 towards Deerhurst Priory, near Worcester. The date was mid November 1958. A narrow lane ended at the churchyard gates, and his wife, Olive, waited in the car, with the family dog in the back seat, while her husband walked up the gravel path towards the church. After a while Olive grew fidgety at her husband's long absence. Sitting in the car outside the church gate, and looking out of the side window, she was suddenly aware of an elderly woman, about a dozen yards away, dressed in clothing that she recognised as belonging to the 1920s. Perhaps she was a church employee, or a verger of the church, waiting for the evening service to begin. Nevertheless, there was some element of menace in the way that the woman continued to stare at Olive and her car. The dog began to growl.

Then there was a strange glitch in space–time, as the old woman, in a split second, suddenly appeared right up against the radiator of the car. Within a minute a yellow car approached along the lane. The elderly lady then turned, unlatched the church gate, and began to walk towards the church door. A woman from the yellow vehicle – who seemed unaware of Olive and her car – began to follow the woman. She was carrying what looked like a bundle of musical manuscripts as if she was the organist about to get ready for the evening service. Almost immediately, and certainly before the two women could have reached the church building, Mr Bryant emerged through the gate, looking a little disturbed. 'Let's get away from here,' he said as he got into the car. 'You could cut the atmosphere in the church with a knife.' Olive referred to the two strange women she had just seen, the one following the other into the church, whom she assumed her husband must have passed on his way. But he said there was only one woman – the organist. After a while, on the journey home in silence, the Bryants looked at each other – both realising that the old lady, in her dated costume, must have been an apparition.[34]

Paulette Isden, 57, was driving along an unlit road near Coventry. She braked sharply at a bend, only to screech to a halt when she saw an old lady standing in the middle of the road. She got out of the car, only to find the road unusually deserted. There was certainly no old lady. Resuming her trip she was flagged down by a policeman who said he wanted to make a 'routine check'. Bemused, Paulette told the officer about the old lady, and he replied that that stretch of road was haunted by a ghost.[35]

In December 2003 a Tracy Boon wrote to the *Kent Messenger* to report she and her husband, travelling to work at 7.30 in the morning, had seen a young female standing on the footbridge over the A229 in a long white frilly nightdress on four separate occasions in the summers of certain years in the 1990s. Perhaps, she thought, she had absconded from a care home, but it was 'totally odd' to see her there, and so often. The sightings ended in 1999.[36] On the A229 somewhere in Sussex, a girl jaywalker in white is seen.[37]

The *Derby Telegraph* of 4 February 2015 reported the ghost of a young woman in an old-fashioned floral dress and with dark hair in a hairnet that had been seen by a woman driver in the Bretby area of Derbyshire two days earlier. The apparition was standing by an old-fashioned bike which had a wicker basket, and watched the woman driver, one Lisa Fisher, as she passed by. The apparition promptly vanished. The newspaper reported confirmations of the female apparition, again by other women drivers. A Matthew Roberts, who worked at the Bretby Business Park, also claimed that a security guard had been asked directions by the ghostly woman, before she vanished. She had been seen, always in winter, walking around the business park or even sitting under trees.

Chris was a member of a motorcycle club in the 1960s, and recalls a fellow member telling how he was riding along a lane in Hatfield, Herts., at about 11 p.m. one October. He pulled up to check a possible engine fault, and became aware of an old lady standing by the road. He was concerned to see her on her own in the cold weather. But she wouldn't respond when spoken to, and remained motionless and staring. After a while the motorcyclist became a bit spooked, and soon drove off. One friend at the motorbike club asked for more details of the old woman, and showed him a local press picture of a resident in the area, who had just that week been killed in a road accident.[38]

- At Wilden, Bedfordshire, in the 1870s, a female figure was said to glide along the grass verge, dressed in the black heavy clothing of the era. Also at Wilden, a phantom old woman in black haunts a village road and is said to have an 'evil face', and was last seen in 1973. At Littlewick Green on local roads, another female apparition is recorded in the Bedfordshire database.

- At Cwmbran, Gwent, Wales, on the road between Llantsarman Abbey and another church, in the early 20th century at midnight, a male pedestrian saw a woman approach him, and then vanish.

- At High Wycombe, Buckinghamshire, along Cock Lane in January 1994, a phantom woman in grey jaywalked across the road. At nearby Hughendon Valley, in 1986, driver Mark Nursey and his girlfriend, following behind him in a car, both saw a female figure by the side of the road near a crematorium. She wore a green jumper – which seemed to be oversized – but no head or hands were visible. Legend has it that she is the ghost of a woman run over in 1978.

- On the A75, at Dumfries and Galloway, on the haunted fifteen-mile stretch between Annan and Gretna Green, a Victorian woman and an old man appeared in the road in a mysterious mist, to cause accidents.[39]

- A woman once reported to Peter McCue that her son confided to her that he had seen a phantom woman somehow enclosed in a 'bubble of mist' on 1 May 2004, near Loch Ashie, Inverness. As he approached and passed through the vision he could see the woman's eyes and teeth were 'lit up'.[40]

- On the M6, south of the Lake District, on one summer late at night, a ghostly woman was seen floating over the hard shoulder, wearing old-fashioned clothing. Her feet were possibly missing.

- At Metheringham, Lincolnshire, at the perimeter of an RAF base, the ghost of a woman killed in a motorbike accident in the Second World War apparently flags down motorists to ask for help in finding her boyfriend on the road, who has had a motorbike accident. Drivers go off to check, leaving the woman – whom they assume to be real – on the road, but inevitably find no boyfriend and no motorbike. And the ghost then vanishes when they return.

- A phantom lady in green caused cars to swerve on Bread and Cheese Hill in Thundersley, Essex, in the 1970s.

- At Blaby Ford, Leicestershire, in April 1995 at 10.30 p.m., two young people in a parked car saw a figure outlined in a long coat standing near a steep bank. Later, at a party, they learned of the legend of a phantom woman in the area who was looking for her drowned husband.

- At York, on the A64 Malton Road, especially on misty evenings, a woman ghost can be seen.

- At Bristol, near the reservoir on the A38, the skid marks of braking vehicles that have tried to avoid a phantom woman in a white coat can be seen. She is said to vanish immediately.

- At Market Drayton, Shropshire, on an unnamed road in the late 19th century, two women driving a mule cart in the month of October saw a woman cross the road wearing an inappropriate light dress in cool weather. She was floating a foot off the ground. The startling vision made the mule, normally a plodding animal, actually 'bolt'.

- On roads approaching the Yorkshire hamlet of Woodhall, not far from the A684 from Kendal to the Great North Road, a ghost known as the Black Lady appears. She is elderly, wears white gloves and carries a walking stick. She appears to be normal, but oddly dressed, and can be seen during both day and night. Passers-by feel the need to greet or acknowledge her, but receive no reply. When they look back they find she has vanished.[41]

- Travelling eastbound to Cold Ashby, Northamptonshire, at 3.30 a.m. on some date in 1999, 'in stormy weather' with few other cars about, a driver saw an old woman actually walking towards him in the road. She was dated both in appearance and in dress, with a bent back, shawl and 18-century clothing, according to the paranormal database. The usual disappearance trick, plus the usual fruitless search.

- At Stalham, Norfolk, on the road to Wroxham, on 3 November 2017, a woman jaywalker ran into traffic, but vanished before being struck.

- In the roads, lanes and foothpaths around the village of Braishfield, Hampshire, witnesses see the wraith of an elderly woman in Edwardian dress. She is said to be hunting for buried valuables and money that she supposedly buried when alive, and while worried about burglars.[42]

- A woman dressed in black Victorian clothes, but holding a modern bicycle, asked two pedestrian friends in Bishops Waltham, Hampshire, for directions to Dean, a small nearby town. The woman then climbed on her bike and disappeared into thin air just moments later.[43]

- A bus driver in Blackburn, Lancashire, picked up a pale female spectre in May 2006 on the road outside Samlesbury Hall, an area where her lover was said to have been killed. The newly opened restaurant inside the ancient Hall has also been haunted with the same girl who would fly past people and disappear into nearby fields.[44]

- On the B339, just off the A39 to Bridgewater, Somerset, the ghost of a woman glides from one side of the road to the other – rather than walks – fading away at each verge. Parts of the vision may be real, but not other parts. She has a filmy, almost translucent, shawl on her head, never quite seen as real as the ghost herself. The outer form and the contours of the head can also seem real, until you catch a glimpse of the frightening face. In this case it was dark grey in colour, with 'horrible glaring eyes'.

- Drivers in the West Country have come across a jaywalking old gipsy woman on the Bath to Bradford-on-Avon road, a notorious spot where vehicles have actually plunged off the road.[45]

- In October 1971 young Clive Thrower was driving on a clear night from Yarmouth to his home in Lowestoft. On the Gorleston Road an elderly hooded woman suddenly appeared in front of his car. He slammed on his brakes, but was convinced that he had run her over. Then the usual scenario: he got out of the car but could see nothing – no mangled body, no blood. Neither did the car show any signs of impact. In the local library he found a story of a hooded woman being seen in the Gorleston Road, attached to a legend that she had been killed in a car accident.[46]

- 'Gerry' was heading slowly one evening at 11.30 towards West Bromwich via Holyhead Road, and slammed on his brakes to avoid hitting a tall, gaunt woman crossing the road carrying an infant or toddler. Her light-coloured mac almost reached her feet. 'Her expression was ghastly, as anyone's would be if they were about to be hit by a car. I was certain I had hit her, and got out. … There was no woman, no child, in fact no one at all. No pedestrians, nobody. I even looked under my car.'[47]

- Jim, a taxi driver, and his wife were driving along the old (north) Dumfries bypass some time in 1990 or 1991 when they saw a woman standing by the roadside. Then she walked into the road, and Jim slammed on his brakes. He turned round at the next roundabout to see if he, or his wife, could find her, but there was no sign of her.[48]

- On the A456, Oldnall a woman is often seen dressed in grey, as is an occasional phantom Cavalier soldier. There is a dip in this road which then rises, causing a momentary loss of vision of the road ahead. A car full of passengers once felt an unusual jolt on this road, and the driver slammed on his brakes, believing he had hit a young woman. He left the vehicle to search for her. There was no one there, and no mark on the vehicle.[49]

- In an edition of the *Western Telegraph* it said a taxi driver for Kitty Cars at 11.30 one night struck a woman in a black dress and a headscarf, an 18th-century costume. There had been earlier reports of this ghost, but this driver was unaware of them, giving credibility to the incident.[50]

- In November 1976 a woman was driving through Waterlooville, Hampshire. It was virtually twilight and her husband, by her side, saw a girl standing in the path of their car which his wife could not see. Startled, he braced himself for the inevitable impact. There was none, and there was no girl. His workmates the day after told him about the legend of the vanishing girl from a council estate in Havant called Leigh Park, who had been killed by a car while hitchhiking to Waterlooville.[51]

- At Alconbury, Cambridgeshire, in the 20th century, a nun jaywalker caused cars to swerve on more than one occasion. There were reports from local people of car crashes being heard, and the strange burning of local brush, or even houses unaccountably catching fire.

- Lorry driver Adrian Moorfield told Sean Tudor that he had parked up for the night at a remote rural spot in November 2007 on the A487 near the Welsh town of Penparc in south-west Wales. He started up his engine again at 4.30 a.m., getting ready to continue his journey, only to see a young woman peering at him through the windscreen! What was odd was the fact that his high cab, like most lorry cabs, was 7 or 8 feet from the ground. And yet the woman's full outline – from head to knee – was level with him as if suspended in the air. She was fair-haired and wearing a light-coloured dress. Startled, he steered round the figure and drove off, and as he did so he could see that indeed her feet were not on the ground. He looked in the rear-view mirror as he passed her, but she was not visible.[52]

- At Peterborough, Cambridgeshire, apparently in recent years, a driver was on the A1 heading north, when he saw a woman in 1950s clothing, carrying a bag and making a dash across the highway from the central reservation. She vanished before she was hit.

- At High Wycombe, Buckinghamshire, along Loakes Lane on an unknown date, the ghost of a woman and her horse was seen. The legend has it that she died after a fall.

- At Great Livermere, Suffolk, on the road towards Thetford, a woman jaywalker was once seen, wearing red clothing. She vanished before impact.

- At Bridport, Dorset, at Gippy Lane in the 20th century, a woman, identified probably as 'Edwardian', was genuinely phantom-like, with a grey face and grey clothes (the phantom image?). And at Charmouth on the road to Bridport, on 11 September 2004, late at night, a woman driver and her passenger saw a woman in white sweep across the road. They said that their car became 'cold'. Also at Bridport, on no particular date, a lady in red was seen on a busy roundabout. She vanished.

- At Abbotskerswell, Devon, a ghostly nun was seen near a priory and on local roads in 2015.

- At Fingringhoe, Essex, on the Abberton Road in November 2009, a motorcyclist watched a distressed woman in white stumble across the road at 2 a.m. She had a blanket over her head, and vanished into a hedge as the witness reduced speed and tried to approach her.

- At Gloucester, along Juniper Avenue in 2016, a lady with a 'blue glow' was seen. And at Naunton, in the same county, a number of paranormal events occurred. In 1998, on the B4068, a ghostly woman was seen was seen by a doctor in his car. She waved to him before vanishing. A monk walked across a Naunton street in 2000 and passed through a car. Other witnesses reported the same phenomenon, and said that their cars unaccountably lost power.

- At North Benfleet, Essex, in the late 20th century, a family hit a jaywalking girl, but no body was found. At Rayne, on the Shalford Road near the Swan pub, three people in a car saw a woman with long black hair, pale face, and purple trousers and a ragged yellow shirt, cross the road, but something about her indicated a kind of unreality. The date was 18 September 2014.

- At Watford, Hertfordshire, at Church Street, a phantom woman crossed the road.

- At Bretby, Derbyshire, on Mounts Road and Ashley Road in 2015, the local paper reported two cases of a woman in a floral dress standing on the roadside; one of the women had a bike.

- At Weston, Hertfordshire, near Lannock Hill at 11.30 p.m. on a night in November 1992, a woman in white was seen. There was rumour in the archives that she was the ghost of a girl who drowned on her wedding day.

# The Lancashire Sightings

- At Fleetwood, in the early 20th century, Theresa, with her husband and chauffeur, saw a woman in what appeared to be a nursing uniform, with an apron and starched cap, run in front of their car. She was knocked down. The car stopped, but she had vanished. Theresa had other ghostly experiences later. It was suggested that the 'nurse' had possibly committed suicide after murdering a patient.

- At Formby, on the A565, between Formby and Ince Blundell, a woman in a green coat was once seen dashing across the road.

- At Golbourne Castle Hill, Manchester, in August 1960, a phantom female drifted across the road in front of traffic. The image was unnaturally large, as if a kind of hologram.

- A cyclist, at another time on Castle Hill, said he saw figure that was 'about 9 feet tall'.

- At Garstang, at Horns Lane on 15 November 2007, a woman in a long black cloak stood in the road causing cars to swerve. She soon vanished. Other reports say that she had a hood, and when approached she revealed her skull-like face.

- At Freckleton, on the road to Kirkham, at an unknown date, a decapitated woman was said to 'drift along'.

- At Longbridge, on the Clitheroe Old Road, a man and his daughter in 2008 saw a Victorian lady on a bike. Surprised at this, and thinking he could be of help, he turned the car around and went back, but the figure had vanished.

## Lincolnshire Sightings

- At Cleethorpes, along St Peters Avenue, an older lady in a green coat was seen at 11 a.m. on some date in May 2015 sitting on a bench. The driver pulled up near her because he had something to do in Cleethorpes, got out of his car and turned to ask the woman if he was within the parking rules. To his surprise, both the woman and the roadside bench she was sitting on vanished!

- In the early 1990s, at Friskney on the A52, three in a car passed a woman in Victorian dress on the roadside. Odd enough, but she would have otherwise looked normal with her long curly hair under a hat, except that her face 'glowed green'. So surprised were they by this, and thinking that some distortion in the daylight reflecting off the road or off other cars was causing this, they halted and turned back – twice – to get a second look. She was still there, and still faintly illuminated.

- At Bourne, in King Street off the A45, a driver and friends tried to avoid hitting a phantom woman jaywalker. It was the winter of 2003, and the time was about 10.30 p.m. The figure vanished, either at the time of the silent impact, or later.

## Other County Sightings

- At Seaton, Leicestershire, at a viaduct bridge on the B672 on 12 April 2007 at one in the morning, a woman with a pale face was standing by, or under, the bridge arch. She vanished from the driver's rear-view mirror as soon as he passed her.

- At South Raynham, Norfolk, in the 1950s, on the road south to East Raynham, a phantom woman with empty eye sockets was seen.

- At Boltby, Yorkshire, on a road heading to the village at midnight in June 2012, a driver saw a woman in an old-fashioned party dress. Even in the darkness, in his headlights he could see that her features were somehow 'blurred'.

- At Flamborough, on Tranmer Hill, two 'female wraiths' were once seen, one apparently without a head.

- At Greasborough, Lancashire, on the road to Nether Hough, there were stories of jaywalking women, some being struck by cars and 'hitting bonnets'. The police were often involved in these alarming cases, but there were never any injured or dead women found.

- At Wigglesworth, Yorkshire, on the road to Tosside, the same young woman jaywalker would always run out into the road on various winter mornings, causing car accidents. She was said to be the ghost of a locally drowned girl.

- At Calverton, Nottinghamshire, on the main street, a lady, described as a 'phantom', was seen at a bus stop in the late 20th century.

- At Watnall, Nottinghamshire, in 1964, a motorcyclist tried to avoid knocking down what he thought was a jaywalking woman, but as he drew closer he realised she was actually floating, by about a foot, across the road.

- At Bomere Heath, Shropshire, in the winter of 2005, a driver and his wife saw an elderly thin lady in grey outer clothing and wearing a headscarf walking briskly along from one side of the road to the other, although the couple were in dispute about which direction she was travelling. But they both noticed that her clothes seemed to be moving slower than the woman herself.

- At Chetwynd Aston, Shropshire, on the A41, two motorists in 1969 saw a white figure near a church, sometimes carrying a baby, and who was later alleged to be the ghost of Madam Pigott.

- At Blythburgh, Suffolk, on the B1125 to Westleton Road, the ghost of one 'Anne Blakemore' reappears every 24 June.

- At Hanham Abbot, Shropshire, 20th-century roads were haunted by a nun, and another woman who could have been the same.

- At Hersham, Surrey, on the Seven Hills Road in November 1966, a cyclist saw a ghostly grey old lady jaywalker. Others described her as a 'misty shape'.

- At Eastbourne, Sussex, on the A22, some time in the late afternoon, a jaywalking ghost alleged to be of a woman who was killed on the road in 1923, was seen. There were some suggestions from disgruntled motorists who had encountered her image that she was deliberately trying to cause a crash.

- At Bulford, Wiltshire, in the 20th century, a lorry driver thought he had struck a woman on the road, only to see her pass through a wire fence.

- At Kilmacolm, Inverclyde, Scotland, a Victorian ghost in a 'sweeping black dress' haunts a road leading into the village, but she floats 3 feet off the ground.

- At Yatesbury, Wiltshire, at a crossroads at some time during September or October 2012, a white 'hazy' woman in 'nun-like' clothing was seen stepping out of bushes. She stopped when a car approached her in the middle of the road, and turned to look at the driver before vanishing.

- In the county of Angus, along the A92 in the late 20th century, a woman driver and her son saw a strange female on the roadside with her head 'illuminated'.

- At Kirkbean, Dumfries, prior to 1890, phantom women used to haunt this road, and one was sometimes seen on treetops!

- At Glasgow, Lanarkshire, in a multi-storey car park in 2007 or 2008, a young woman was seen to walk across and leap onto the edge, before jumping off. But no body was found, nor was there any evidence that someone had fallen or jumped. Yet the woman car driver who saw this happen was talking to friends in the car park, and pointed to the woman who was walking towards the edge, although they may not have seen the actual drop itself.

- At Llanerchymedd, Gwynedd, a ghost of a woman was seen at the edge of a main road, alleged to have been killed in a riding accident. No date was given for this.

- At Battlesden, Bedfordshire, a location for earlier paranormal events, a jaywalking nun was seen in June 1996 at Dowty Avenue, but vanished before a car reached her.

- At Salisbury Plain, Wiltshire, in the late 20th century, on a road where his wife had been tragically killed at an earlier date, a lorry driver saw an apparition of a woman floating in front of his vehicle, which he recognised to his horror as being the exact image of his dead wife. He braked and stopped, but at that very moment a child ran out across the road, and could have been killed – as if the vision of his dead wife was a warning signal.

- At Church Minshall, Cheshire, on 15 December 2004, it was past midnight when two people in a car saw a woman in 1960s clothing, plus a distinctive red scarf, and with 'sunken eyes'. This was possibly a time warp, because the road looked different and dated, too.

- At Handcross, Sussex, on the A23 between the town and Crawley near a motorway junction, in the 20th century, a woman waited for a lift, but vanished. Sometimes a male phantom is at the same spot, or nearby.

- Derek McGall had a collision with a phantom on 12 December 2010 at about 8.30 at night on the western fringes of Dumfries. An elderly woman, who was at first at the side of the road, wandered directly into his path. He hit the brakes, but there was no time to avoid a collision. The figure vanished, and McGall saw nothing in his rear-view mirror.[53]

- At Whiteacre Heath, Warwickshire, a cyclist swerved to avoid a jaywalker on some date in the 1930s – but he passed right through her, and was told later that she was a ghost.

- At Calne, Wiltshire, on the road to Derry Hill in 1968, a 'white figure', assumed to be a woman, was seen by a driver and his passenger in front of their car at night. Again there was a local ghost legend.

- At Potterne, Wiltshire, in 1936, a driver offered a lift to a woman in green standing by the roadside. She vanished.

- Andy Doyle was driving over the roadway section of a rail bridge near Corringham, Essex, on 29 January 2005 at 2 a.m., when he saw a young woman actually on the bridge. She was clearly a phantom, dressed in a puffa jacket, jeans and boots, and with a pair of earphones and a rucksack. But the ghostly give-away was the fact that she was walking above the surface, and appeared to move suddenly around his car – first one side then another – before finally vanishing.[54]

## The Hampshire Sightings

- At Aldershot, on the road between Tweseldown and Aldershot, in November 1990, the ghost of a a homeless woman, who was killed years earlier, was seen.

- At Emsworth, the Hordean Road is said to be haunted by a 'distressed' woman killed by a vehicle. At Fareham, on the Saltern Road, a 'misty' figure of a young girl jaywalker was seen by three persons in a car, in the year 1999. She disappeared into a verge on the other side.

- At Fleet, along the Bagwell Lane, a 'woman in white' phantom occurs, who crosses a field and vanishes into a pond.

- At Oakley, along Sheardown Lane, a woman runs up to a horse rider, and stares at the rider and the horse before turning and vanishing.

- At Rockford, in the area around the Alice Lisle pub (itself possibly haunted by Alice's ghost – the last woman to be executed by the notorious Judge Jeffreys), Alice's ghost rides around in a driverless coach with headless horses – her coach can also be seen along Winchester roads.

- At Southsea, on Alan Grove, a driver stopped at a zebra crossing in 2010 to allow a woman to cross. She was judged to be in her thirties or forties, and wore a short skirt and knee-high boots. While staring at her, the driver was distracted by an impatient car horn and glanced in his rear-view mirror 'for a second'. Returning his gaze to the road, the woman on the crossing had disappeared.

# Chapter 14

## The Blue Bell Hill Legends

The most remarkable combination of hitchhiker and phantom female ghosts is centred around north Kent and became one of the most iconic hitchhiker legends in Britain. Some investigators believe that the A229 from Kent to Sussex is one of the most haunted roads in Britain, not least because of the Blue Bell Hill incident. A woman in a white dress regularly disappears just before a driver hits her. Pluckley, near Ashford in Kent, is also known as a haunted spot, with twelve claimed ghosts, male and female, all locally related to Blue Bell Hill.

Sean Tudor has checked into the numerous Kent local press reports of the accidents and hauntings, interviewed many surviving witnesses of the Blue Bell Hill female, and reviewed many police and other documents concerning these sightings, which seemed to have grown in number after 1980, when most of the earlier ghost stories seemed to peter out. Tudor has also relied on email contacts about these ghosts with occult investigator Neil Arnold.

Blue Bell Hill is a village that effectively occupies the mid point between the M2 and M20 and Maidstone and Medway towns, with the wide snaking ribbon of the A229 providing a link road between them. There was also a familiar pub in the area, which featured in the ghost scenarios – the Lower Bell – but this often adds to some confusion when a woman is picked up from there.

The complicated connection between hitchhikers and conventional ghosts is always evident. What is odd is that the earlier ghosts – in the 19th and early 20th centuries – in Kent history seem to predate a dreadful car accident of 19 November 1965. The accident involved a Mark 1 Ford Cortina containing four young women, and a Jaguar containing two people. Three of the women in the Ford died, including the one who was driving, although it was not clear what happened to the victims in the Jaguar. They were all going to a wedding; three were the bridesmaids, and one was the 'bride-to-be'. There was considerable confusion about who the bride actually was, at the time of the first reports of the accident and the later ghost reports, and whether it was her ghost that keeps turning up on numerous Kent roads. The apparition is seldom considered to be that of one of the bridesmaids, also dressed in white.

Sean Tudor, dating the road hauntings back to the 1960s and 1970s, thinks drivers are influenced by the press stories, especially the later one of 1974 when different behaviour was included in the stories.[1] The first sighting seems to have been in autumn 1966, when the Maidstone police had a frantic call from someone convinced he had killed a woman pedestrian. The earliest published story about the Blue Bell Hill ghost appeared in the *Kent Messenger* of 8 December 1967.

Throughout his major book on the subject, Tudor refers to two types of road ghost – the hitchhiker and the 'spectral jaywalker' – the 'knock-down' scenario – the woman who deliberately runs into the road or in front of a speeding car of the kind we have already discussed. He ponders whether the two types seen in Kent might be aspects of the same phenomenon, or instead whether they are separate female ghostly episodes, with most of them being the result of over-zealous interpretations.

Drivers had come forward to tell the phone operator at the switchboard of the Oakwood Hospital, near Maidstone – where the two other victims were taken and who died there – of similar happenings, often in the main streets of the town. Some ghosts were aiming for other nearby Medway towns like Chatham. There were confusing ghostly end-games: motorists travelling between Maidstone and Chatham, generally after 11 p.m., reported a young girl thumbing a lift from the roadside at Blue Bell Hill. They all happened late at night, and all appeared as real, solid figures. Some of them thumbed a lift outside or near the Lower Bell pub, and then vanished when they got to the centre of Maidstone. Similar calls were made to the police during the 1970s, with the resigned officers on duty actually telling the callers not to worry – they had only collided with a ghost.

So the spooky scenarios come together – the haunted bride, the hitchhiker, even an orb light (see Chapter 19), and the bloodied woman in a party dress.

At the inquest concerning the deaths of Judith Lingham, 22, Patricia Ferguson, 23, and Suzanne Brown, 24, it was said that Judith Lingham died probably instantaneously in the collision, and she was the only one of the three girls to have clear links with the area, while Patricia died an hour after being admitted to the West Kent Hospital. The actual bride-to-be, Suzanne Brown, died five days later.[2]

The inquest into Judith's death had been given local Kent press publicity, and in the process she was confused with Suzanne. And Judith's name was the only one people remembered. This may also be because she was the only girl to die on the spot, and had the local Maidstone links, thus giving rise to the erroneous press stories. But drivers picking up female ghosts occasionally added to the confusion and misidentifications. In the process the 1965 car crash became poignant in its own right, and the 'bride-to-be' factor became part of a new oral tradition – a mainly inaccurate one that became both independent of, and combined with, the other earlier ghost girl stories. But this was largely because of the similarity of the girls, all in white garb, and the various Medway locations the ghosts were supposed to be heading for. Further, both Judith and Suzanne were dark-haired – the usual description given. In other words in dwelling on the tragic bride-to-be, in a high emotional and happy state, they focus not on Suzanne but on one of her companions, Judith, indicated in a picture in a *Maidstone Gazette* article of February 1975. Two of the deceased did not have permanent addresses in the main Blue Bell Hill area. Patricia was staying with friends in Rochester and Suzanne was not from Kent.

In fact the entire Blue Bell Hill area tends to facilitate ghost sightings – it acts as a kind of liminal junction, where town, suburbs and country change over, where the street lights end and dark pools of periodic light take their place. A raft of ghostly confusions, legends, and anniversaries of various deaths and hauntings have resulted. Judith lived in Maidstone, so if a hitchhiker gave that as her destination, it was assumed to be her. Indeed, prior to 1992 the story of the ghostly girl probably generated more notoriety than other road ghosts, such as the penchant for appearing in the back seats of cars. With the female car-rider legend it is always the return journey that was significant. The driver is going home, and the woman also wants to be taken home, either to the same town or just nearby.

One ghost researcher, a Dennis Chambers, believed that only two of the victims of the 1965 crash were haunting Blue Bell Hill. One girl said she had been involved in an accident and asked to be taken to Albany Road in Rochester, but disappeared from various cars. This may have been Patricia's ghost. Several drivers experienced this and went to the address and were told that the description of the girl didn't quite match. Chambers describes how the phantom would often wait at the bottom of the Hill where the A229 joins the M20 at Junction 6. She would hitch a ride and say that she was involved in an accident, and vanish. Mr Lingham was so distressed by these motorists calling saying they had picked up his daughter that he threatened to have a service of exorcism conducted at Blue Bell Hill, although, oddly, Judith's sister said they had never had motorists knocking on their door to specifically mention Judith.[3]

## The Legacy of the Blue Bell Hill Ghosts

The difficulty with the Blue Bell Hill ghosts is because of the earlier ones that date from before the 1965 tragedy. An elderly woman was killed on a Kent main road in 1959, according to police. She reappeared to drivers of at least two other cars.[4]

A ghost rumour had grown up years earlier – the 1916 murder of a girl at the top of the Hill called Emily Trigg. But the eerie connection derived from the fact that her remains were buried in Burham churchyard, near Rochester, and could actually have been the origin of all the later ghost stories, where the description of the girl – average height and build, dark hair – was also similar, as was the fact that Emily was about to be married, and there was a connection with local cemeteries. The ghostly connection with a woman in a blue dress, rather than white, is often mentioned, and is the kind of garment Emily Trigg was wearing on the night of her murder. And nearby Lower Warren Road is also associated with the death of a female naval secretarial officer who died in a car crash not far from there.[5]

Male ghosts also figure in the Blue Bell Hill saga. On a misty morning in December 1968 Richard Marchant was driving westward along Grange Road, near Sandling, at the foot of Blue Bell Hill. He had just turned a corner when in his dipped headlights he saw a cyclist crossing the road ahead of him. But this was a real ghostly experience, because the cyclist, wearing a cloak of some sort, seemed to exit from a solid wooden fence that had no apparent openings. He recalled that the man's bike wheels were at least three inches below the level of the road, and everything was in slow motion. He was 'faceless', and Richard could see through his body as if it was transparent. Richard later said that the figure was perhaps a ghost from earlier than 1965, when the fence either had a gate or an opening at the time, 'because the figure came straight out of it', which could also be the cause of the ghost appearing lower than the existing level of the road.[6]

But female ghosts predominate. And those seen in the 1970s along the A229 all seemed to wear costumes that were clearly dated to before the year 1965, hinting at the accuracy of ghost stories not connected with folklore rumour about the 1965 and later-publicised events. As with the earlier happenings, the fact that one of the 1965 victims was preparing for a wedding, and had been trying on wedding clothes, could include other recorded female deaths in accidents involving weddings and bridal parties.

The year 1934, in fact, was a seminal one for the ubiquitous female ghost, assumed to be Emily. A Mrs Renee Hughes, of Barming, Maidstone, as a young cyclist, had an experience halfway down Blue Bell Hill in September 1934. It was about 9.30 p.m. when a 'dark cloud' seem to fall across her path, and was assumed to be Emily. She blacked out momentarily as she was knocked from her bike.

Jack Woodger was a lifelong resident of the Hill, dating back before the Second World War. He worked at the Aylesford paper mill, and was travelling home on a motorbike one night after an evening shift in that year when he came across a young woman standing in the road outside the Lower Bell pub, probably to attract attention to herself after she had missed the last bus from Maidstone. She wanted to go to the nearby village of Burham, and he gave her a lift and dropped her off at her street, but then she disappeared. Woodger's elderly wife, who worked in a café for fifty years, would tell of cab and lorry drivers who, in the 1960s, had the same experience of being flagged down by a girl, taking her back to her parents' home, and finding she has disappeared.[7]

The early post-1965 dates tended to create more anxiety, and were growing more commonplace. They were becoming more like the hitchhiker legends. Bob Fearne was driving his lorry at some time in the mid 1960s from Faversham, Kent, to New Ash Green in 'dark and dusky' conditions about 4.30 one November evening. It was at a footbridge at the Chatham Road intersection, near the bend of the former 1965 crash. Around the middle of the bend he encountered a blonde on a pedal cycle, but without lights. He swerved to avoid her, and a fellow driver in a lorry behind saw this erratic manoeuvre but couldn't see any cause of it.

A Ron Thomas was surprised to see a young woman in a light-coloured coat standing on the verge as he rounded a bend at the Hill area in 1968. It was about 4.15 in the morning in mid November. His passenger in the car wanted to stop and talk to the girl, but Ron drove on fast as he was in a hurry. But he later realised that, being aware of the Blue Bell Hill ghost stories, he may have been secretly frightened to pick her up. Joe Chester, pushing his bike up a steep hill on his way home to Chatham from Maidstone on a Friday night in October 1968, abruptly came to a halt when he saw a young girl of about twenty in a nightgown or frock, soaking wet for some reason, dash out of a hedge and head straight for his bicycle. She halted, stared at Joe, then ran past him and disappeared into the hedge again.[8]

While motoring at night on the road between Chatham and Maidstone in 1968, an unnamed man picked up a young woman at about 1 p.m. He was at the crest of Blue Bell Hill itself. She said she was to be married next day, but on the outskirts of Maidstone she vanished from the car. The driver was travelling at a moderate speed, and he heard no car door open. He went to the address and learned she had died three years previously, on the eve of her wedding, on the very day and hour he picked her up.[9]

Peter Leadbetter, aged about 30, was driving to his work at Rochester airport in 1967 or 1968, at about 8 a.m., when he gave a woman a lift at Blue Bell Hill, just beyond the Lower Bell pub. He was speaking to her while driving only a short distance, when he realised she had disappeared from the front seat without being observed.[10]

Mr and Mrs Gowers were driving down Blue Bell Hill in the summer of 1968, when they saw a young woman at the side of the road. They stopped and asked if she needed a lift. She gave them an address in Maidstone, which they went to, and turned to find the girl had disappeared. Upset and disturbed, they went straight to the Maidstone police station, and were informed of the ghost stories about the 1965 crash down at the Hill area. The police said the description the Gowers had given them matched one of the girls killed in the accident.[11] And the Gowers were the first named witnesses to identify Maidstone as the destination of the girl ghost, and theirs was the second published story of the Blue Bell Hill ghost (the first was the *Kent Messenger* report of 1967) which helped the later crystallisation of the ghost legend.

# The 'Spectral Jaywalker' Legends of Blue Bell Hill

The 'spectral jaywalker' events seem to have started, in the Kent area at least, in the spring of 1967. Leon Posner was a taxi driver based in Chatham but lived in Rochester. At 1 a.m. one day in Blue Bell Hill, he saw a woman in a long dress and with her head covered walking towards him in the middle of the road. He swerved to avoid her, but thought he might have struck her. He got out of the cab and found, of course, nothing there. He contacted the police the following day, who merely said that he had 'seen the ghost'.

Malcolm Grant, the pseudonym of an Aylesford businessman, told Sean Tudor that some time in the late 1960s he was travelling with his girlfriend towards Maidstone. They were flagged down by a young woman. Again, the usual scenario; she got into the back of the car, and soon vanished. He said his girlfriend became 'absolutely hysterical' at the girl's disappearance.

A couple in the early 1970s, driving towards Rochester on the B2097 at night, saw a young woman in a pale dress walking along the verge on the opposite side of the road. They were concerned for her being out alone at that hour, and turned round in order to offer her a lift. But they could find no trace of her.[12]

In May 1975 an article in the popular magazine *Reveille* said that a pop musician named Richard Studholme was travelling back to London from Maidstone in the early hours, probably in 1973. He was four miles north of Maidstone, at the Hill, and stopped to pick up a girl hitchhiker. She asked to go to West Kingsdown, three miles to the west. She asked Studholme if he would additionally go to her parents' home in Swanley and tell them she was okay. But the man who answered the door in Swanley said his daughter had been killed two years previously at 'the very spot' where Studholme had picked her up.[13] Studholme thought he was the victim of a hoax.

The girl seemed quite normal, and he recalled touching her, and he took her bag from her, and helped her into the car. She was not ghostly in the usual sense; 'there were no peculiar sensations like coldness', he said in the article. She didn't vanish, and exited the car in the usual manner (but many other hitchhikers have also exited normally, only to vanish immediately afterwards). But when Studholme read about the strange happenings in the Hill, all of them in the early hours after midnight, he began to believe that perhaps she was a ghost. In fact the heading of the article declared: 'I gave ghost a lift, says pop star'.

Mr John Dawkins at around 6.30 a.m. at some time in the year 1975, near the Hill area on his way to work, stopped to pick up a blonde woman who flagged him down. She sat in the front passenger seat, and said she had been up most of the night spray-painting a motorbike with her boyfriend, and was on her way home. He saw that she had green hands. He let the girl out at a bus stop situated along a deserted road, with grass verges and bushes on either side, and then realised she had vanished.[14]

Joy Gammon was on her way back home to Maidstone one night in the mid 1970s, at 50 mph, when half way down Blue Bell Hill a female figure suddenly loomed up from the grass verge, wearing a flowing white dress ('that you expect of ghosts', she said to a newspaper reporter).

## Other Ghostly Blue Bell Hill Encounters Reported by Sean Tudor

- Wendy Lang was a passenger in a car one late autumn in the late 1960s, on the A229 in the Blue Bell Hill area. A girl of about nineteen or twenty in a white but noticeably dated long-sleeved dress, banded at the waist, was standing dream-like, illuminated in the car's headlights. 'What's she doing here at this time of night?' she muttered. Her partner pulled the car to a stop, and they both got out to search for her. She had vanished.

- A man working at the paper mills at Aylesford around 1969 was driving home in the rain when he passed a young woman at a bus stop at Blue Bell Hill, close to a turn-off for his destination. He turned round to offer her a lift, and she climbed into the back seat, and then vanished.

- A former employee in the Bridgewood café near Aylesford told Tudor of a 1960s event when a lorry driver entered the café to tell of a girl he had given a lift who asked to be taken to Eccles, a mile south-west of the Hill, but who vanished.

- Neil Arnold, Tudor's occult collaborator, also spoke of a woman who came forward after one of his talks and said her brother-in-law, while driving along the Old Chatham Road, saw a woman in a white dress first lying in the road ahead, and then just standing up and floating away.

- In 1972 a passing motorist picked up a girl on the Hill, only for her to vanish. The story was related to drinkers at the Upper Bell pub, where he ordered a stiff drink and told his story.[15]

But there are still puzzling discrepancies that centre around the various deaths, and the identities of the young women connected with the Blue Bell Hill legend, especially that of Judith and Suzanne. In the early hours of 13 July 1974, Maurice Goodenough, a 35-year-old bricklayer from Rochester, had actually knocked down a girl of about ten or eleven, with shoulder-length brown hair, and who seemed to be in a school uniform. She had suddenly appeared in his car's headlights. He had picked her up and wrapped her in a tartan blanket. He then left the girl in a grass ditch by the roadside, rather than taking her in his car to the police station, to which he reported the 'accident' at 12.15 a.m., an extraordinary move on Goodenough's part, especially as he told the police that she may be in danger from passing traffic.

In fact the police could find no damage to Goodenough's car, and when they arrived at the spot the girl was nowhere to be seen, but they found the abandoned blanket under which Goodenough had left her. It is not clear from the various accounts whether she was conscious or not, or the true extent of her injuries. One assumption was that as she was not badly hurt, she had crawled away from the scene in a distressed manner, and tried to flag down motorists for help. In any event the girl had vanished, and no one had found her or reported her missing after the police called on several houses, and there were no reports of injured girls being taken to the local hospital.[16]

Goodenough said he had not heard of the Hill ghosts at the time, and was only aware of the legend later. But the young girl herself became embedded in the ghostly legends, just another hapless and accident-prone female seen at night. There was later some suggestion that the girl was indeed the ghost of someone knocked down the day before at the same spot. A young Gladys Painter, who was travelling with her parents at Blue Bell Hill on the A229, saw a young girl run into the path of their car and seem to get run over. She had long hair, a long pale-coloured skirt and a white blouse, and was 'youngish' enough to be Goodenough's vanishing girl. Mrs Painter pulled on the steering wheel because she thought the husband had not seen the girl, nearly causing an accident.

But Goodenough's girl wasn't a ghost – at least not then – as she was not killed, or (therefore) in the process of becoming a ghost. There was also some confusion about whether Goodenough had picked up an older girl, despite his victim wearing white ankle socks. The height of the girl is not clear, and white ankle socks could have been a teenage fashion in the 1960s and 70s. A policeman who went to the July 1974 crash scene, a Ted Wright, said in his memoirs that the victim was a woman who had walked out in front of the car, and was thrown over the top.[17]

Both Goodenough and the police regarded the event as real, and not part of any ghost legend, although the local and national press tended to suggest a ghost explanation, with some linking it to the earlier cases. That a phantom might be capable of adopting all the physical characteristics of a live human being is often not believable – weight, form, skin texture, speech, even the warmth or coldness or wetness of the skin of the hitchhiker when it is accidentally touched by the driver. In fact the differences in height between the 1965 victims and the young girl in the Maurice Goodenough case has raised queries. Other ghost experiencers on Kent roads said they were not aware of the Goodenough encounter, so it did not, apparently, influence their description.

Nevertheless, the road deaths in north Kent were soon linked after the 1974 incident, with both hitchhikers and the spectral jaywalking incidents becoming part of the same syndrome, either coming later or earlier, or spatially related in some way.

In fact the Blue Bell Hill saga gained credibility with major accounts that occurred in the later 1970s, some within just weeks of each other. John Gear was returning home from his work in Tonbridge one evening in the winter of 1976. Approaching his street he saw a girl standing in freezing weather in a blue summer-style dress. He pulled up, but she declined his offer of help or a lift. When he glanced back she was not there.[18] In the late 1970s Neville Butteris, a coach trip courier, accompanied the driver of a 13-ton coach. They were returning to the depot in Maidstone in the early hours and had just crossed a bridge at 55 mph near the Lower Bell when a woman suddenly appeared in the headlights. But there was no impact as they hit her, and the coach skidded to a long halt. She was wearing a long reddish dress, with dark hooded headgear covering her top half, including her face, although her legs were not visible because of the height of the coach cab. The woman vanished, and both men struggled to rationalise their experience.[19]

One story came from James Skene, with his account that seemed to combine the spectral jaywalker with the hitchhiker syndrome. In fact Skene, a bus inspector at Gravesend, had two phantom experiences. In the autumn of 1977 he was on his way home to Maidstone after midnight when a young woman suddenly appeared in front of his car. He was by then at the bottom of the Hill, somewhere near the Lower Bell pub. He could not recall whether she had stepped out, or simply appeared. She had brown hair, was of medium build, and was wearing a dark coloured velvet dress which was, he thought, quite unsuitable for the damp weather conditions at the time. He was doing about 40 mph, veered round her, and pulled up intent on scolding her for nearly causing an accident. He opened the passenger door to his left, so that she could clearly hear his loud reprimand, when she suddenly appeared in the seat, as if she had jumped in for an uninvited lift. She asked to be taken vaguely 'to Chatham', i.e. in the opposite direction to Skene's, but Skene decided to turn round and take her there, assuming she had already been in some kind of hitchhiker trouble and fearing she may be vulnerable if he simply kicked her out.

When reaching Chatham Skene dropped her off at the old cinema, which was as far as he was prepared to go. Then the girl just exited the car, but he could not remember whether she opened the car door in the usual way or just vanished through it. The street, lined with shops, was lit but deserted at that time of night. Skene reversed his car round for the return journey and glanced out of the window, but the girl had simply vanished, although there was nowhere for her to go.[20]

Skene later said there was nothing unusual about her, she did not actually fit the folk version of the girl in white, nor was she dressed in the light clothes mentioned by others. Even so, Skene's experience fitted very closely to the legend of the young woman seeking a ride from a lone male driver who, somehow, is 'persuaded' to stop and give her a lift, and then gets out of the vehicle and promptly vanishes without being directly observed to do so. However, the endings are not always quite right, especially when there is no onward journey to the relatives to learn that the girl is a ghost, so this aspect of reality versus the paranormal is still debatable. The inappropriateness of the road and weather conditions hints that such female ghosts may be in a time warp – not actually there at that instant.

In James Skene's second ghostly experience he was approaching the entrance to a familiar petrol station in the Blue Bell Hill area in 2001. It was a particularly wet night, and the woman, with long blonde hair and a black coat, seemed to have no car and wasn't carrying a petrol can to be refilled. She nevertheless looked very happy, and was walking gaily down the slip road entrance, with no umbrella, as if unaware of the wet conditions. Then she could no longer be seen.[21]

Another account came from a Mrs Ann-Marie Austin and a female friend who saw a passive female figure standing near a bus stop near the Upper Bell pub about 1976 or 1977. She reported the similar unreality – someone without a proper substance – about the woman, who had long hair and a deathly white face. The vision was only a short distance from Emily Trigg's former home. It was also the scene of a road accident in July 1939 in which an Edna May Yearsley sustained fatal injuries in a motorcycle accident. Were they distinct apparitions, or one and the same?

A third 1977 account was on 27 August. Barry Collings, and passenger Steven Pope, both from London suburbs on the fringes of north Kent, had turned off the M20 onto the A229 at the foot of Blue Bell Hill, on the outskirts of Maidstone, at around 12.40 a.m. Their headlights picked up the figure of an attractive young woman standing opposite the Veglios Motel, now demolished. She wore a white evening dress (which could have been mistaken for a wedding gown), which appeared to be in some disarray, and made them think she might have been in some sort of trouble. They pulled up and asked if she wanted some help or a lift, and she simply smiled silently in return, but on closer inspection there was an uncanny stillness about her, and her long blonde hair was not blowing about in the rather stiff breeze. Feeling spooked, the two men drove off, and the following day they learned from colleagues about the ghostly legends of the Hill.[22]

## Later Blue Bell Hill Sightings

Around 2 a.m. on a November morning in the year 1979 or 1980, a driver describing himself as 'JST' was driving home to Sutton Valence and was heading for Blue Bell Hill where he was to drop off a girl he had been with at a nightclub in Maidstone. When they both saw a young woman in a long hooded cloak or cape standing in front of them in the road, he braced himself for the impact, which never happened.[23] 'I got out of the car shaking like a leaf, not helped by the girl with me yelling "you hit her, you hit her". There was no one there, the car was undamaged. I had hit nothing.'

John Hippisley of Canterbury was driving up the familiar A229 to the Chatham Road at Blue Bell Hill in March 1983 at about 12.30 a.m., intending to take the turn-off for the M2, when he picked up a male hitchhiker carrying bags. He got into his car and Mr Hippisley had to put the seat belt on for him. In this instance the man disappeared within minutes, with Mr Hippisley having driven no more than 40 yards. But the seat belt was still attached to its bracket – the hitchhiker had passed right through it.[24]

A male ghost on Blue Bell Hill was seen by a 'Sarah M' in the winter of 1987. She was returning home to Walderslade when, around midnight, a man ran across the road waving his hands and wearing a white butcher's-style coat (he was assumed by some to have been the ghost of a local butcher, alleged to have been crushed by his own cart in 1848). She was unable to stop in time, and she assumed she went right over him while he stared at her oncoming vehicle. She looked in the rear mirror and of course there was nothing there. On her arriving home her partner, Stephen Watts, noted she was obviously distressed, but said that she had just imagined it. Neither had heard of the Blue Bell Hill legends at the time.[25] A hotel employee and companion were leaving the Aylesford area of Kent in October 2002, and they saw a woman at the bus stop in Chatham Road (i.e. near the scene of the 1965 crash), although the last bus had gone. She was wearing odd attire. She moved in front of his vehicle, and he braked hard. She vanished. They got out to vainly look for any injured woman.[26] Darren and Christine Green had reached the foot of Blue Bell Hill at some time in the mid 1980s, again late at night. They had just come off the A229 southbound at the Aylesford turn-off in their Fiat 127. Suddenly they saw the figure of a girl. It was all over very quickly: Darren stamped on his brakes, and both braced for the impact that never happened: there was no physical being.

Two important ghost sightings in November 1991 gave another impetus to the Blue Bell Hill saga. Ian Sharpe, a 54-year-old coach driver, was travelling home to Maidstone shortly before midnight on 8 November 1992. He noticed a woman standing in the outside lane of the road, just before the Aylesford turn-off for Eccles and Burham. She seemed to be in her early twenties, and had shoulder-length fair hair rolled inwards at the shoulder. Then she ran straight out in front of Mr Sharpe's car, and turned to face him before apparently being run over. She was solid, with normal skin tones and big eyes. He braked to a stop, and fruitlessly searched around the car and the nearby bushes. 'I honestly thought I had killed her,' he said. 'You can't imagine how it felt, I was so scared to look underneath the car.' He did, but found 'nothing there'.[27] He attempted to flag down two other drivers for assistance, but they failed to stop. Shaken and white-faced, he then made for the police station to report the incident to officers, who were aware of the spooky legend. They accompanied Mr Sharpe back to the scene, but found nothing. They said that if he had hit somebody they would have found a body, and the front of his car would have been caved in. She would have gone over the top, not underneath.

The experience of 19-year-old Christopher Dawkins also had similarities with the Ian Sharpe incident, but was some distance away up the Hill. It was 10.55 p.m. on Sunday 22 November 1992, and again occurred near the anniversary of the 1965 crash. He was on his way home, just passing Robin Hood Lane when a woman wearing a red top suddenly ran into the path of his car, and spookily vanished beneath it. 'She ran in front of the car. She stopped and looked at me.

There was no expression on her face … It was as if the ground moved apart and she went under the car.' She seemed, he said, perfectly solid and real, and he implied that she was not 'ghostly' as he couldn't actually 'see through her'.[28] The usual happened; he got out of the car to look, but found she had vanished. But assuming she had run off in distress somewhere he found a nearby public phone box and called his father, saying that he thought she might be trapped under his car but he was too afraid to look. The police, when they came, found no damage to the car, and inevitably found no woman under it, and concluded that the famed ghost was abroad that night. According to *the Kent Today* paper, the ghost was that of Judith Lingham. The police involvement in both Ian Sharpe's and Christopher Dawkins' encounters, both of whom could testify that they were shocked or disturbed, perhaps proves the credibility of the accounts.

There sometimes seems an anniversary connection with the 1965 deaths, perhaps Ian Sharpe's and Maurice Goodenough's is one, although the local papers, such as the *Gazette* or the *Kent Messenger*, are not always clear as to which death anniversary is involved, if any. Possibly they wished just to exploit the media content of the story. Perhaps the newspapers themselves were becoming confused by police interpretations of recurrent events.

Gillian Barry was driving on the A229 at around 1 a.m. one day in January 1992 towards Maidstsone between the Hill area and the Lower Bell pub, when she saw a dark-haired, pale-faced girl standing on the central reservation, but wearing only a black dress on the very cold night. Concerned, Gillian pulled up some yards ahead, and looked in her mirror to find the girl smiling 'malevolently'. In an instant the girl, about twenty, had vanished. Gillian then suspected that the girl was a ghost. 'It really did shake me up,' she said, when she arrived home in a shocked, trembling state.

Joan Masters and her husband had a similar experience. They were heading to Hempstead, Kent, from Maidstsone at some undisclosed winter date in the 1990s. Mrs Masters saw a gaunt, white-faced girl on the verge, passively hoping for a lift, but they drove by. Mr Masters, though, when Joan mentioned the woman, said that he hadn't seen her.

Tudor's colleague Jacquie Hopkins thought she had run over a shapeless black figure on the northbound carriageway way of the A229 at Blue Bell Hill, after midnight on Sunday 25 October 1992, under or near the footbridge. According to the *Chatham Standard* it was on the Chatham Road. This was only a short distance away from Ian Sharpe's encounter just two weeks later. She said, 'I felt the car shudder and thought I had run over something. I definitely heard a knock. I stopped almost immediately, and was quite badly shaken.' She searched around and beneath the car but found nothing. She thought she had hit an animal, but later realised that whatever she saw was too far up in her windscreen view. In fact it reminded her of somebody going down, putting their hands up in the air.[29]

Paula Cooper, 24, was on her way home in the early hours of Sunday 20 June 1993 after a night out with friends in Larkfield, Maidstone, and was driving up the Hill on the dual carriageway at the point where the Chatham Road joins the A229. Suddenly someone of an unknown gender ran out in front of her car. 'It felt like I went over something, I really thought I had hit the person,' she said. She stopped, remained in the car, and looked around, but could see nothing. She was fearful of getting out to investigate, and drove straight to Chatham police station to report the incident. Again the police found nothing, and no damage to Miss Cooper's car.[30]

Clare Bush, aged 17, had just passed her driving test in the1990s, and her college pal Tanya asked for a lift in her VW Polo. Later, cruising along Blue Bell Hill between Chatham and Maidstone, the rear end of her car began to lurch wildly, and she crashed into a lamp post. Clare was injured, but saved from death by her safety belt. But, through the shattered windscreen, she had an apparition of a woman with long black hair on a nearby verge who just stared blankly at her before disappearing. The woman was strangely dressed in what appeared to be a white summer dress, although it was cool autumn weather. After she had recovered, Clare told her parents of her unnerving experience. She was startled to learn from her dad that the Blue Bell Hill area had a reputation for a female ghost, and that the local police knew this. Clare later wrote that her premonition had probably saved Tanya's life as she was in the more vulnerable passenger seat, and the woman in white had been 'watching over me'.[31]

Barbara Selwyn, a resident of Blue Bell Hill since 1987, knew nothing of the ghost legends when she encountered a mystery woman on the Hill on an undisclosed autumn night, presumably in the early 1990s. She had just passed the petrol station on the A229 when the young woman of medium height stepped out from a narrow scrub verge with her left hand raised towards her. Barbara thought the woman, in a creamy white dress but no coat, had broken down and needed a lift. The woman smiled as she moved towards Barbara's nearside. The episode lasted only a few seconds, but the figure seemed perfectly solid and real. However, as so often with phantoms that can seldom actually be seen in the process of disappearing, the girl was lost to view somewhere near the middle pillar of the car, as if she was heading for the back seat (where such lift-riders or hitchhikers seem to prefer to sit so that they can dissolve away unnoticed). Strange, thought Barbara at the time, but perhaps the girl had changed her mind and slipped away unseen.[32]

# Blue Bell Hill Sightings in the 2000s

There was no end to the sightings. Again the extraordinary road victim who looks directly at the oncoming driver, even smiling at him. At 6.45 a.m. on 6 January 2000 a 53-year-old coach driver on his way to work at Wye, near Ashford, was confronted – as so often when rounding a bend – by a woman standing in the middle of the road. The driver, a Keith Scale, was on a route that took him routinely down White Hill, a wooded and narrow escarpment of the North Downs, 25 miles distant from Blue Bell Hill. His car struck the woman, and he actually saw her roll over the bonnet. 'Shaking like a leaf', he leapt out of the car, obviously expecting to see a seriously injured person. He described her as in her early thirties, with shoulder-length hair and dressed in a long, dark overcoat. Inevitably and routinely, there was nothing there. He searched everywhere, and even climbed the high bank at the roadside on the assumption that she had been thrown up there by the collision. 'I definitely hit her, I felt the thump on the front of my motor. She didn't try to get out of my way but just looked at me and smiled as I hit her. She bounced over my bonnet and disappeared.' Continuing to his workplace, he phoned the Ashford police, but their search of the scene revealed nothing.[33]

Elderly ladies have been seen in broad daylight actually walking down the centre of the A229 Maidstone Road towards Bridgewood. This happened to Andy Reeds of Gillingham some time in 2001. He swerved desperately, but when he looked round the woman he had seen was not there. She was dressed in a Victorian-looking long shapeless dress, with long hair tucked into a bonnet of sorts, and was 'completely grey from head to foot', but looked solid and real. No other car in the busy road seemed to have hit her, or had swerved or stopped. Later he surmised she *could* have been a ghost. However, he later said to investigator Sean Tudor: 'I just couldn't believe that something like that might be visible in full daylight ...' Lorry driver Paul Lowing also saw a young woman, at some time in the early hours of an autumn morning in 2008. She was in a white dress and white hat, but with no coat, and was walking along a cycle path along a slip road off the A229 that led to the M2. As he passed her he looked in his side mirror and found that she had vanished.

One of the most extraordinary stories was related by two male teenagers, who were driving slowly into the Blue Bell Hill area at 12.15 a.m. on Sunday 10 June 2012, when a young woman ran out in front of them, stretching out her arms to block their path. She placed her hands on the bonnet, preventing them from moving forward. Then she came round to the side window. She was dressed in a white blouse and dark skirt, with a white face, large dilated pupils and running mascara. Her general demeanour was that she was the worse for wear, having just come from a party. 'Can you help me?' she repeated over and over, and it was difficult for the boys to get any sense out of her. She tried to get into the car, but they simply drove off. Oddly they saw her twice more, once near the Upper Bell pub, and another time when they saw her stepping out from some bushes, attempting to flag them down again.[34]

Another account, related again by Sean Tudor, is just as peculiar. Glenn Jones, a cyclist, had to pass by the Lower Bell pub on his way home to Walderslade from Maidststone. One wet evening, Friday 14 February 2014, he dismounted to push his bike up a hill called Warren Road next to a wooded area appropriately known as Fright Wood. It was then that, through the trees, he could just make out in the dark a young woman in an old-fashioned white dress dancing around a tree, and as he got closer she vanished. Instead he could hear women laughing! This could, of course, he surmised, have been a prank, or some youngsters skylarking, but surely not on a cold wet night in such a secluded spot.

We could still ask: was the Blue Bell Hill ghost the same young schoolgirl run over by Maurice Goodenough in 1974? There are, to be sure, remarkable coincidences involved in Ian Sharpe's and Christopher Dawkins' weekend ghost encounters of the early 1990s. It soon became evident that the Blue Bell Hill story was more than just embellished folklore. There was a pattern emerging, with three named witnesses, lone motorists, undergoing similar experiences at around the same time in the same area, and in each case with no damage to the vehicle, as confirmed by the police, and all seeming to be around the anniversary of the 1965 crash.[35]

Sean Tudor, searching for a plausible reason for these disappearances, and on the look-out for cruel hoaxes possibly connected with the Halloween period, was curious but also concerned. He suspected, perhaps, the embellished imaginations of tired drivers. He dismissed this event as some kind of prank played on John Dawkins because of the early time of the morning, and her unusual 'green hands' suggested proof of the spray-painting episode. But he is uncertain about whether the sightings are real phantoms, and part of folklore, or the more psychological explanations – say some form of unconscious projection. He seems to seldom take the reality of phantoms seriously. There were so many common denominators – the spectral jaywalker, the lone homeward-bound motorist in the Medway region or heading towards Maidstone, the woman staring at them as their vehicles struck her (Ian Sharpe and Christopher Dawkins), the late hour, the absence of a body, lack of vehicle damage.

## More Blue Bell Hill Hauntings – 'Old Hags'

Drivers cannot be absolutely certain, but an old lady at night with dated clothing and carrying twigs could be either the real thing or a manifestation of 'old hag' legends, so often reported. The ghosts of old women in shawls and bonnets, and carrying a basket, crop up in other ghost and folklore anthologies, particular in the north and west of England. An old lady ghost in the north Kent area, known as 'paraffin Lynn', wanders over a dual carriageway in the region, searching for a petrol station at night near the scene of the earlier encounters mentioned. But as the petrol station was not built until 1972, it could be the wanderings of another old ghost haunting the uninhabited brush at that location. A lady apparently used to live in the woods there, and other rumours were spread about a reclusive old woman in the area in the 1950s, named Emmeline King, who lived in a shack in Weeds Wood, near Blue Bell Hill.

Relics of folklore, such as the jaywalker and the hitchhiker, also fit in with the old hag, 'a very strange game played to a particular set of rules', who would, late at night, in the same Hill area location – Rochester, Chatham, Maidstsone, Aylesford – be standing in the road to attract the attention of motorists. The only difference was that the old woman would vanish while being directly observed, whereas with the others you somehow noticed that they were no longer there.

These hags must be a variety of phantom connected with the darker forces of the supernatural, as it would be hard to connect such hideous apparitions with the spirit of a normal departed person, no matter how odd their character and habits in life. In several other instances the old hag turns and scowls at passing motorists, waving a bunch of twigs at them, and hissing at them in an uncanny way. Tudor mentions that many of the corroborating details of the frightening sightings were relayed to him personally, and were all remarkably similar and were not reported in the media.

Again on the A229, Angela Maiden, travelling with her husband in January 1993, on a dark and frosty night, said she saw an elderly female figure walking slowly across the highway on the Maidstone to Chatham section, as did two others in that month. So did another couple, a Mr and Mrs Rayburn, who, on 5 January, saw 'an old face and horrible eyes and no lips' (although, oddly, she was described as having long blonde hair).[36] Mr Rayburn contacted the Chatham police, who came and found nothing. This elderly female apparition was a disturbing event for Mrs Maiden, resulting in sleepless nights, and traumatising her for a year afterwards. She saw 'very small, black beady eyes … a wizened face. The worst thing was the mouth. It opened and was like a black hole … I've never felt evil before and I've never been so terrified.' Similarly, Alan Matthews saw an old woman late on a Saturday night in September 1994. He was approaching the Aylesford, turn-off when he thought he saw a 'gypsy' with a shawl, and carrying long twigs. He never saw her face, but learned that it might have been the hag when he looked on Tudor's website. But as for them all being facets of the same phenomenon, they are also the mirror opposite: a polarity, the early evolution of the ghost girl in her prime, and the frightening and dark character of the old hag as she aged.[37]

Construction worker Donald Gallagher saw the old hag ghost in Victorian dress in late September 1983 or 1984, on his way home to Aylesford, near to the Lower Bell crossroads. As he came off the motorway onto the A229, going down a dark tree-lined avenue, he was confronted with the figure rushing towards him in the middle of the road, seemingly unaware of her surroundings or other cars (and the drivers of those cars also seeming to not see the woman).

He slammed on his brakes, but the woman had apparently passed right through the car, as Gallagher could see in his mirror the figure running up the hill behind, illuminated by the headlights of other cars coming in the opposite direction. She turned up Chatham Road and was lost to sight.

Taxi driver Colin Eacott and his four young passengers also saw an 'old hag' on the A229 at Blue Bell Hill in the winter of 1991. It was about 9.15 p.m. and raining hard, and the figure was wearing a black cloak and long hat, and walked with a stick. The young men in the cab opened the window and catcalled the figure, which didn't make it turn around. Then it simply disappeared.

John Arnold and his girlfriend were driving up the Chatham Road one summer's evening in 1990 at about 11.30 p.m., travelling at about 40 mph. An old woman with straw-coloured hair simply walked into the middle of the road, stopped and 'looked at us', before resuming her walk across the road.[38] This figure could indeed have been the ghost of a 71-year-old pensioner who was killed on 16 October 1980 on the centre white line while attempting to cross that same stretch of road.[39]

James Shoebridge and his college student friends – two lads and two girls – had a particularly chilling encounter with a local hag in January of 1990 or 1991. James decided to travel to Aylesford to drop one of the girls off, and was heading for a route that took him via Blue Bell Hill. But his car engine cut out, after which a strange figure stepped out into the road. 'It was clearly an ancient woman,' he said later, 'with a shawl which half concealed lanky long white hair. I can vividly recall her features. Her face was nut brown and looked like a prune, it was the most wrinkled countenance I have ever seen.' He said she emanated a sense of evil, with penetrating eyes. 'She was clutching a bunch of twigs and she had a mouth opened in a black maw.' He said the whole car was filled with a horrible hissing noise, and the car 'just cut out, just stopped dead – everything, lights, dashboard'. The car swerved and slid on the icy road. The hag advanced on the car, with the apparent aim of swiping it with her twigs, when she suddenly vanished, and then the car kicked in and started. James said one of the girls in the car became hysterical when she saw the hag staring through the windscreen.[40]

A party of five women had a similar experience at about 1 a.m. some time between 1992 and 1994. Driving home to Gravesend from a night out in Maidstone, they saw a woman walking northward on a verge pathway. She was slim, and wore a long, light-coloured dress that looked particularly old-fashioned, with a white floppy hat, and carried a basket over her arm. The women thought she might have come from a fancy dress party, and one woman said, 'Fancy being out like that on your own.' A moment later she vanished.

# Chapter 15

## High Strangeness on the Highways

As well as ghosts, there is an extraordinary range of other weird beings and uncanny experiences that motorists have encountered. Many of them are frightening and menacing aberrations of the ghosts themselves, redolent with the suffering of those who have lost their lives on our roads.

But many of them simply involve bizarre and difficult to explain incongruities. For example, a young driver was giving his friends a lift back home in the Warrington area of Cheshire in the small hours of a rainy morning some time in 1991. On the way to Latchford the friends noticed something extremely odd. For one thing, a white Toyota was parked incongruously on the central grass mound of a traffic island. But inside were two frightening occupants with huge heads, one looking like 'a giant upright raisin' without features, and the other even weirder, 'whose head in profile was shaped like the African continent'! And both were wearing dark glasses![1]

We have seen earlier the phenomenon of steering wheels being wrenched out of drivers' hands, with the spiteful ghosts of dead motorists being blamed. Many think this is a sure sign of invisible entities at work. These stories emerged when few people had actually died on the roads. In the early years of the 20th century, when wealthy people started to buy cars, some spooky events happened to drivers in the Dartmoor region, such as losing control of their steering wheels, causing them to swerve unaccountably off the road. A doctor at Dartmoor prison was killed when he lost control of a motorbike combination in June 1921, although one of his two daughters in the sidecar, who both survived, said that some invisible force caused the accident. A few weeks later a coach driver lost control, resulting in injuries to passengers. An army captain just months later claimed a pair of invisible hands forced him and his motorbike off the road.[2]

An unnamed woman wrote to Sean Tudor to tell of the frightening experience of her 30-year-old daughter who was with her boyfriend in January 2010. They were stuck in traffic near a roundabout at the top of Blue Bell Hill. Out of boredom she was gazing at the falling snow on the grass verge when all of a sudden she saw deep footprints appearing, actually running or trotting along. The footprints then turned to the right to face the car window, as if whatever was there had stopped to peer into the car. 'She screamed,' said the mother. 'Her fella jumped out, and went round to her side of the car ... there was no person in sight, just footprints, as if someone had run up to the car window ... no prints led away from the car either, they just vanished.'[3] This location was only about 300 yards from the late Emily Trigg's home (see Chapter 14).

In a similar incident, a Mr A. and his girlfriend were parked in his Mini Clubman under a street lamp in Oxford Road, Birkdale, South Yorkshire, around midnight in the summer of a year in the early 1980s. They were situated outside a home for blind children which was near the site of the allegedly haunted Palace Hotel. As they sat chatting, they both could hear a man's heavy footsteps walking along the flagged pavement from behind them. Mr A. looked around, and could see nothing out of the car windows, nor anyone visible in the rear-view mirror. But the footsteps continued, reached their car, passed right beside them and beyond the bonnet. Mr A. got out and stood with the car door ajar, looking around. There was no one. His girlfriend had now become somewhat disturbed and asked to be taken home quickly. Mr A. later told Rob Gandy that he was very familiar with acoustics and ran his own company in that area. He was convinced there was no misperception on his and his girl's part, or any unusual sound effects or 'echoes'.[4]

A young couple, driving back to Nottingham from Darlington, County Durham, in the 1980s, got lost at 3 a.m. The man decided to sleep for a short while in the car, and the woman kept watch, with the aim of waking him within half an hour. She then saw what she thought was an ageing leprechaun with a beard, about 3 feet high and hooded, walking towards their car, and dragging a sack over his shoulder. The woman's boyfriend then woke, and was startled to see the same being. He started the car and shot off down the road. But he had got no further than 100 yards when he cried out and brought the car to a sudden stop, having seen another leprechaun – the same hooded figure, the same bearded face. He then confided to his girl that he had seen such creatures before near his home in Nottinghamshire. 'They were always by the road and dragging sacks.'[5]

Some cyclists, exposed to the elements, cannot account for the strange noises they hear, as at Dorstone, Herefordshire, at a place known as 'Arthur's Stone', in the 20th century, where a strange humming sound was heard.[6] Gavin Lloyd Wilson, one warm night in the summer of 1985, was cycling back home on rural lanes to Wantage, Oxfordshire, passing numerous empty fields on the way. It was odd, then, that he could hear an incessant low droning sound that seemed to be coming from all around – it had no definite point of origin. There were no factories or workshops in the area that could be causing the droning sound; not at 2 a.m. Gavin saw a lone police car, and wanted to flag it down to ask questions about the sound. He didn't do so. 'I found the whole situation so surreal and thought, probably irrationally, that somehow the authorities might be implicated.'[7]

At Milford Haven, at 10 p.m. on 2 February 2012, an unusual booming noise lasted for two minutes. Nearby was the Castlemain firing range, but the MoD said this could not have been the cause of the noise.

In 1986 someone waiting for a bus in the early hours of the morning at Lewisham clock tower, south-east London, near the station, heard someone calling for help, apparently from the top of a nearby tall building. He called the police, who heard the voice, and told the witness that he was not the only one who had reported voices. It was suggested that they came from those who were killed in a notorious train disaster in the St John's area nearby in December 1957.[8]

At Dowlais in Wales, on 20 October 1978 at 8 p.m., a loud explosion was heard outside a mission hall.

In Norfolk, on 21 July 2010, two people in a stationary car on North Repps Hill, a fairly deserted location, were surprised to hear 1960s music, possibly being played on a radio. They looked around, even getting out of the car, but found no source of the music, which abruptly fell silent.

## Alarming Phantom 'Humanoids'

A couple travelling through Longstanton, Cambridgeshire, saw a grey humanoid creature jump across the road, kangaroo-like. The entity stopped on the road to stare at their car before turning back into the grounds of a cemetery.[9]

Arthur Shuttlewood reported how Leonard Denman was driving a lorry along the Coventry–Oxford highway at 2.30 in the morning of 24 September 1971. Near a flyover at Bodicote, Oxfordshire, he saw what appeared to be an 8-foot-tall greenish figure. He pulled up and got out to look, but found nothing. Yet when he got back into his cab, he again saw the humanoid walking towards the vehicle. But this time he noticed it had red eyes reaching round to the side of its head. Mr Denman sounded his horn, which frightened the figure (a common reaction of humanoid or alien encounters reported in the Ufo literature), and the figure leapt over a 3-foot hedge.[10]

- At Martlesham, in the Ipswich area, on 25 March 2006 in the early hours of the morning, an old-fashioned policeman, clearly not real, was writing something down, and 'seemed to "glow"'. Other glows occurred, the one at Lakenheath, in the mid 20th century, being a weird example. A ghostly cyclist was seen, and alleged to be glowing a deathly green.

- At Atworth, Wiltshire, on the present A365, during the winter of 1944, a driver braked hard when a horse and rider emerged from a hedge and crossed over. They vanished into a wall on the opposite side.

In Co. Down, N. Ireland, some young guys had halted their car in a country lane to let other friends in another car catch up. It was then that they heard heavy footfalls heading for them over the nearby fields. When they started off again, rather alarmed, they could see a giant humanoid, about 8 feet tall, actually running parallel with them. They could see the entity in the adjacent field through the gaps in the sparse hedges, even though by then they had reached 30 mph. It seemed to lope on muscular legs, and from the side it looked like a buck rabbit, but full faced it looked like a goat with two horns, but was on two legs. It was covered in shaggy light brown hair. (They mused that it might be an Irish 'pookie', or a hob-goblin.)[11]

Lisa H and her family were driving northwards along a meandering road in Langdon Hills Country Park, Essex, in early February 2003 at 6.30 p.m. As they emerged from a strip of woodland towards a bend they noticed an illuminated entity of sorts, a foot long. 'It was not a shape you could describe, not a human or animal shape. When it noticed us it darted off towards the church, where it vaporised completely.'[12]

It is likely, of course, that a misinterpretation of normal phenomena is occurring. For example, a Ms W was travelling back from work at Ormskirk, West Lancashire, one dark early evening in November 2013. She was doing 40 mph when for a split second a shadow of a human enveloped the whole car, as if someone had moved past the rear of the vehicle. She thought at the time it had been merely shadows caused by telegraph poles, trees or a barn on the corner she often passed. But it happened again in September and October of the following year, along the same stretch of road, at roughly the same time as the first experience – just the three times, in the space of one year: the same mysterious enveloping shadow.[13]

But many horrible experiences concern phantom humanoids with scary appendages or missing body parts. In fading light a Neil Pike saw similar entities in the small town of Cradle Hill, Wiltshire – three of them – just two months later. He got out of his car and noticed that the figures seemed ghostlike and unclear. But Mr Pike had come across a bizarre scene, because the figures seemed to have had no legs, with their bodies ending in mid section. Further, the upper portions seemed to be transparent. One of them immediately disintegrated when Pike shone his hand-torch at it, only for it to reappear at another spot closer to him. He flashed his light on the two others, and the same thing happened – they advanced menacingly towards him. In fear, he rushed back to his sports car and fled down the hill at breakneck speed. But on his way back home the road ahead seemed to have right-hand loops and bends that did not in fact exist, one of which he travelled along. Arthur Shuttlewood wrote: 'It was as if a false trail was being laid as a pitfall to affect his capable driving. Luckily (Pike) knows the road to Hilperton very well, but was much puzzled by the false allure of the deliberate distortions …' [14]

- At Cummers, Dumfries & Galloway, at the junction with the A175 road, a car was waiting to move across when someone saw a 'long pair of legs' run past, disconnected from any human body. No date was given.

- At Corsham, Wiltshire, in the 20th century, a lorry driver saw a figure in the road. He became frightened when its head seemed to become disconnected from its body, because what can only be described as the skull of the figure, grinning maniacally, sprang onto the side of his cab. And at Limpley Stoke a similar event happened when a ghostly face appeared at a driver's windscreen at a bend in the road.

- On 4 February 2015, on the A4076 between Milford Haven and Haverfordwest in Wales, there were reports of strange encounters, when two women nearly collided with a 'dark shadowy human shape with long arms and legs'. Just four days later another two ladies travelling to work had a similar experience in Steynton, Pembrokeshire, in the early morning, a road which had a spooky reputation, they were later told. A tall but extremely fast-moving shadowy figure suddenly raced across the road. The same tall sprinter was seen by Luke Mayhew on 11 February along the same road.[15]

- At Moreton-in-Marsh, Gloucestershire, along the B4455 on 9 October 2005, a couple driving at 9.30 p.m. saw the top half of a figure run across the road. It was light grey, and had no head or legs, and because of its strange elevated posture was possibly riding an invisible horse.

There is a recognised cynical aspect to police officers which protects them from feelings of gullibility when confronted with stories like this. Yet police special constables Dick Ellis and John Beet were not afraid to tell their colleagues that they had encountered a hooded figure on a section of uncompleted bridge at Stocksbridge, South Yorkshire, on 12 Sept 1987. They were checking up on an earlier ghostly sighting and remained stationary in their car when the figure suddenly appeared first in one car window, and then moved over to the other in a split instant. They described its face as 'wizened', with piercing eyes. Then they heard a series of thuds and bangs, like angry attacks on their vehicle.[16]

- At Rougham, Suffolk, heading towards Bradfield St George, a taxi driver saw a large black shadow dimming his headlight beam. The date given was September 2016.

- At Kingsley, on the road towards Frodsham in 2014, a driver saw a hooded figure without visible legs. It crossed the road, regardless of the traffic which seemed to be totally oblivious to the entity. It was as if the vision was apparent only to the one driver.

- At the strangely named town of Pool, Cornwall, on a road close to the South Crofty mine, two people in a car felt a menacing pressure. It was late 1995, at 10.45 at night. They saw a dead horse blocking the road, and they halted with the aim of moving it. But as they approached it, it vanished.

- At Leven, Yorkshire, near the White Cross pub, a headless woman was seen. No date was given.

- At Hangley Cleave, Shropshire, a hairy creature, described as a humanoid or a 'Neanderthal ghost', was seen, although no date was given. And at Kingston St Mary, 'fire breathing dragons' were once seen.

- On the Humberside–Lincolnshire border a little creature, described as a humanoid with a seal-like face and long hair, was seen travelling on the River Trent in a 'large pie dish'.

- At Vange, Essex, at a level crossing on the A13 near the Five Bells Inn, a driver saw a fuzzy humanoid shape which vanished from his rear-view mirror. It was the summer of 1990.

- At Little Hallingbury, Essex, at the junction of Church Road, a motorist had to brake to avoid hitting a floating black figure at some time during the 2010s.

- At Peasehall, Suffolk, near a well-known church, a wild hairy man was seen by a motorist.

- At Avening, Gloucestershire, it is alleged that 'ghosts', standing at the roadside, wait for people and motorists to see them.

- At Tuddenham, Suffolk, at 10.30 p.m. on the night of 23 June 2011, a woman walking her dog along Finon Lane heard a cyclist pedalling behind her. She turned, and quickly moved aside to let his looming figure pass. But he then vanished.

- At Gosport, Hampshire, along Green lane, a taxi driver on 7 November 1999 braked to avoid a faceless entity, which slowly dissolved before his eyes.

- At Tarland, Aberdeenshire, fatigued tourists sleeping in their car in July 1992 were woken up by a hooded figure passing by the car window.

## Other Entities and Abnormalities on the Road

Two police officers in a police van, on an unspecified date, were travelling to Highworth in Wiltshire, when suddenly a dense column of vapour appeared in the road just ahead, and nearside to the van. The two cops speculated on what it was, and both actually used the word 'ghost'. They turned back immediately to discover what it might actually be, but there was no steaming drain hole or any natural mist in the air. When they returned to the police station they learned that there had been fatal accidents on that particular road.[17]

- At Birmingham, West Midlands, along Ickfield Street in April 2014, a couple in a car watched a grey humanoid jump across the road. It stopped and looked at the car before moving back to nearby cemetery grounds.

- At Thornton Cleveleys, Lancashire, people in a parked car in the autumn of 2008 saw a white mist in the shape of a person pass right in front of them.

- At Ingleborough, Yorkshire, at Geping Hill, at an unknown date, a pedestrian saw a glowing light behind him. He said later it was in the ghostly form of a monk. At York Road, heading towards Killingbeck, Leeds, in a summer in the mid 1990s, two people in a car saw an 'armoured' figure on the side of the road.

- At Willoughton, Lincolnshire, a cyclist saw a bipedal creature rush out in front of him.

- At Sexhow, Yorkshire, a 'fire breathing dragon' was once seen, according to the database.

- At Longdendale Valley, Derbyshire, on the road to Glossop, a motorcyclist, named as Mr John Davies, stopped and let a 'giant slug' cross the road. The year was 1950.

- At the Malvern Hills in Herefordshire, in the late 20th century, a large eagle-like figure appeared and 'terrified' witnesses.

- At West Bilney, Norfolk, first in 1898 and then ten years later, 'glowing' barn owls were seen.

- At Falmouth, Cornwall, a creature was seen in bushes and trees walking on its hind legs during dates in the late 2000s.

- At Beckermet, Cumbria, in January 1998 just after 1 a.m., a 7-foot-tall creature covered in ginger hair and drinking from a pond was observed. Also, in the same small town, a large 'pterosaur' was seen flying over Nursery Wood in January 2006.

- At Bakerstead, Cumbria, on the road passing from Barenmoor, a phantom pony with a coffin strapped to its back was seen several times.

- At Looe, Cornwall, a white creature was seen running down a hill, disappearing when it reached the village of Talland. Often, it was alleged, strange sea creatures and mermaids were seen on the beaches of Cornish coastal towns.

- At Canewdon, Essex, in Gardeners Lane in the summer of 2008, a black mist darted out in front of a car. And at County Lane, in the same town during the 1980s, a 'demonic entity' chased a motorcyclist at speed.

- At Bovingdon, Hertfordshire, at an unknown date, a 'gleaming entity' was seen.

- At Scunthorpe, Lincolnshire, along Cemetery Road in the mid to late 20th century, a cyclist saw a white cylindrical shape on the road.

- At Denchworth, Oxfordshire, on 14 January 2006 at about 9 p.m., a phantom horse dashed out from a side road in front of a car. It then galloped ahead of the car before vanishing.

- At Ipswich, Suffolk, along the A12 in November 2013, a driver saw a pile of smoke morph into a young man.

- At Winterfold, Surrey, on 16 December 1967, a driver stopped and got out to wipe his smeared windscreen, made worse by the windscreen wipers. It was then he saw a strange creature some 4 ½ feet tall, he guessed, and 'glowing', and with an odd-shaped head. He noticed that it had an acrid smell.

- At Salisbury, Wiltshire, in June 2005 a hybrid creature, said to look half kangaroo and half monkey, was seen.

- At Slindon, Sussex, on the A27 on 29 June 2011, a lorry driver saw black misty circles with white centres appear just above the road, which actually passed through his windscreen to exit at the rear of the cab. His engine cut out.

- At Seaton Burn, Yorkshire, circa 1990, a 'flying pterodactyl' with an 18-foot wingspan was seen hovering some 18 feet above rooftops.

- At Slingsby, Yorkshire, on the road to Hovington, a 'great lizard' was killed by a local hero and his pet dog, who both died later. No date was given.

- At Monmouth. Gwent, Wales, early in the 20th century, there were several reports of invisible horses galloping by.

- A young American male, travelling at night in the County Dublin area of Ireland in the 1990s with his Irish fiancée, saw a shapeless white form moving up the mountainside. It was like a large pillowcase or bag. Perhaps it was something that was blowing about, but the couple noticed that it was moving against the wind. They halted the car, got out and stared. The object, whatever it was, then started to jump from tree to tree, heading towards them. They could then estimate it was about 3 feet square, and had a matt bluish-white colour. The couple said they sensed something menacing about the entity, 'So we jumped back in the car and hightailed it out of there.'[18]

- At Eton, Berkshire, on the road leading to Windsor, a sense of evil was once detected along a dark road in December 2012 at 7.30 p.m.

- At Beaulieu, Hampshire, near the New Forest in 1951, a family driving past a mist-covered lake found that the lake disappeared when they drove back on the return journey, never to reappear. Also in the New Forest area, near Burley, a motoring couple came across a mysterious patch of blue smoke hovering some 6 feet off the road on Boxing Day 2005. They stopped, turned the car round to check into it, and found the smoke had gone.

- At Ruskington, Lincolnshire, on the A15 in February 1998, a driver tried to escape from an olive-skinned man with a pitted face that clung on to his bonnet. Eventually the entity let go and disappeared down the road as the driver increased his speed. This was apparently a recurring event dating back to the 1970s. At Scopwith, on the road that runs parallel with RAF Digby, two men in a car, driving just before dawn on 29 January 2007 towards their destination of Waddington, saw a figure with a long cloak or tailcoat disappear into a hedge. It was transparent and shadow-like.

- At Malmesbury, Wiltshire, on the Burton Hill on the A429 early one morning in January 1967, a man in overalls was spotted in the dim morning light. The driver was unable to stop, but as he veered round the figure he noticed a pale face and raised arms – perhaps in alarm or beckoning for help or a lift – before the figure vanished.

- At Llyswen, Mid Glamorgan, on the A470 to Builth, a driver and passenger saw an older man at the side of the road at 7 a.m. on 12 January 2008. He had a long grey overcoat, and an 'oval head' which was 'faceless'. Alarmingly, the figure had a faint glow which the driver said gave him strange sensations – like sudden shivery, flu-like symptoms – which disappeared as soon as he passed the entity.

- At Bedford, at the junction of Tavistock Street and Union Street, a figure in dated clothing – thought to be someone in fancy dress – was seen staggering along the highway at some time in the 1960s, before vanishing. The description of this figure and his gait, at the very same spot, suggested that the same entity had appeared 'at Christmas' on an unspecified date in the 1990s.

- At Fazakerley, Lancashire, at Higher Lane in February 2006 – and occasionally earlier – a 'smoking entity' appeared in front of cars, resulting in accidents.

- In roads at Wesham, Lancashire, a floating apparition was seen.

- At Bearle, Yorkshire, on the A684 to Leybourn, a grey misty figure once appeared. No date was given.

- At Hopwas, Staffordshire, a 7-foot hairy creature was seen at 7.15 p.m. on 24 January 2015. At nearby Gentleshaw, teenagers travelling through the wooded area in June 2007 claim they saw a hairy humanoid.

- A Sebastian Cliffe, on the road from Bath to Warminster, Wiltshire, found his dashboard gauges had stopped functioning. He then felt a sudden chill, and a ghostly face appeared at his windscreen. The horrible image slowly faded, and his gauges began to work again.[19]

- Referring to an accident at Welford, Berkshire, on the M4 in 1970, the database said that 'mishaps' happened on the motorway possibly due to the ghost of a 'local wise man' who was uprooted when the M4 was built.

- At Elksley, Nottinghamshire, on the A57, a bus struck a dark entity that 'screamed'. Nothing was found on the road afterwards.

- At Newark Castle, Nottinghamshire, in the 2000s, mysterious stones were thrown at cars, accompanied by flashes of light.

- At Parsons Grove, Cambridgeshire, a woman and her son saw a creature with a single yellow eye – some time in the 1980s – which watched them from behind a bush. They said it was 'the size of a calf'.

- At Horbury, Yorkshire, early in the 20th century, a strange malevolent creature with glowing eyes was seen near the roadside. In local legend such creatures in Yorkshire were known as 'boggarts'.

- At Haywards Heath, Sussex, in 1995 one day at 1.15 p.m., a driver saw a WWII bomber descend towards a railway line, and thought it had crashed. When he got out to check he found nothing. (A number of other phantom plane sightings are mentioned in my earlier book, *Our Holographic World*.)[20]

# Chapter 16

## Beware Fairies on the Road

A woman who goes by the name of Felicity Fyr Le Fey, from Brighton, wrote of her experiences of, and belief in, fairies. They date back to her childhood years, and she refers to them as The Fae. In a feature in the magazine *Chat It's Fate* she said they could give her premonitions of future events by popping pictures into her head. One was about her boyfriend Scott's red car 'crunched into a lamp post'. He took Felicity's warning seriously and drove ultra-carefully. But within days another car driver tried to goad him into a kind of road race. She begged Scott not to be provoked, and he pulled over to let the other car pass, which promptly crashed into the lamp post that Felicity had been warned about. 'We stopped the car and leapt out to help. Luckily, nobody was seriously hurt – but it was then that it hit me. This car was exactly the same colour, make and model as Scott's car …'.[1]

Simon Young, writing in *Fortean Times*, says there has long been an association among occultic writers of 'fairy lore' with 'alien lore'. They are both associated with strange lights and the notion of superior or paranormal beings that come in various sizes and forms and adopt different behaviour patterns. The connection with small entities that may have been goblins, fairies, pixies – or even aliens – is illustrated in the event that happened on 12 August 1983 at 1 a.m., when presumably a Ufo was seen by an elderly man walking along the Basingstoke Road in Aldershot, Hampshire. He later said he saw two 'little men' in tight green outfits, who had 'visors' covering their faces (presumably spacemen-type visors). These entities shone a light at him before saying he was 'too old'! This story, from the Hampshire archives, may have been apocryphal.

Even so, these tiny entities might be ancestral folklore memories of an ancient race of dwarves, or perhaps witches or fallen angels. And they often indulge in the same kind of abductions as the experiences of people who claim to have met aliens – in the case of fairies it is usually children who are supposed to have been kidnapped by them.[2] The mysterious stone circles that can be found on moors all over the UK were believed to be gateways to 'fairy land'.

According to the county paranormal databases, most fairies were likely to be seen at certain well-known fairy sites, and often by drivers of horse wagons and carts in the days before automobiles. A 'pixie' was seen on the road to Hawes from Ingleton, Yorkshire. It, or he, would loiter by the roadside and leap onto carts. At East Chelborough, at Castle Hill, Dorset, a legend has it that fairies were disturbed by an ancient church being built there, so this might have been hundreds of years ago. Local people driving carts in the 19th century would also pass Cauldon Low, in Staffordshire, where a round barrow was a recognised landmark and known home, so it was said, of 'dancing fairies'. A Burpham, Sussex, at Harrow Hill, fairies were said to have 'chased away archaeologists' in the 1900s. At Stowmarket, Suffolk, on Tavern Street, fairies were seen dancing in a ring. They were 3 feet tall, but ghostlike, wearing 'sparkling' dresses.

- At Shurton, Shropshire, motorists in the 20th century would see, as they passed by fields, another fairy barrow, also known as Pixies Mount, and some said they actually saw the little people moving or sitting around it.

- At Bincombe, Dorset, car drivers would often see – on certain recurring middays – groups of fairies 'singing' (the folklore name for Dorset pixies is 'Hobs'). The little folk were also seen along a roadside at Thorncombe Wood, Dorchester, in the year 2006. Fairies at Bridport, specifically on Langdon Hill and Lasingdon Hill, on unspecified dates, were seen by motorists in a nearby clearing. Fairies were also seen at Lewesdon Hill, and near Portland, dancing and singing, and 'causing mischief'.

- Motorists saw 'fairies and pixies' at Burnsall, Yorkshire, on the Elbolton Hill, and at Holme in the Wolds, when drivers were negotiating difficult or unfinished roads during building work, which fairies were apparently annoyed about. Others would describe the fairies as 'little humanoids'.

- Fairies seen at Kettleness, at Claymore Well, circa 1750 and sometimes seen in the 20th century, 'when they do their washing'.

- At Kilnsley they are 'dancing fairies'. They were also seen at Melsonby, at Diddersley Hill, and at Rungwick Bay (regarded as 'helpful'), and at Reeth, at Surfitt Hall. The latter were regarded as 'domesticated', but they left the area after feeling insulted when offered a new set of clothing! At Spaldington, prior to 1838, when they were last seen, there was a troublesome elf. At Wold Newton there was often a 'pixie party', with human gatecrashers not welcome!

- Drivers passing a churchyard at Corsham, Wiltshire, in the 20th century, said they saw a 3-foot-tall fairy sitting on a gravestone that was near to the road. At Hackpen Hill, Wiltshire (the site of several crop circles), fairies were seen.

## Welsh Fairies

- Travellers near the Black Mountain, at Dyfed, or around the Lyhn y Fan Fach mountain lake, say they have seen fairies.

- At Aberystruth, Gwent, fairies exist along Church Lane.

- A Newcastle, Monmouth, and Cwmbran, where cars negotiate the site of a former castle, more 'little folk'.

- Around Risca, along the Barwyn mountains, motorists say they have seen fairies.

- On 1 May, virtually regularly, fairies are seen on the Brecon Beacons, in Powys. They are also seen around the castle at Penmaen, West Glamorgan. Again, they often seem to be complaining, or demonstrating, against the rebuilding of certain areas that they have long inhabited.

- At Clocaenog Forest, Clywd, 'little people' were said to exist.

- At Brynberian, Dyfed, fairies were seen in military uniform, 2 feet tall!

- At Crymech, Fyded, more fairies. At Llangua, Gwent, there were dancing fairies.

- At Trellech, Gwent, at Cwmy Llan, Gwynedd, and at Beddgelert and at Maesteg, Mid Glamorgan in the 19th century, they were all described as 'water fairies'.

## Other Fairy Sightings

- Fairies in 1897 at Dartmoor, Devon, on the Shaugh Bridge, dressed in red and blue, some 18 inches tall also on the River Tavy, and at New bridge.

- Fairies seen in the woods at Capel St Mary, Suffolk, near an old house.

- At Clacton, Essex, in 1982 a fairy was seen 'digging in the school playing field'. At Fyfield a female elf, named 'Lavina', was seen on Gypsy Mead, heading a singing session at sunrise.

- At Staining, Lancashire, fairies were seen washing clothes at night in a stream, and at Worsthorne, at the 'Arm Hole' well – described as 'little folk making butter'.

- At Formby, Lancashire, small entities like gnomes and elves, as well as 'humanoids' – known as boggarts – were seen in Foulbridge, Grindleton and Houghton, where fairies and rabbits were seen side by side in warrens. Fairies were seen at Goosnargh, Lancashire, and pixies heard at night.

- More fairies or pixies at Puxley, and Great Melton, Northamptonshire. No specific date, but prior to the 20th century.

- At Long Compton, Oxfordshire, at the Rollright Stones area, where fairies were seen 'dancing'. No date.

- At Storgursey, Somerset, pixies at Wick Barrow.

- At Walsall, Staffordshire, near St Matthew's Church, fairies appeared in recent times apparently as a reaction to the moving of a foundation stone.

- At Frensham, Surrey, fairies in church grounds. No date.

- Fairies were seen at Alfriston, Surrey, near the Burlough Castle.

- At Durness, Aberdeenshire, at Fraisgell's Cave, fairies.

- At Annandale, Dumfries, fairies were seen at Brunwalk Hill.

- At Skye, Aberdeenshire, fairies.

- At Alva Glen, Clackmannanshire, 'pesky' fairies were encountered.

# Chapter 17

## The Alien Black Cat Sightings

There are an unnerving number of big cat sightings on British roads – known as Alien (or Anomalous) Big Cats (ABCs), a bizarre subject that has been written about by Janet and Colin Bord[1] and by Merrily Harper.[2]

On 18 July 1963 police officers in a patrol car saw a large ginger-coloured animal jump over their bonnet, clearly not a domestic pet. Checks were made to zoos and circuses for any missing animals.[3]

An Adrian Grier thought he saw a lioness at 1.30 a.m. on 9 June 1981 while driving in Bedfordshire. It loped its way into a nearby field.[4]

Susan Stritch, with a woman friend and their families, while driving in Somerset, encountered an ABC in a lane. It was black, with massive teeth. Snarlingly aggressively, it hurled itself against their car. Ms Stritch stopped and got out, and saw the creature dash into some bushes. There was no blood, although the creature had left a 'huge dent' in their car.[5] At Nether Stowey, Somerset, in a field off South Lane, ABCs were seen 'with kittens' but inevitably a bit on the large side. This was late August 2007.[6]

Merrily Harper, driving in Gloucestershire on a summer's evening in the 1990s, saw a smooth black huge feline-looking animal lope across in front of her car and launch itself up a steep bank.[7]

Cannock Chase, Staffordshire, is a scene of many ABCs, and has also been the location of bigfoot-type creatures. A Jackie Houghton in 1995 is said to have seen one of the latter. While driving near the village of Slitting Mill she saw a lumbering 6ft 8in dark-coated creature.[8] The same one, or another, was seen by other drivers in December 2003 and April 2004.

- Black Cats seemed to proliferate in Suffolk in 1996, specifically at Kesgrave, at Shelley in March, and another at Tuddenham Road in Ipswich in June. At Pakenham in the winter of 2003 one ABC crossed the road in front of a van. At Elveden, on the A134, an ABC was seen, as it was at Honington in April 1985, and it appeared at the town of Hartest, and in the Ipswich area in 1996, specifically in Kelly Road and Felix Road. Foxhall Road, in the same area, had an ABC visit on 21 August 2006.

In fact the ABCs in Ipswich had quite a long pedigree, seen almost entirely in the 2000s and often along the A12 bypass. Those at Felix Road were described as 'very black' and 'large'. At Holton St Mary they were seen in May 1998. At Glemsford, in a corn field in the summer of 2006, a large cat-like animal had left a huge pawprint. Were these Suffolk ABCs all of one family? At Akenham a large black cat was seen on 18 December 2009 at 9.50 a.m., and attacked a deer, as did another – or the same one – earlier at Bures in February. A Jimmy Freeman says he saw a large shape, probably a big cat, while driving in the Rendlesham Forest area, Suffolk, on a dark night in the 1970s.[9]

- An ABC was seen at Assington, Suffolk, early in 1966, at Martlesham in 1996, at Melton in May 2004, and at Red Lodge in the summer of 2008 and November 2014. This latter sighting was described as a 'huge feline, sandy in colour'. At Sudbury, along the Henry Road, it was seen again by a driver who saw it run out of a hedge and along the road on 28 September 2010, at 5.30 in the morning, before vanishing into another hedge.

- In May 2001 a woman was driving with her young daughter near Ringwood, Hampshire, when an ABC confronted them in the middle of the road. It had huge paws and a tail that was looped at the end, a surprising feature that was often reported in ABC sightings. This one was panther-like with amber eyes. It eventually sauntered away.[10]

- At Abberton, Essex, an ABC was seen near a reservoir in 1996, which was probably the same entity seen at Braintree, near a golf course, in May of that year, as well as at Galleywood. It continued to be seen elsewhere in the county up to 1999, especially at Colchester. It was seen at Rochford in April 1978, and at Tolleshunt Knights in January 1996. It was observed at Dunmow in 2007. At Wivenhoe an ABC was seen in the early hours outside a police station on 27 January 2009. At Pitsea, Essex, an ABC was seen in May 1976. At Great Wigborough, an ABC was seen in January 1996, although its colour was 'dark fawn'.

- At Barrow-upon-Soar, Leicestershire, in the high street, a large white or ginger cat was seen 'suddenly' in April 2001. It was run over, and passengers in the car felt the impact. But nothing was found, on the road – no carcase or traces of blood. There was no database indication of the time this occurred, but there was something extra odd we can deduce about the event because apparently the lighting conditions were poor or failing, yet the animal was ' too large and visible for the lighting conditions'.

- At Wokingham, Berkshire, in the Forest Road area, 'a large cat' was probably wrongly described, as it had similar ears to a fox, and had light brown fur and a long straight tail. It was seen in June 2004.

- At Wendover, Buckinghamshire, in May 1983 and in 2005, a 'puma' was seen on an RAF housing estate.

- At Willingham, Cambridgeshire, another was seen in February 1996, and at Isleham on 25 August 2008. At Melbourn, along the Foulmere Road, cyclist Gavin Elliot-Turner saw two ABCs in the snow at just before 6 a.m. on 5 December 2012, but they left no footprints.

- In August 2001 on the M5 near Taunton, Somerset, an ABC was seen more than once. And at Allithwaite, in 2009, a large ABC was 3 feet high at the shoulder. At Drigg, in the summer of 2005, an 'adult puma' was seen.

- At Beeley Moor, Derbyshire, in March 2016 which already had a 'phantom horseman' haunted reputation, an ABC 'the size of a small horse' would dart out in front of cars. At Kniveton an ABC was known about in the 1990s.

- At Barnstable, Devon, in the late 1970s, a large ABC. At Exmouth an ABC was seen periodically between 1982 and 1990. There were also allegedly 'panthers and lynxes', which were probably the same entity. At Spreyton, during 2006, a large ABC with a bushy tail was seen. Dr Richard Freeman, Zoological Director at the Centre for Fortean Zoology at Exeter, wrote that in May or June 2011 while travelling by coach to Bristol on the M5, he saw a 'massive cat standing completely still in a field'. It was the height of an Alsatian dog but somewhat longer, with a tail as long as its body. He said it had a rounded head and ears, and looked like an adult puma.[11]

- At Mevagissey, Cornwall, in January 1995, giant red cats were seen.

- At Dorchester, Dorset, an ABC was seen in August 2006 and 2007 in a field. Another strange creature was spotted in a park in March 2013. On Yellowhorn Hill, another creature was seen on no particular date.

- Driving along the Liverpool Road, Chester, in July 2003, Malcolm Pennicord heard cats meowing in his car.

- At Chorleywood, Hertfordshire, on the M25 between Junctions 18 and 19, Karen Thomas saw a huge ABC on the edge of a field, 'ten times higher than a dog'. At Welwyn a local ABC, once seen in 2005, was described as the 'Beast of Brookmans Park'.

- At Mundesley, Norfolk, in August 1936, a phantom creature was reported – it travelled fast through the water of a local river or lake. At Thompson, an ABC was seen at midnight on an undisclosed date in 2004, described as having a sleek body and long drooping tail (although cats' tails do not 'droop', even when they are running). An ABC at Horsham, at St Faith's Church in April 1996, and at Roughton in the summer. At North Walsham in June 2010 four witnesses in a car saw an ABC in a wheat field at Spixworth; also the same witnesses in 1998. At Snare Hill at Thetford in April 1985, this time the Big Black Cat had 'red glowing eyes'. A brown ABC had been seen at Claxton, Norfolk, since 1962, and there was a solitary sighting at East Runton on 19 March 1964. The big cat was seen at Crostwick in February 1996 and at Claxton on 9 June 1996.

- At Winestead, Yorkshire, in January 2000, police were called to investigate an ABC case.

- At Leeds, at the side of an outer ring road in the spring of 2013, an ABC terrified a drivers. It was 6 feet tall, fur-covered, but had no eyes, although witnesses sensed it was looking at them.

- At Church Fenton in July 2006 there were two reports of big cats to the police. A 'sheep killer' was reported at Demby Dale, and at Denshaw, Greater Manchester, along the M62, driver Helen Morris saw an ABC in the middle of the motorway on 19 January 2009. She said it had a tawny coat, and a long tail, lioness-like.

- At Halifax there were perhaps more than one of them seen since 2005, because of the slight variations in the descriptions given to researchers.

- At Huddersfield, in the suburb of Meltham, one was seen in the spring of 2005, described as a 'ten year sighting' – perhaps a decadal occurrence.

- At Northallerton, on the Hallstone Moor, North Yorkshire, a 5-foot-long ABC was seen in December 2011.

- At Warter, near a priory, in 2001, an ABC was seen at 3.30 in the morning, and was said to have 'frightened a dog'.

- At Whitby, in several areas of the town, strange black giant cats were seen from 2001 onwards. At Wombwell, South Yorkshire, it was seen again in the Pontefract Road when it darted in front of a car in 1998.

- At Great Hilton, Oxfordshire, an ABC was seen on 30 April 2008 by a woman driver. It was 3 feet high, and had a long black tail drooping downwards. The vision lasted only about four seconds.

- At Ellesmere a large lion-sized albino cat was seen in August 1997.

- At Farnham, Surrey, there is a 200-year legend of sightings of ABCs. At the Heath Park reservoir one was seen, specifically, at 7.45 a.m. on 16 July 1962. At Wallis Wood, Surrey, along a footpath in the late 1980s and early 1990s, a 4-foot-tall (or 'long') ABC would sit in the pathway preventing mothers and children from passing.

- At Eastbourne, Sussex, along the Faversham Road, a large ABC was seen on 1 July 1979 ('the size of a pony'), and also at 10.30 p.m. on 8 January 2007.

- At Podsmead, Gloucestershire, in 2012, a fawn-coloured creature may have been mistaken for a big cat because it had a feline-shaped head. This was probably the same creature that was seen at Winchcombe in April 2002, with its 'flecked brown coat'.

- At Old Trafford, Greater Manchester, at the area around the canal and the Pomona pub, an ABC was seen regularly in the 1990s.

- At Pershore, Herefordshire, an ABC was seen in April 2006 and again on 1 June 2012, sometimes described as a 'black panther'. And at Storridge in the autumn of 2003. At Worchester, near the Old Talbot pub, a ghostly cat was experienced, sometimes brushing against people before vanishing.

- At Hinckley, Leicestershire, an ABC was seen at 5.15 p.m. on 15 December 2014 in the fields along the A5. And at Measham, one was seen in 2000. In fact 'puma' sightings were reported in Leicestershire towns and villages from 150 witnesses, around the turn of the 21st century.

- At Barnham, Merseyside, a big cat was seen in woods on 19 April 1985. One was seen again at Attleborough on the A11 in February 1996.

- At Aspley, Nottinghamshire, along Trentham Drive, a puma-sized 'tabby' ABC was seen in 1984. This was clearly described as paranormal because a loud noise was made before it disappeared.

- At Shrewsbury, Shropshire, one was seen in August 2003 in a field. It was 'large and long', and the police were called. In the town of Bamwell Hill an ABC was running 'very fast', frightening off both a woman and her pet dog. This took place in September 2007.

- At Saltford, Somerset, on a path that was not far from the border with Bristol, an ABC was seen in August 2001.

- At Norton Bridge, Staffordshire, an ABC in August 2008.

- At Lighthorne Heath, Warwickshire, in the Lean Road area, an ABC was seen in May 2006. It stopped to watch witnesses watching it!

- At Biddestone, Wiltshire, they were seen in the 2000s, and at Marlborough in July 2003.

- In Scotland, one seen in the 1990s at Bennachie, Aberdeenshire, and at Mintlaw late in 2006. They were seen also at Greenock, Inverclyde, in January 2016, and at Glen Prosen, Angus, in the month of June in the 2000s; this, incidentally, was a very large big cat, with its shoulders higher than its body, with a long thick tail.

- At Carmyllie, Angus, on the A92, a tall creature was seen, 6 foot from feet to shoulders, in 2005. At Turin, Angus, in the summer of 1989, a mother and daughter watched a white cat as big as a deer. In the Borders, at Earlston, Berwickshire, one was seen 'large and golden' in 1983. And at Airdrie, Lanarkshire, in September 2008.

- In Wales a 'sheep killer' was seen at Clyro, in the county of Powys, in the summer of 1989. At Anglesey, in Gwynedd, an ABC that attacked horses in October 2011 and again in April 2004, had inevitably a 'long bushy tail'.

- At Trellech, Gwent, in August 2000 an ABC attacked a child. At Aberystwyth, Dyfed, in the 1990s, another sheep killer, along with a 'shuck' (see Chapter 18) later), supposedly killed some sheep. No date has been given.

- At Haverfordwest, Dyfed, an ABC in March 2005, seen by a cyclist. At Margan, in West Glamorgan, police were called in December 2005 after a strange animal with unusually long legs was spotted.

# Chapter 18

## The Wolf-like Apparitions

Entities are often grotesque, and some are just bizarre because they look dog-like – either a recognised breed of hound or a wolf type of hybrid. There are stories of 'hounds' chasing cars at amazing speeds, actually leaping through car windows and mauling drivers in their seats. These legends exist in profusion alongside the familiar one of the pale woman in white apparel. They are characteristically regarded as part of the paranormal: they are similar to the ABC legends, and have the same mystical landscape properties. Sometimes unusual or unknown creatures of medium size and fur-covered – and with apparent ghostly or paranormal powers – could be either ABCs or shucks.

But the most obvious fact is that – like the big cats and indeed like everything else in this book from jaywalkers to cars – they simply and unaccountably 'vanish'. One singular difference is that the phantom dogs often have 'red' and 'glowing' eyes. Then there are the phantom black dogs, which are occasionally seen with balls of orange light, as in West Yorkshire once. Peter McCue believes that some of these sightings are hallucinatory, or connected with ESP or the death of a close relative.[1]

The common name for these entities is 'shucks' or 'shugs', but when shucks are mistaken simply for large stray dogs, there can be confusion, with shucks being listed in the paranormal database in a speculative fashion. The Black Shuck was referred to by folklorist Jennifer Westwood, who had compiled a list of a great many sightings of this creature, with many connected with death or misfortune.[2] They are sometimes known as 'hellhounds', with long shaggy fur and glowing eyes. The 'Barghest' is a shapeshifting hellhound peculiar to Yorkshire, where it is headless and called *Yeth*, and its wailing can be heard at night. One phantom dog used to rush through Devon and Dorset villages, destroying buildings in its path. Norfolk, Essex and Suffolk have shucks usually with just one glowing red eye in its forehead. There are several spectral shucks haunting the East Anglian region. The Black Shuck, familiar to Norfolk, is derived from the Saxon word for the devil, and legend has it he can be seen crossing the A1151 at Barton Common. He can alter his dreadful appearance, and is often seen with just one eye in his head, or even minus his head. Wales' hellhound is called the Cwn Annwn.[3]

The Cornish ghostly animal is not the hound but the hare, the sacred animal of the Celts. Yet yellow-eyed demon Yorkshire dogs would actually attack moving vehicles, and slash their tyres.

Jemma Waller was driving with two friends through the village of Halsham, in August 2016, when she encountered the legend of Old Stinker or 'the Beast of Barmston Drain'. It was a 'werewolf over 8 feet tall, with light grey fur'. She saw a beast on all fours that began trotting towards her moving car. Then it reared up to walk on two legs. 'It looked like a big dog, probably bigger than my car, but it had a human face.' Then it ran off.[4]

As a 16-year-old in the late 1970s, Andrew Long had an evening paper round in a village near Swanley, Kent. Returning home one autumn evening along the B2548 he saw a large greyish-coloured dog walking along the side of the road in the same direction he was travelling on his bike. It looked like a lean Labrador, and was illuminated by street and car lights, but 'soon faded and disappeared'. Surprised, he dismounted and tried to find the 'dog' to no avail.[5]

Derbyshire has had its share of alarming shucks, or stray dogs that could have been mistaken for them. They are sometimes alleged to be the ghosts of dead persons. At Buxton, there was often a werewolf type, very large and moving fast, and it could date back to the 16th century, when it is said the last wolf was seen in England. At later dates a shuck was seen at Barber Booth and at Bradwell. No date was given for either event but the latter sighting was by coal-miners playing cards at the town gates. Another was seen in the vicinity of the Peveril Castle at Castleton. Here, it is interesting to note that a ghostly and motionless 'knight' is said to stand on the ramparts of the castle. At Chapel-en-le-Frith, in a phenomenon which dates back to the 9th century, according to the database – but presumably continued into the 18th and 19th centuries after the railways were built, and perhaps later – a shuck sits on the corner of the road near a railway bridge, apparently waiting for its owner, who never comes.

What makes the Derbyshire database bring this dog into the paranormal is the fact it just 'vanishes'. But there is invariably a problem with stray dogs having shuck-like attributes because of some perceived peculiarity attached to them, as in the case of the animal seen at Mappleton which was 'friendly'. Indeed as this stray was taken into someone's home and 'ran around bedrooms and hid himself', it seems that it was not really a shuck. But at Upper Booth, in 1930, a shuck passed through a wire fence, indicating it was a paranormal phenomenon. Motorists cruising around the byroads east of Buxton are likely still to see a fast-moving werewolf, or an enormous jet-black hound, often baying in pain or terror. At Ladybower, near a reservoir, on the roadside of the A57, a tall creature was seen in 1991 and early in 2006. Any car approaching caused it to vanish, on both these occasions, into nearby woodland.

Heather Webster, 49, related in *Fate and Fortune* magazine how she, her dad and her son Chris were taking a late caravan holiday in Towyn, North Wales. It was a recent November when the weather had turned rainy, but they decided to put up with it for the sake of the peace and quiet it provided. Family members had often holidayed in the caravan, but not at such a late date. She had her blind dog with her, named Jock. Chris and Heather decided to take him for a walk at 7.30 one evening, when they both sensed something uncanny. By the look of it the site owners were putting in new clubhouse and pool in the dark and rain. Heather's arms then, for no reason, 'felt heavy'. They decided to return promptly to their caravan. Suddenly a few feet ahead a 'huge black thing' lurched out in front of them from between two vans. 'It was covered in black hair, unlike anything I'd ever seen,' she said. From the front it looked like a mastiff, while its shaggy hind legs reminded her of a lurcher. But the creature had enormous oversized knees that quivered. Jock, although blind, was frozen with fear. The entity didn't walk or trot but hopped like a rabbit: that's when real fear overcame Heather.

But it fitted in with all the other shuck stories – it slowly turned to look at Heather and Chris with shining bright-red eyes. Despite Grandad, Heather and Chris going back to search for it later, it had gone. In January, Chris told his family that a 'black mass' had leapt out of his wardrobe, 'freaking him out'. But the family, including Heather's mother, recklessly had another holiday in the same caravan at the same site in January despite their experiences and, surprisingly, Heather saying to *Fate and Fortune* magazine that she knew of stories of 'hellhounds with glowing red eyes'. She even suggested that the building work at the caravan site had somehow disturbed the shuck. When Heather later checked up on the Internet about Welsh hellhounds, she was surprised to see reports from 'all over the country'. That was it: 'My days of staying in the caravan are over. I've sold it to my parents. Whatever it was we saw, I don't want to risk coming face to face with it again.'[6]

## Norfolk Shuck Sightings

- At Wells-Next-the-Sea, a shuck was seen in a lane leading to marshes.

- On the A7075, between Thetford and East Wretham on 22 December 2007, a large creature with long greyish-white fur and small ears, long snout and large eyes was seen. One witness had to drive past three times just to prove to himself that he was not seeing things. On the third go the creature rose up on its hind legs, almost forming a human shape, and was at least 7 feet tall when it did this.

- At Buxton, in a churchyard in the 1930s, a black shuck would vanish if approached and patted on its head.

- At Coltishall the shuck was headless.

- At Great Massingham in the 1960s shucks were just bad omens causing traffic accidents.

- At Great Yarmouth, on the Southend Road, the shuck had an 'old face'. On the Sheffield Road in 2006 it had 'long legs' and disappeared when seen.

- At Hernby, in the summer of 1996, at midnight, the shuck had glowing red eyes and was growling 'unlike any dog I heard before'. This one was an omen, giving the family bad luck.

- The one at Hempnall, seen in the 20th century, just vanished in front of a cyclist. The one at Heathersett, on the Mill Road in the 19th century, was tall, with large eyes. At Gillingham, in 1927, the shuck had the familiar glowing eyes. The shuck at Gorleston was first seen on 19 April 1942, and in 2006 it just vanished on its remarkable long legs.

- At Ditchingham in 1938, a shuck disappeared when a witness allowed it to pass.

- At East Dereham in November 1945, John Harries, who has written on this subject, was once cycling to an RAF base in November 1945, when he was stalked and chased by a black dog.

- At East Runton, on 19 March 1964, a shuck was seen, and at Old Costessey, in 2005, it was seen near a pub. At Thurton, in November 1944, a shuck leapt out at a cyclist.

## Suffolk Shuck Sightings

- A Keith Flory in early 1973 was travelling home by motorbike to Woodbridge from a night shift at his work when he found a Great Dane-sized black shuck bounding along after him. It was an extraordinary feat of endurance on the part of the animal – if that was what it was – as this went on for over a mile all the way down the town's Old Barrack Road. He finally lost his eerie pursuer when he reached a coastal road alongside the A12.[7]

- The Woolpit Wolf is the legacy of the pre-Norman era when wolves were common in the neighbourhood. It haunts motorists as it prowls around the A45 around Bury St Edmunds and Ipswich. The Upware hound is named after the village, and the huge and uncanny Black Hound has a large red eye as bright as a rear car lamp! It haunts roads near the villages of Reach and Newmarket Heath along the A11 and A45.[8]

- At Elveden, on the A134 on 19 May 2011, a driver saw, through the grass, a hairy entity on all fours. It had forward-facing eyes, a long snout, upright ears, and stood on its hind legs at times. It moved like an ape towards the halted driver, then dropped on all fours and ran off, peering over its shoulder as it did.

- At Bungay a shuck that suddenly emerged on 4 August 1577 actually killed people at Blythburgh Church. At Burgh, the shuck was white as was the one at Beccles, seen in 1974, which 'faded away'.

- At Barham it was seen in the 1960s. At Dunwich it was seen in the years prior to 1924, its last sighting. At Stowmarket, at Clapham Hall, a shuck 'stood guard over a crock of gold', said to be a monk's buried treasure. Walbedswick, from very early centuries, had a reputation for shucks, right into the 1980s. It was seen also at Wissett, along Mill Road.

## Essex Shuck Sightings

- 'M', on 10 July 2016, describes how he and another passenger in a car on a clear, sunny day saw a figure and a dog near the middle of the road in the north of the county, about 80 yards ahead of them. When they reached the spot both figure and dog had vanished, and there was nowhere they could have gone to without being seen. The man even appeared to look back at the car when it was just yards distant.[9]

- Not far from Rettendon, heading towards Hanningfield, can be seen on the A130 a ghostly pony and trap with a black dog running alongside it, possibly either East Anglia's Black Shuck or a version of it.[10]

- At Alphamstone, in the late 1940s, a shuck ran through wire netting when shot at, yet no holes in the netting could be found.

- At Tollesbury in the 1920s a very large shuck chased a woman on a bike. The one at Tolleshunt D'arcy, seen on the B1026 in the 1960s, was black and snarling.

- At Buckhurst Hill, in the summer of 1989, a shuck in a graveyard jumped over the retaining wall and landed on the bonnet of a car.

- A notorious shuck was seen Manningtree in 1938.

- At Southend in 1991 a 'calf-sized' shuck patrolled the Rochford Road.

- At Hockley the shuck was only seen on misty nights and disappeared suddenly each time, causing 'shocks' to the witnesses.

- At Ingatestone, in the 1970s, a large shuck was said to be the enlarged ghost of a small dog that died in 1914. This transformational nature of shucks is well known. At Theydon Bois in the 1970s the well-known shuck was said to be the human victim of a burned out house.

## Devon Shuck Sightings

- At Cheriton Bishop, on the A30, in the 20th century, a 'dog' leapt out in front of a car. This was also regarded as a shuck because of the uncanny experience of not finding a body.

- At Lydford, on 5 April 1983, at 3 a.m., a farmer reported a dog-like creature which had a snout like a pig's, and slits for eyes.

- At Molland, on a road leading to the village on 31 October 1984, a driver saw what he thought was a Great Dane in the road. He stopped and watched as the dog walked along and suddenly vanished.

- At Uplyme, near a pub, a shuck 'turned into vapour' and disappeared.

- At Okehampton, in the spring of 2006, another shuck was seen.

## Dorset Shuck Sightings

- At Bournemouth, in 2005, a puma-like shuck was seen on West Cliff Road.

- At Bridport, at St Mary's Church, a shuck was seen sitting in in the church grounds, even in the church itself.

- At Broadwindsor another black shuck often lurked. On the Isle of Portland a 6-foot-tall shuck was seen and at Leigh the shuck was regarded as 'evil'.

- The phantom dog at Shipton Gorge had a stick thrown at it, which passed right through it. The one seen at Lewesdon Hill was 'headless'. Another was seen at Puncknowle. The date that the black shuck was seen at Lulworth Cove was given as being in the '19th century'. At Seatown, the only knowledge about this shuck was that it was 'charging along' the A35, and it was at an intersection near a graveyard.

- The last shuck seen at Lyme Regis was in 1959.

- Philpots Camp reported one in the early 20th century.

- At Belchalwell people often saw a shuck at a particular gate of someone's house. In Sturminister Newton, and at Woodcuts, in the early 20th century, shucks were seen, one very large and black with 'saucer-like eyes'.

## Berkshire Shuck Sightings

- At Horton, in Bognor's lane, a black shuck with 'red eyes' was seen, and assumed to be an ill omen.

## Staffordshire Shuck Sightings

- At Brereton a shuck was seen in 1972 and 1985, with glowing eyes. At Ipstones it was seen outside a farm.

- At Stafford itself it was seen outside a German war cemetery in April 2007. It was large, black and hairy, and it stood on its hind legs to become 8 feet tall. A shuck was seen at Swinscoe and again at Rugeley, near the Britannia Inn. The shuck also appeared at Boxford.

- It was at Woodseaves in January 1879, again had the glowing eyes, and was again black. There were signs that the shuck was paranormal when a horseman on a cart cracked his whip at it and the whip passed right through it. The database said that the creature then leapt up onto the cart to attack the horseman, but did not say whether the phantomness continued, or whether the creature actually caused harm.

- Similarly, at Reydon, in the 1900s, a couple in a trap said the dog ran under their horses. Again the driver tried to hit it with his whip, but it passed straight through. At Wednesbury, Staffordshire, a shuck was known as one of the 'Gabriel Hounds', who could fly like angels.

## Yorkshire Shuck Sightings

- At Baildon, on Slaughter Lane, a shuck was seen with eyes 'the size of saucers'. At Brigham, a large animal seen at the local crossroads was 'Willie Sled's Dog'. At Egton the shuck was seen prior to the death of a local person. At Flixton, the 'werewolf' had glowing red eyes.

- At Grassington, at an unknown date, the shuck had 'rings of colour' in its eyes, and made 'rattling sounds' when it moved. Surprisingly the shuck at Grindlesford Bridge could be easily frightened off with a shout.

- At Hillsborough, on the Taplin Road, a shuck was seen in the 1960s, and, as usual, soon vanished in front of a witness's eyes. A shuck was seen in Huddersfield, in the Milnsbridge area in the 20th century.

- At Ilkley, on the moorland, a shuck was seen. At Sheffield, shucks were seen with humanoid faces. At Bunting Nook, in 2012, a shuck with large eyes was seen, and became 'misty' if approached or threatened.

- At Skipton, in the early 19th century, a black dog the size of a horse was seen. At Skipwith Common, in February 1975, a 'dark brown bear', 5 feet tall, was seen. At Wreghorn a black shuck would howl when a well-known local dies, setting off other dogs. On York side roads a shuck with glowing eyes was seen.

- Another shuck was seen at Wharfdale in the mid 20th century. On the A684, running between Kendal and Ellerbeck, named as one of the UK's most dangerous roads, in the summer of 2001 after 8 p.m., a woman driver saw a black dog pass through her car. It had no facial features and floppy ears, and was 'shadow-like'.[11]

## Nottinghamshire Shuck Sightings

- At Beckingham, on the Old Trent Road at an unknown date, a shuck with glowing eyes was said to fade from view. But according to legend the sight of this creature drove a farmer mad and paralysed him.

- In a field near Kimberley, in September 2012, the black shuck was horse-sized.

- At South Muskham, at Crew Lane in the 19th century and once in 1910, a black shuck trotted alongside horsemen and their horses, cyclists and even motorcyclists. At Worksop, along Blythe Road on 11 May 1991, a black shuck with glowing eyes was seen by a woman driver, possibly dragging something.

## Shropshire Shuck Sightings

- At Church Stretton a large glowing-eyed shuck. At Clee Hill, a shuck was outside a pub.

## Somerset Shuck Sightings

- At Batcombe, on Gold Hill, another shuck. At Bedminster Down, on Dead End Lane, in 1908, a shuck was transformed into a donkey, and stood on its hind legs. In 2004, in the same lane, a shuck passed through a car.

- At Selworthy it was seen on the road to Tivington.

- At St Audries it was seen on the road to Holford. At Stogursey it was seen near 'The Witches Tree'. Seen again at Watchet. At Wellington the shucks seemed to change from black to white; they were described as 'albino'.

- At Yeovil, on the road to South Petherton in the 17th century, a 'glaring-eyed' shuck enlarged itself into a huge bear.

## Wiltshire Shuck Sightings

- In this county there were many oversized, even 'tall', shucks, or other creatures assumed to be manifestations of the legendary large black dogs, such as the one at Atworth, and the one at Allington, both seen in the early 20th century, described as 'very tall'.

- At Cholderton, at Welbury House, the shuck was 'friendly'. At the roadside in Coate, in 1938, the creature had saucer eyes and was regarded as an omen, likely to appear at the time of someone's death. The same goes for the one seen at Wootton Bassett.

- In the 1950s it was seen again at Donhead St Mary, athough it was not clear that the invisible creature heard galloping along the Salisbury Road at Durnford was also a shuck. At Wilton, in the early 20th century, the shuck could only be heard panting.

- At Knighton Down, it was near a barrow. At Lascock, usually at midnight, the shuck 'accompanied' walkers. At Ludgershall, it was seen in the woods. At Manton, during World War I, the shuck was headless. At Foxhams in 1936, at a crossroads and near a church, another black shuck, and another at Urchfont.

- At Chapmanslade, on the A36, a shuck with glowing red eyes. This sighting was said to be an omen.

## Welsh Shuck Sightings

- At Denbigh, Clwyd, in the 18th century, a horse-sized werewolf was encountered. At Buckholt, and at Cwmbran, Gwent, in 1961, a shuck. At Bridgend, Mid Glamorgan, a shuck reoccurs at midnight, and trots along before vanishing. At Cold Knapp, South Glamorgan, at 11 p.m. on a date in February 1997, and again in September 2013 at midnight, the black dog reappeared. In Mid Glamorgan the black shuck was seen virtually every night in the late 19th century. In South Glamorgan, at the village of Natgarw, near Cardiff, the areas had a haunting shuck legend.

## Scottish Shuck Sightings

Scotland, sharing the Norse traditions, also has ghostly dogs like the black shuck, only grey. One pads along the B7009, a lonely road between Selkirkshire and Dumfriesshire.[12] In the Highlands at

Creag Innis an Daimh, along the B869 to Lochinver in the early 20th century, the shuck had a devil's or a human face, and was regarded as an omen. It was seen again at Knockand, Lothian, along the B9008, in the 20th century.

At Ayr, near woods, unusually, a shuck attempted to warn off a wolf that was attacking an infant. The shuck seen at Selkirk, in the Borders region, was regarded as 'scruffy.' At Mainsriddle, Dumfries, prior to 1890, an invisible shuck was sensed.

## Cumbria Shuck Sightings

- At Beetham in the 1820s, a shuck could morph into any other recognisable four-legged animal. Also at Leece, a couple driving in winter in the late 1990s saw a large black animal in the road, measuring, they said, an astonishing '6 foot by 3 foot'. It was neither cat nor dog, and it had black, bristly hair. They stopped the car to watch it, and it eventually moved over to the verge.

- At Shap, a town on the A6, at a place called Shap Fell, a large black shuck ran across the road towards a cliff top several times in the 20th century. It was regarded as a bad omen for serious road accidents, some of which occurred. Another shuck was seen at Eggholme.

## And Elsewhere

- At Edale, in the area around 'The Tips', some time in the 1930s, a large black and 'ghostly' shuck was seen, and then a sheep-killing werewolf was seen in 1925, with a 'howl like a foghorn'. At Turnditch, on 2 September 2008, another shuck.

- At Tring, Hertfordshire, prior to 1863, a black shuck with red eyes was seen. It would stand in the middle of the road, and sink into the ground if it was approached. It was said to be the ghost of an executed person.

- In Lancashire, on the Formby coast on 31 October 1962, a black shuck bounded along the sand dunes but left no tracks. At Godley a shuck the size of a cow was seen.

- At Warwick Castle, a servant woman 'bewitched the place' with her own pet black shuck, to create havoc. At Crockerton there was a headless horse, and at other times 'ghostly hounds'. Shucks were seen at Bishops Cannings, Swindon, in the Toothill area.

- At Deane, Hampshire, in 2008, at Waste Bottom, it was black, with a shiny coat and spiked collar.

- At Birstall, Leicestershire, a shuck had a glowing mouth, and at Kilby the shuck had bright eyes and a large-fanged mouth. No dates were given.

- At Algakirk, Lincolnshire, in local trees seen from the road in the 20th century, a tall, lean, long-necked shuck with a protruding muzzle was seen lurking. At Barnoldby le Beck a shuck the size of a donkey was seen. Some shucks were seen near bridges at Manton.

- At Soulbury, Buckinghamshire, a black shuck was seen in 1880. At Aylesbury, in the 19th century, a large black shuck blocked the path of a farmhand working with cows, who struck out at it. He became paralysed as a result. At nearby Fingest, on a local road, a black shuck stood under a tree, snarling at travellers. Legend has it that this was the ghost of an executed man.

- At Barwell, Cambridgeshire, on the road leading up to the A11, a large black dog was seen, although probably this was in the 20th century. At Prickwillow, in the 1930s, and in the late 1970s, and again in 1996, a large black shuck was seen, at the nearby village of Reach, at a place known as 'Devil's Ditch'. This creature was said to be an omen, as witnesses to it experienced unfortunate occurrences. A shuck was seen in Arbury Road, Cambridge.

- At Winsford the shuck slowly dematerialised, leaving only its glowing red eyes behind.

- The shuck at Moortown, Yorkshire, on the road to a well-known country house, always vanished when spotted. Down this particular road other strange animals were reported, along with fairies. Pet dogs refused to walk down it.

- At Willingham, Cambridgeshire, in 1933, 'Hairy Jack' was well known, and on local bridges there were yet more shucks. At Northorpe, Yorkshire, near a churchyard, early to mid 19th century, a black shuck was seen.

- In Norfolk, on the A1067 between Fakenham and Warwick, a driver saw a black wolf with yellow eyes and black matted fur. The year was given as 2006.

- At Cottingham, Northamptonshire, in the Old Corby Road area, a shuck walked alongside lone pedestrians, but vanished if touched. At Thornby, the shuck that reoccurred in the woods, often in the in summer, was the 'size of a pony'.

- In Surrey, at Cobham, near St Andrews Church in the 20th century, a 'discoloured creature' was seen. At Great Bookham, on 3 August 2010, it was brown and shaggy, and three feet high. It dematerialised.

- In Sussex several shucks were seen at Brighton. One was even seen on the beach in the spring of 1977, 'the size of a small horse'. Another was seen at the junction of Mill and Dyke Roads on 23 December 1982 at 10 p.m. At Alfriston, often at a time of a full moon, a shuck is said to stare at passers-by over a flint wall. At Ditchling, on the road to Westmeston, a headless shuck was seen. Three large black dogs were seen at Willingdon. Another was seen at Jevington. At Henfield, in nearby woodlands, the shuck had 'burning eyes'.

- At Warndon, Herefordshire, in 1979, a black creature emerged from under a parked car. Then it morphed into a man with a long cloak. Similar stories were about in the 2000s.

- At Keresley, Warwickshire, along Watery Lane, a person saw a shuck with the usual glowing eyes, squatting on its hind legs.

- At Millbrooke, Bedfordshire, a shuck was seen with red eyes, but no date was given.

# Chapter 19

## The Car-Chasing Orbs

Theresa Cheung, in her book *An Angel Spoke to Me*, gives considerable attention to orbs that appear in photographs as real spiritual entities, ghosts of loved ones who have passed on, but are not actually seen at the time. She says she has received many orb pictures from her readers. Scientists who examine the pictures say they don't always match the commonly recognised image of reflection patterns of dust, pollen, moisture or obvious camera lens light flares. 'In other words, they don't know what is causing them to appear.'[1]

Many of these are seen in haunted mansions, homes and dwellings, and people have managed to take pictures of them which are often reproduced in occult magazines, like *Chat It's Fate*. But they are also seen at night along roads. In fact one of the most likely abnormal events reported by motorists is the bobbing ball of light (known as the 'BOL', or 'orb'). Next to the vanishing hitchhiker and the black shuck is the mysterious light that is either low down in the sky, or actually on the road. They are often regarded as the manifestations of the ghosts of the automobile dead who, for some reason, have become malign or spiteful spirits.

BOLs can descend from a high altitude to road level and literally chase motorists long the highway. Theo Paijmans, a Dutch investigator of unusual phenomena, questions whether road orb phenomena are the same as Ufos. Elongated Ufo-type objects, with their frequently observed phantom lights, all masquerading as vehicular transport, have occurred throughout history, and they are invariably accompanied by weird paranormal effects.

Two Scottish mothers, in their thirties, Mary and Jane, realised they had run out of certain grocery items. They got into Mary's car at 8 p.m. on an evening in September 1996 to drive to the nearest late-opening shop with their two young children. To get there they had to travel down a remote country lane in the dusk. But then two powerful beams of white light illuminated an adjacent field. As Mary got closer she could see the lights were coming from a dark shape in the sky. The two women soon saw that it was triangular in shape, estimated to be 80 feet across, with three red lights on at each angle. The Ufo seemed to sense aircraft pursuing it, and suddenly shot away across the valley.[2] On their return journey from the shops, Mary stopped the car at the place where they first saw the Ufo. It hadn't disappeared – it was now a faint red dot. To their astonishment it shot towards them and hung in the air over the car 'as if aware of our presence', Mary said later. The women and children naturally became very frightened. When they got home they called a Ufo hotline, who rather unhelpfully told them to return to the area with a camera and binoculars, which they did not have. Nevertheless Mary and her young son, Peter, and daughter, Susan, did go back unaided by any Ufologists, and found the Ufo still, after some time, actually waiting for them, this time materialising as some kind of capsule giving off a powerful blue glow, and with pulsating multi-coloured lights.

They then saw silhouettes of thin small alien entities inside the craft, and others outside moving around on the ground – dozens of them, appearing to be doing various tasks. Mary and the children then appeared to have what is usually known as an abduction experience, being dragged aboard the Ufo and given an examination.[3]

## Ufos – the Naturalistic Explanations

Ufos themselves are often confused with 'spooklights'. These are small orbs seen alongside roads or in fields or near lakes and ponds. They are like the flickering will-o'-the-wisp, said to have natural or organic origins. Paul Devereaux drew attention to something that occurred in April 1977. At 9 p.m. a couple parked in a car near Loxley Edge, in the Pennines, saw a 'bright orange light' accompanied by a crackling noise. Devereux, perhaps desperate to avoid allusions to Ufos, included this sighting in his book about earth lights. But clearly something more than natural phenomena was involved when the couple described a 'half-moon or dome-shaped object', a fact that must have become obvious when a large 'humanoid' figure appeared, surrounded by a white haze.[4]

All sorts of other odd scenes are associated with the orbs, and could be misinterpretations of natural phenomena. The attractive A684 running from Northallerton across the Pennines to Kendal can experience spooky BOLs, but unusually large and bright. Rabbits, foxes or tree branches can swing into the probing rays of the headlights, and light bouncing off obscure clouds abruptly illuminates acres of fields and copses – only to vanish in a flash. The night-time road can be suddenly illuminated as if a full moon has emerged from behind clouds. At other times motorists think they are being blinded by an oncoming car with undipped headlights, only to realise that the BOLS are not moving and then abruptly disappear.

The most common scientific claim for BOLs is that they are 'marsh gas' – a term much derided in the US where this has been the explanation for Ufo sightings. They are supposed to ignite methane, although they are seldom actually seen near marshland but are encountered virtually anywhere in the countryside and along roadways. John Harries is also sceptical about most of them, which he says have naturalistic or 'ball lightning' types of explanation. Nevertheless, some strange whitish orbs seen above the road or low down in the sky do themselves have an automobile origin, attributed to lights from car and truck headlights being beamed, refracted or bent from low elevations behind hills, often miles distant. The famed 'Min-Min' lights in Queensland, Australia, are often cited as an example of this phenomenon.

Although in Ufology commentaries the orbs are shapeshifting aerial phenomena, on haunted roads some orbs seem to morph into human shapes. For example, on the A266 going south from Margate at night a glowing light moves flickeringly along the road, and momentarily takes on the image of a robed figure.[5]

Albert Budden suggests that Ufo experiences in the lanes of Blackpool, Lancashire, were some kind of optical phenomenon brought about by the existence of a 'corridor of electromagnetism' running from a nearby quarry to the coast, and which might also have been due to the large ferrous structure of the nearby Blackpool pier which could have acted as a huge magnet, and he suggested the pier is also associated with geosounds and earthlights.[6]

The East Anglian coast that includes parts of Suffolk, Essex and Norfolk is notorious for strange little lights that have been seen for centuries, and assumed to be alive or sentient, variously known as will-o'-the-wisps, jack-o'-lanterns, or 'corpse candles' – all mostly associated with ghostly spirits and churchyards. There is also a tradition of Ufos and orbs in the west of the country. Some can be seen near Glastonbury on the A39, not far from an ancient battlefield.

Nevertheless, it is odd that similar-shaped Ufos seem to plague certain counties, and one wonders if a heptagon-shaped Ufo seen at Croydon was the same one seen at Bagshot, Surrey. The one seen at Croydon, along the Purley Way in the 1970s in the early hours, hovered with a red underbelly, with bright rotating silver sides. The road was strangely empty while the Ufo was at road level, and the driver gained speed in an attempt to chase it. The Ufo, of course, greatly outpaced him and soon disappeared, presumably into the sky, and then the 'traffic returned to the road'. In the Bagshot case a driver saw a saucer-shaped object with a heptagon rim in January 1985, at Junction 3 along the London-bound motorway. It had white lights at the front and blue at the rear. The sighting lasted eight minutes.[7]

In County Carlow, Ireland, in 1884 a witness saw 'two men ride out of the carriage shed. They were sitting in a fire which carried them along to the graveyard, where they disappeared.' In the late 1920s one English account related to a motorcyclist being pursued and passed by an 'ultra-modern type of motor coach' with pipe-smoking men, all identical, as if from a cartoon, holding a lit match to their pipes. Then the coach seemed to turn into a ball of light, explode and vanish. A 'high-powered motor-car ablaze with lights' was seen noiselessly zooming along roads near the village of Athleague in Ireland.[8]

Ken Wooton, in October 1951, was on holiday with parents and relatives, and was driving near Eastbourne, Sussex. In the late afternoon they saw a silvery disc in the sky outlined against the setting sun. Ken stopped the car, and the passengers and he took it in turns to look at the motionless object through binoculars for half an hour. Then it suddenly shot off in the direction of Newhaven, travelling in a straight line, faster than any aircraft could.[9]

## Wiltshire Ufo Sightings

Arthur Shuttlewood wrote memorable books on the sightings of Ufos in the 1960s in the Wiltshire area, and had been on observation vigils with Ufologists and saw Ufos for himself. He noted how paranormal events have occurred to Ufologists, with personal possessions having gone missing from their cars only to turn up when they got home, or radios or tape recorders that would not work properly. One driver, Neil Beverly, saw a shadowy figure inside his locked car which he had left on the outskirts of a Ufo hunt, yet he found no one inside. Ex-policeman John Bennett told Shuttlewood in 1970 that while he and his Ufo friends were sitting in his van in fading light at Cradle Hill in Wiltshire they heard heavy plodding footsteps in the brush and vegetation, which seemed to go round the back of the van. They found nothing in the vicinity, and they knew that no animal could have produced such heavy sounds.[10]

Lorry driver Terry Simpson was cruising along the Westbury Road in Warminster at 5.25 one morning in 1966. He was suddenly confronted with a blinding light to his left. He braked hard and skidded to a halt. He jumped out of his cab and stared at the light. 'It seemed to be a thing of substance. It was overhead and shaped like a ball. It was dancing about. There was no shaft of light beneath as you'd get from a searchlight gleam.' The light seemed to 'blow out', like a candle, but with 'funny, frizzling noises'.[11]

A Dennis Tilt and his wife had a Ufo experience in the village of Chitterne, not far from Warminster. It was 22 October 1966. They both saw orangey-red lights in a triangular formation on nearby farmland. Mr Tilt briefly stopped his car and got out, before driving off again within minutes. The Tilts noticed, looking back, that the object seemed to morph from a confusion of lights to a flattish metallic object in a flying saucer shape, but still somehow radiating colours.[12]

John and Joan Lewis were driving along the Shaftesbury to Warminster road on 18 May 1972, and were just a few miles from Longbridge Deverill. It was after 7 p.m. when they saw three lights appear low on the horizon over Cow Down Hill. At first Mr Lewis thought the sun was merely reflecting off seagulls, but then they both could see that the objects were silvery blobs of pearl-shaped light. The couple got out of the car for a better look. John later described the lights as 'incredible, quite uncanny and unworldly'. Soon there was only one light, and it drifted slowly downwards, but shortly after, nine more luminous orbs appeared. The vision lasted for three minutes, before the Ufos flew off or vanished. Police in the Warminster area took the Ufos seriously, because they 'may prove important one day in the future'.[13]

At Devizes, in fields near Oliver's Castle, oval BOLs were seen on 11 August 1996. At Eastcourt, at dusk, a blue BOL was seen in the main village street. No date was given. There was an explosion over the village of Ford at 3.45 a.m. on 23 February 1977. It was accompanied by a turquoise flash (turquoise is a familiar Ufo or BOL colour). At Laverstock in the 1990s motorists and pedestrians saw a 'glowing loaf of bread'. At Upper Scudmore, on 9 October 1976, a small orb in the sky was seen from the road.[14]

## The Hertfordshire Sightings

- On 2 September 1977 at 11.40 a.m. at Hadley Wood, on the border with Enfield, Greater London, and Hertfordshire, a driver and his passenger saw a small fluorescent green ball manoeuvring directly in front of their car before disappearing. Two days later, at Potters Bar, Enfield, at 11 p.m., a young couple spotted a bright object moving slowly from a nearby copse. It hovered for a while before dimming, brightening and pulsating, and even 'spitting flame' from its left side.[15] And just a week after that, south of Potters Bar, a family of four travelling along Stagg Hill noticed a bright orange triangular light hovering in the direction of Enfield. After stopping the car they viewed the object through binoculars and noted that it was actually boomerang-shaped, and the light was coming only from the edge of it. Two days later, at Dancers Hill, again in the Potters Bar area, a couple were driving along a country road when they saw a circular object hovering low near a road junction on the edge of Wrotham Park Estate. It had two orange-red lights and one green one. The object soon shot away into space.[16]

- At Rickmansworth two policemen saw a bright green light pass over their patrol car in February 2010.

- At the place now known as St Albans, a 'bright coloured ship' was seen in the skies on 1 January 1254.[17]

- At Besford, Worcestershire, in the early 20th century, a motorist pulled up when he saw a bright phantom light outside Dower House. There were other reports in the database of paranormal shadows and faces near Dower House. At Pershore, Worcestershire, near the River Avon in August 1965, a large team of ghost hunters were surrounded by a misty shape, and they also saw a glowing square object. Not far from it a humanoid-type figure, 6 feet tall, was floating

3 feet off the ground, and may or may not have been associated with the misty shape. Again, in Pershore, circa 2005, a green flash in the sky startled many witnesses, as did another light that was 'swirling'.[18]

- And at Welwyn Garden City a triangular craft was seen over a lake in 1992.

- At Ballachulis, in the Highlands, an orb was seen by a driver. No date was given, but the database for the Highlands said that such orbs were an omen from a clan chief. On the Isle of Skye, in one winter in the mid 1990s, three men walking on a road in Glendale watched a bright BOL descend into a field and disappear in a flash of light. They said it was white in the centre and had coloured edges.

- On the Isle of Arran, Ayrshire, a mushroom-shaped Ufo was seen by a driver and his family on 5 February 1985. They said it had a blue light at its base. At East Kilbride, South Lanarkshire, in the 1960s a BOL was seen to emerge from a graveyard and travel into a nearby road. At Glasgow, Lanarkshire, in December 1752 the database records exploding fireballs, giving off sparks and stones. A bright orange shimmering Ufo was seen in the city on 2 January 2011. There was some confusion from various reports that the light might have come from fighter planes roaring overhead, although no aircraft sounds were heard. In any event the light 'shot upwards'.

- At Tarbrax, Lanarkshire, on the A70 to Balerno, a black shiny Ufo was seen on 17 August 1992. This was presumably during daylight hours, as no light was seen. However, the motorist who saw this implied that an abduction may have taken place because one and a half hours was unaccounted for when he or she returned home.

- At Paxton, Lothian, a driver stopped when he came upon a yellow light in the road that lasted '30 seconds'. The date was 12 March 2007.

## Derbyshire Ufo Sightings.

- In March 1978 a van driver travelled home to Risley on the M62 motorway, and then took a short cut off the motorway, and travelled for a short distance on an unmarked road of overgrown land, and was not far from a nuclear research plant. It was then that he saw a 'glowing white mass' (later described as a vaguely humanoid silver-white shape, and even later as a 'silvery man'), cross the road in front of his vehicle.[19]

- At Bonsall village a Ufo was seen in the year 2000. It was the classic type often shown in Ufo images on websites – it had a small segment missing from its circular edge. It was videoed.

- At Buxton during 1973–74 a Ufo or phantom aerial vehicle of some sort was seen several times, invariably at night.

- At Glossop, on the road between Chapel-en-le-Frith and Glossop, a Ufo 'flying box' was observed hovering over the moors. The date was August 1962, and the object was glowing and had four windows. It vanished from view after traversing several miles of sky.

Mrs Laverne Marshall was driving home to Glossop on 14 February 1995 with members of her family. She was approaching Longdendale when a group of small cavorting balls of light appeared on the dashboard of her car. Then they performed routines like moving into the interior of the car, splitting up into groups, going back to the dashboard in single file, and so forth. They vanished after a few minutes.[20]

## In the Meantime

- At Brixham, Devon, on 28 April 1967 a Ufo was seen hovering over the town for several hours. At Torbay, on 26 May 2004, a 'flying cigar' was seen, and a picture taken of it. In recent years a driver along an unnamed Devon country road saw an object just twenty yards distant, hovering motionless and silent, just above some nearby trees. It was very large, a 'flying saucer' with lights around its outer, lower circumference, 'and gothic in style, with lighted windows in its inner, upper circumference'. He assumed a secular explanation for this vision, and speculated whether the nearby electricity pylon had any connection with it.[21]

- A Peter Day was driving on the road to Aylesbury, Buckinghamshire, just after 9 a.m. on 11 January 1973 when he saw a pulsating orange light in the north. It travelled more or less parallel with him until he eventually stopped to look at it. Fortunately, Peter always carried a movie camera with him which he found useful in his work as a building surveyor, and managed to film the orange blob before it disappeared suddenly. Local schoolchildren at Ickford, also Buckinghamshire, had also seen the object that morning, as did a teacher who was driving to the school. The film itself was analysed by Kodak laboratories in Hemel Hempstead, Hertfordshire, and confirmed to be genuine, and to probably be a 'fireball' or 'ball lightning'. Atmospheric scientists were called in by Kodak to determine this, but although they concluded the Ufo was not a natural phenomenon they had no idea what the object was.[22]

- In the spring of 1976 a group of people on a bus travelling to Sale in Greater Manchester saw a massive Ufo the size of a football pitch (some 300 feet) hovering over a former large industrial site. It had large white lights arranged in a kind of grid pattern. Police officers, further away, also saw it.[23] There were other Ufo sightings over this industrial area, often large black objects with beaming columns of coloured light, often appearing as semi-solid. And they were frequently very low down on the roads and fields.

- Along the banks of the Mersey river, south Manchester, an oval orange/pink Ufo was seen at 9 p.m. on 19 August 1979. It dropped into a field, morphed to a grey colour, rose again and hovered close to a road.

- At Bury BOLs of different sizes, fast and zigzagging, were seen in the late 1990s.

- At Reading, Berkshire, on 14 April 2006, when they had reached Basingstoke Road, two teenagers saw a red glowing orb on the horizon.

- On the March Fens, just south of Torney in Cambridgeshire, drivers could see a 'ghost light' deep in the fens. At Peterborough on 23 March 1999, a 'large airship' was seen travelling fast.

- At Rings End, Buckinghamshire, a Ufo was seen in the skies over March Road on 10 April 1008 at 11 p.m. The witness, one Andrew Warren, said it was a diamond formation of lights, accompanied possibly by other similar shapes.

- At Mawnan, Cornwall, on 3 May 2007 in a wooded area close to a church, a camper saw two BOLs shining through the fabric of his tent. At Redruth on 9 July 1976 a driver saw a spinning and pulsating white disc.

- At Caldbeck, in Cumbria, on 4 March 1954, a father and son saw a disc-shaped Ufo disappearing over the horizon, and it was assumed that it had crash-landed. According to the county's paranormal database, both were detained in custody for two weeks on the assumption that they had witnessed a secret project of some kind. In fact local people who had also seen the aftermath of the Ufo event said they had seen alien bodies with 'devil-like' faces being removed.

- At Briantspuddle, Dorset, along Roges Hill, a patrol car team saw a single headlight approach a bend on a date in 1983. The driver dipped the headlights and turned the bend, but the other light could no longer be seen. Similar reports of the orb flitting along the hill had been made, and there had been several fatal accidents in earlier years. The police also chased a Ufo along the road at Holworth in October 1967, where it was originally seen hovering over Moigne Down.

- At Blackmore, Essex, on 18 March 1985 at 7 p.m., a hexagon-shaped Ufo was travelling fast with two beams of light at the front, and clusters of other colours on its underside. At Coggeshall a strange ball of light was seen outside Guild House, on Market End. No date was given. At Colchester children said they saw a BOL in the autumn of 1976.

It apparently stopped, and returned along the A12 to be seen by others later.

- At Hainault, Essex, in the Forest County Park, a red light was seen over the lake on 5 May 1977. When police were alerted and travelled along the road leading to the lake, it vanished. Also at Hainault, on 8 May 1977 two men walking their dogs saw a blue figure, some seven feet tall. It promptly vanished.

- At Langenhoe on 14 September 1965 a Ufo was seen 'flashing its lights'. At Ramsden Heath, the Ufo seen in February 1965 was a 'zigzagly rugby ball', surrounded by red lights. At Rochford, along Acacia Avenue, on 30 August 2005, several witnesses reported orange BOLs, undulating like 'jellyfish'. At Southend on 14 September 1954, a local pilot reported a near miss with a fast-moving domed disc.

- At Market Harborough, Gloucestershire, an orb, actually flitting around in a car, was caught on camera at 9.20 p.m. in February 2009. The town already had a reputation for ghosts and poltergeists.

- At Snettisham, Norfolk, a dark-grey craft, looking like a 'stretched plectrum', emerged from a cloud on 22 August 2016.

## The Hampshire Sightings

- At Bordon, along the Forest Road/Hendon Road area, a Ufo was seen in June 1999 by friends driving from a hospital. This was normally a two-minute trip, but unaccountably lasted more than forty minutes. There was no sense of unconsciousness or any awareness of 'jumps' in time. The same trip was done by pedestrians in March 2001, when this time three hours were lost.

- At Chawton, a white orb was seen at 9.30 p.m. on 22 June 2002. It was filmed, and was seen morphing its shape and size. It vanished behind a dark cloud. At Sopley a Ufo was seen passing over the A338 that runs between Avon and Sopley, and generated such heat that it melted the tarmac surface. This happened one night in November 1967 and was witnessed by two separate groups of people. It was reckoned to be 25 metres long, and affected cars' lights and electrics and highway lights.

- At Winchester, on the Chilcombe Road near the A272, a cigar-shaped Ufo was seen on 14 November 1974, and had 'three faces peering' out of its 'windows'. A halted car was said to have been approached by an alien humanoid with a beard, making the car vibrate. Then the alien presumably returned to the Ufo, which promptly vanished. The car was then able to drive away normally. Also at the city, in January or February 2004, councillor Adrian Hicks reported an 'alien entity' walking along a busy street. It was what Ufologists call a typical 'grey', with large oval eyes, 'almost human' and wearing a tutu! He noted it shuffled along like a penguin.

## The Yorkshire Sightings

- At Skipton, a Ufo was seen on roads in the late 20th century. At Byland Abbey, North Yorkshire, a 'large radial silver object' was seen in 1290.

- At Chapel le Dale, in the 20th century, in a cave system, a Ufo was seen, but also large flying creatures which may have come from it.

- At Cleveland, in November or December 2003, a cigar-shaped Ufo was seen, some 18 feet long. Motorists watched, amazed, as it was forced down by RAF fighters.

- At East Scrafton a 'light' was seen floating down the middle of a main road at night, causing motorists to swerve.

- At Filey, said to be a 'hotspot for Ufos', forty-eight reports were received by one group in a year. The database records one in 2004.

- At Gilling West, a rotating orange/blue object was seen by campers at 1 a.m. on 2 August 2007. It made a 'washing machine sound'.

- At Bridlington in March 2007, a David Hinde saw two BOLs emitting reddish glows.

- On the Moors on 1 December 1987 a strange creature was seen running away with a large silver disc on the ground in the distance. The Ufo flew off, and the witnesses said they lost two hours, and there was possibly an abduction experience.

- In Myers Lane, Loxley, in 1977 a couple in a car was pursued by a Ufo. They actually saw a figure in the craft – 'large with frizzy hair'.

- In July 1793 orbs were seen dancing around an empty grave in St Thomas's Church, Penistone, at the time a young boy was being buried.

- Over what is now the Woodthorpe area of Sheffield, in December 1731, a 'cloud' shot out beams of light. Strangely another cloud did an identical thing 286 years later in February 2017.

- At Todmorden, from the 1960s to the present, there have been endless experiences of BOLs, and a famous case of a Ufo involving a police patrol car is mentioned later.

- At West Wilton on the A684 to Swinithwaite, in the 20th century, a BOL, presumably when it was hovering at road level, vanished when cars got too close to it.

- At Anlaby, near a school on 18 January 1978, three figures in 'golden clothing' were seen to climb out of a round Ufo. The Ufo soon flew off.

- At Skipton, North Yorkshire, a Ufo was seen on roads in the late 20th century. A 36-year-old woman, given the pseudonym Christine Smith, was driving home on the A65 to Skipton on 4 March 1982 at about 10.15 p.m., and had reached Coniston Cutting. She saw this car with a blue light on one side of it, while other blue-green lights actually seemed to be following it.[24]

## The Norfolk Sightings

- On 30 May, reoccurring, blue lights are seen over a particular area at Bircham Newton, where regular 'flying machines' had been reported. At Gorleston, on 24 August 2007, a 'flying wheelie bin' was seen with flames or lights coming from its base.

- At Great Ryburgh, Norfolk, in the mid 1990s, a large flying saucer with flashing lights was clearly observed by many witnesses, the lights going both clockwise and anti-clockwise according to several reports, while one report said another set of lights pulsated.

- At Ingoldisthorpe in 1961 and also specifically on 1 July 2013 at 11.30 p.m., a 'glowing lantern' was seen down at the bottom of a hill known as The Drift.

- At Hemblington, some time in 1997, motorists slowed down to see a Ufo illuminate an entire field with its intense flashing red, purple and green lights.

- At West Harling, in July 2014, after 11 p.m., a turquoise light was seen in nearby woodland, turning at speed. The five people in the car who saw this had 'negative feelings', and said it was 'scary'.

- At Thorpe Market, south on the B1436, a disc-like craft was seen on 13 January 2012. It had two window lights and one red light. It vanished in a flash of white light.

- At Saxlingham, on the Halt Road at it nears the B1145, a Ufo some 15 feet wide was seen in 2010, hovering some 60 feet above the road. It was seen by two motorists, who both drove away fast.

## The Suffolk Sightings

- It was recorded in the database that at Bury St Edmunds, at 9.30 a.m. on 20 April 2007, the 'MoD', presumably military personnel and Suffolk police, saw four black spheres in the sky. Over the cathedral, a year later at night, an illuminated 'grey' Ufo was seen.

- At Brantham, on Slough Road, a driver saw a 'metal' Ufo with blue and red lights along its side, and it hovered over a field before disappearing. The time was 10 p.m., and the date was some time in 1986.

- At Felixstowe two orange orbs were seen falling to the surface in July 2006, and two months later people saw Ufos near the coastline, one being 'dark and round'. At Eyke, not far from the RAF Bentwaters incident[26] and prior to it, other strange craft were seen in the skies in the 1980s.

- At Hollesley Bay in January 2010 a motorist saw a greenish BOL which 'danced around'.

- At Ipswich in the 1990s, a family driving home saw a bright BOL. At the city's Orwell Bridge, on the A12, at 2 a.m. on 26 August 2006 a teenage driver reported two dull spinning BOLs in front of her car, turning corners as she did. These BOLs were also seen by others at Nacton Road. At Nacton itself, in 1998, one night at 1 a.m., two friends sitting in a car park saw a triangular Ufo, after their car failed to start. It is possible the same triangular object reappeared at Ixworth, on the road towards Diss, at dusk at some date in June 2000, when again another 'two in a car' saw a triangular Ufo, 'the size of a house', hovering over a field. Other vehicles slowed down to look. It was described as having soft lights on its underside.

- At Orford Ness in the 1970s, two lights hovered close to 'water', presumably a lake or a pond. There was some suggestion that witnesses were seeing radar waves that went into the visible spectrum and came from a nearby military base that was conducting 'Operation Cobra Mist' experiments.

- At Sudbury, on the A1092 that runs between Long Melford and Haverhill, Roselyn Reynolds was reported in the county database to have been abducted by aliens from her car in September 1982. The aliens were described as being a mix of the classic humanoid, with 'messy blond hair', and accompanied by several classic 'greys'. Later Roselyn went on, we are told, to develop a psychic talent.

## More Ufo Sightings Gleaned from Various County Databases

- At Anfield, Lancashire, a pilot said he saw a flying saucer, a 'mile long' on 25 July 2007. On Manchester's Golbourne Castle Hill BOLs of different sizes were zigzagging, fast. They were seen at Oldham, on Saddleworth Moor in December 2006, and also, on and off, on Saddleworth Moor since 1978. At Scratton Wood, Nottinghamshire, dancing blue lights were seen on a road after sunset.

- On 5 July 1989 Andrew Billing was driving his cab towards the sea front at Blackpool when he noticed the familiar orange-red brightly glowing sphere over the sea to the south-west. Then it shot over at a fast clip to another part of the sky. It hovered, repeated the manoeuvre and then disappeared out of sight into the north-west.

- In Leicestershire, dating right back to 1388, three spinning 'balls of flame' were listed.

- At Stanton in the early 2000s a circular object had two small flashing lights that soon became 'blinding', before vanishing. It made a strange sound. At nearby Stoney Stanton a saucer-shaped object travelled slowly across the sky at 7 p.m. on 1 October 2011. It had small lights on either side, and a larger one flashing one on top.

- At Grantham, Lincolnshire, a family were frightened in their car when they saw a Ufo in either 1980 or 1981. Other drivers saw it and reported it to a local radio station. When radio journalists contacted the RAF about possible planes in the area they said, unconvincingly, that it was crashing Russian spy satellite. At Idestone, Oxfordshire, in February 1985, a driver and another saw an orange oval light, although it is not mentioned whether this was in the sky or at road level.

- At Weston, Shropshire, in January 1869 people saw a Ufo that produced what would now be described as shockwaves.

- On the A39 on a village street near Bridgewater, a white light was once said to be following drivers. It vanished if the drivers turned back to check out the source of the light.

- At a town called Warmly, a Ufo 'fireball' was seen on 6 March 2012.

- In 2008 Joanne Kyte, in her early 30s, was out with two friends who were interested in the paranormal. They were driving through rural Derbyshire with the actual intention of trying to capture some ghosts on their cine cameras. They pulled up in a wooded area near to East Midlands airport. It was then that they all saw a hovering Ufo surrounded by an orange glow. They got out of the car and started filming it, a fuzzy still picture appearing a decade later in a woman's occultic magazine. Joanne wrote in the magazine that she noticed at the time that the Ufo moved as if it was trying to avoid an oncoming plane.[27]

- At West Bromwich, in the West Midlands, on 25 July 1997, some twenty Ufos were seen with zigzagging lights. Some were yellow and had a red centre; all were largely transparent and all moved towards Walsall.


Hanbury, Staffordshire, has a reputation for BOLs, and three were seen over the Malverns – a range of hills covering Worcestershire, Herefordshire and Gloucestershire – at an unknown date. In February 1985 a family watched an orange glowing 'mushroom for an hour hovering above Buckhall'.

A BBC cameraman separately recorded a Ufo in Hanbury in 2005.

A couple were driving along Cannock Chase, Staffordshire, at night in August 1988. They saw a circular glowing and pulsating reddish mass. A semi-solid object seemed to emerge from it. The mass then moved further away within seconds, before vanishing into a hedge, which was later found to have been damaged by something physical. The object, or mass, seemed to induce a sense of calmness in its witnesses rather than fear. Jenny Randles, a renowned Ufo investigator, suggested it might have been a ball of plasma or an earthlight in an area known to have geological fault lines.[28]

- At Guildford, Surrey, at 8 p.m. in October 2006, two police patrolmen drove under a flyover on the A3, and on emerging could see a black triangle with three white lights at each corner, and a dim red pulsating one in the centre of its underside.

- At Bury, Sussex, on the A29 at 8.30 p.m. on 24 August 2012, a van driver saw a bright BOL on the road. At Burgess Hill, in September 1995, multi-coloured circular BOLs disappeared and reappeared. Similar events happened on 8 July 2017 but this time accompanied by something like 'TV white noise' from the sky. It lasted twenty minutes.

- At East Dean on 1 February 2008 a 'silver plane' Ufo was seen which darted off at an 'incredible' speed. At Uckfield, on the London Road in October 2007, some sixty Ufos with red lights were seen, it was alleged, in 'close formation'.

- At Dubbenhall, Warwickshire, along the Stoneleigh Road, a flashing orange disc was seen landing in a field by a couple in a car on 11 February 2008. At Compton Wyngates, Warwickshire, in 1924 a yellow and blue light was seen 'dancing about'. In the town area, prior to this, the phenomenon of 'lights' seen in the vicinity was part of the legend of a phantom with glowing eyes.

- At Stratford 100 people saw a Ufo on 21 July 2007, within the space of 30 minutes. Various descriptions were given – some were triangular craft, some BOLs, some hovering and others darting around.

- On 8 May 2018, Jerry Glover was returning from Aylesbury on the A418 with his family, when they noticed what they thought was a large aircraft as they drove through the hamlet of Rowsham, Bedfordshire, located less than ten miles from Luton airport. But it was much larger than any normal commercial airliner – at least 100 feet long. It was silent and appeared to be motionless – and 'unnervingly low' if it was actually flying. He could see a row of large 'windows', tall and surprisingly rectangular. But the entire object had no wings, being largely cylindrical in appearance. He thought that his angle of vision was wrong, or flickering light as the sun shone through nearby foliage might have caused a misperception of size and shape.[29]

• Two related women spotted a bright, triangular light hovering over Bromley, south-east London, in 1978 as they drove home after a concert. The resulting local press article gained the attention of Soviet scientists.[30]

• A family – two parents with their two children – driving home towards Brockworth, Gloucestershire, on the night of 19 June 1978, claim they were abducted by aliens. They noticed a white light in the sky that seemed to keep pace with them. It was a giant glowing white saucer-shaped object with its undercarriage lit by a circular rim of coloured lights. John gained speed, but seemed not to be on the correct road, and had the sense that his car was being guided. Road signs were either missing or different. Arriving home later than expected, John found about an hour had gone missing. Over the next few days all of the family discovered heat rashes or skin problems. Under hypnotherapy, John revealed that he had been 'floated up' to a Ufo, and medically examined in a 'circular room' by three humanoid aliens in close-fitting silver suits.[31]

• Mrs Lillian Middleton, 33, was driving across the Northumberland moors in the early hours of 21 August 1980 to rescue a friend whose own car had run out of petrol. Then she saw a bright flash of light, and thought that a plane had caught fire or exploded in mid air. She peered out of the window to see a huge rugby ball shape, giving off a brilliant light and hovering. Then, as it zoomed down towards her, she frantically drove away at speed, reaching 70 mph, with the Ufo tailing her. When she reached the petrol station, she realised there were still other witnesses observing the Ufo. With the can of petrol she set out for the stranded car, with the Ufo still in pursuit. Later, after she rang the police, she learned that they had also seen the Ufo. The experience left its mark. 'I was in a state of shock for several weeks.'[32]

- In a similar incident on the evening of 13 March 1980 a contract driver on a job near the village of Haselor, Warwickshire, saw a cigar-shaped apparition. It didn't seem to have a distinctively solid outline, but was a reddish-white haze or mass. As it passed in front of his car the steering wheel became too hot to hold. Luckily he was able to manoeuvre his car off the road. The Ufo had disappeared and the steering wheel gradually cooled off.[33]

## The Welsh Ufo Sightings

The amazing litany of the paranormal experiences of the Coombs family (see Chapter 20) has become embedded as the most notorious of Welsh Ufo accounts, of which there are a surprising number. Two lorry drivers in 1974 saw an enormous black cigar object with lights down one side when they were travelling to their home area of Maentwrog, North Wales. When they got home that night at 1 a.m. they found that three hours of time had gone missing.[34] Soon weird events involving lights and explosions in the Snowdonia area and other parts of Wales came to the attention of the police and the military. Only a few days later residents of Llandrillo and Llandderfel heard a loud explosion, and saw orange lights in the distance on the remote mountainside of the Berwyn range, near Snowdonia Park, which they thought was a plane crash. Some said they saw a BOL descend before the explosion. A local woman and her two teenage daughters drove along the B4391 to investigate – where they eventually saw a glowing pink and pulsating Ufo for twenty minutes.

They returned home in fright. Police and army vehicles were soon on the scene, and roads got sealed off. There were heightened security issues in the area because sometimes military drivers had to deliver equipment and chemicals to the Porton Down facility which had a base in Llandderfel.

- A farmer with property just outside Aberystwyth, fifty miles south on the coast of Mid Wales, heard an explosion and found a swathe of pine trees demolished. Other Ufo happenings occurred in later days. In Snowdonia a family saw a saucer-shaped craft hovering over the road. It had cobalt-blue lights around it and coloured beams shining downwards.[35]

- At 9.55 p.m. on 1 September 1978 Vivienne Roberts was nearly home at Llanerchymedd on Anglesey Island, North Wales, when she abruptly brought her car to a halt when she saw a yellow light nearby, low down in the sky, seeming to switch itself on and off at intervals of one or two seconds, only to reappear at different locations. Then a solid-looking, triangular blue and purple aircraft of some sort suddenly appeared, with distinctive yellow lights on its body. Perhaps, she thought, this was the same craft she had seen in the sky moments earlier. She got out of the car and watched it as it glided slowly southwards over a nearby churchyard. By now its purple colouring was glowing, casting a strange, eerie light everywhere. Miss Roberts was aware of some commotion being caused by this Ufo, with horses whinnying and strange 'voices'.[36]

- At Halkyn, Clywd, a brief account of a 'monster', and a 'Ufo close encounter', was mentioned in the database for 1982.

- At Nannerch, at the Moel Arthur Hill, a BOL was recorded, along with 'paranormal' weather events, both regarded as omens. At Llandilo, Dyfed, spectral lights were seen, again considered to be an omen for the following day's drowning of three men. No date was given for this. Another omen was the small BOLs seen at Ramsey Island, Dyfed, sometimes mentioned in the occultic literature, as well as in this database report, known in occultic literature and the database as 'corpse candles'.

- At Blorenge, Gwent, on the B4246, at 10.30 p.m. on 9 April 2016, a driver and passenger saw a white/blue cloud on the road, but it was in a 'humanoid' shape.

- At Dylife, Powys, near some mine tunnels in the 1950s, blue lights were seen. At Llanddfetty, prior to 1800, witnesses said that as they approached a chapel on foot they could see BOLs, which, according to what was interpreted at the time, were expanding or enlarging.

- On 23 November 1977 a number of rugby players were driving towards Carmarthen Town along an incline known as Nantycaws Hill when they collided with a Calor Gas tanker at about 10 p.m. There had been earlier reports of other accidents in that road caused by lorry drivers encountering aliens. This particular tanker driver, with his colleague, said his lights picked up two huge entities seven feet tall. They were reddish-orange in colour and appeared to be wearing single-piece celluloid suits. They had long heads, as if wearing a busby-type helmet. The figures remained standing as the tanker careered by, the startled driver having lost control of his vehicle, which jack-knifed and overturned across the three-lane highway. Most of those in the car were killed, and the tanker driver was severely injured. The driver later said: 'I had a weird feeling. I wouldn't call it fright. It was a sort of cold tingling as we were approaching and passing them ... I've never seen anything so weird or ever felt so weird.' It was then that he braked hard and had the accident.[37]

## Notable Scottish Sightings

- A Mr and Mrs Procek were driving along the A80 heading for Cumbernauld, not far from Bonnybridge, Falkirk, in the late evening of 15 January 1993. Mrs Procek pointed out some aerial lights to husband Ray which seemed to be attached to two large triangular craft, about 300 feet off the ground. They were jet black, but both had pinkish lights on their undersides.[38]

- Vera Prosser, 51, was driving near Falkirk with her husband and daughter in October 1995, when they noticed a large light in a field. She slowed down, but the family noted with alarm that the light had approached their car, hovered just 6 feet over it, and shone its light directly into the transparent sunroof. It soon zoomed off into space.[39]

• An Andrew Swan, in the West Lothian area, was caught in a thunderstorm late at night on 30 July 1994. He pulled up, worried about his and his car's safety, and watched the display. It was then that he saw a large pyramid-shaped Ufo behind some trees in the near distance. He started to drive off again, only for the Ufo to come down towards him. Swan made an emergency stop, got out, and noted that the object had now flown to an industrial waste tip. He then found he could not restart his engine, and contacted the local police, presumably by using a mobile phone, at shortly before midnight. The police arrived after a considerable wait, and it later turned out that they had recorded his call at 2 a.m. So a whole two hours had gone missing.[40]

# Chapter 20

## The 'Car Stop' Phenomenon

Many Ufos interfere with car engine and electronics, with motorists reporting that their car's electrics and engine fail when the Ufo is anywhere near their vehicle, say hovering nearby or beginning to approach them on the road. Often the car simply grinds to a halt, known as the 'car stop syndrome'. Arthur Shuttlewood pointed out that a common phenomenon at the Warminster Ufo sightings was car engines seizing up. There were unaccountable stalls and stops after skywatching, even while going downhill. Car radios would cut out, and there were strange scratching noises on the roofs of the cars, all invariably after Ufos had been seen.[1] Again, in virtually every car stop case, as we have seen, time has become distorted – minutes or hours of journey time have gone missing.

A doctor had to take a patient, as an emergency, in his own car to a nearby hospital in Bexleyheath, Kent, in July 1955. As the car travelled, the passengers – the doctor and young patient and his mother – sensed a dark shadow looming over them, with the shadow actually turning with them as they negotiated corners. The car soon spluttered to a stop, and the passengers, now standing outside, could see a concentrated mass of 'grey cloud' barely 18 feet above their heads. This phenomenon began to morph into a bell-shaped craft, with ball-bearing type 'wheels' and a pewter-coloured exterior. It flopped and manoeuvred across the road before zooming off.[2] The local paper said the Ufo had also been seen by a policeman and other residents.

Jean Bradley, 79, and her husband, John, from Rugby, Warwickshire, were driving past a place called New Inn, near Rugby, in January 2018 when their car's electrics, lights and engine suddenly cut out. They were brought to a standstill on a busy main road, with lorries hurtling past. It was then that they noticed bright lights in a field that was right next to the highway, and assumed a farmer was working late. But as soon as the lights went out their car started working again.[3]

Mr Wildman worked for a car dealer and was driving a new vehicle, an estate car, to the customer who had ordered it in Swansea, Wales. It was 9 February 1962. It was early in the morning and still dark, and he was just at the end of the deserted Ivinghoe Road at Aston Clinton, Buckinghamshire, when he noticed a moving oval-shaped object suspended some feet off the road ahead of him. Along its side he could see twenty black markings spread out, which were possibly, he thought, portholes or vents. The craft was about forty feet in width. As Mr Wildman got within 60 feet of it his car engine decreased his momentum to about 20 mph, and he couldn't increase the speed by dropping down a gear and using the accelerator. However, his headlights remained on. He continued with the journey while the Ufo came ever closer to the road. Then it developed a white haze around its exterior, and shot off into space. But he noticed some air displacement when this happened (which seldom occurs in other Ufo manoeuvres) because some frost particles from treetops landed on his windscreen.[4]

Terry Pell was driving his lorry to Warminster, with his wife and young daughter in his cab, on 10 August 1965. It was near Colloway Clump, a hillside copse to the north of the town. He saw an arcing red light zoom out of the hillside, hover 50 yards in front of his vehicle, and then come down to virtually touch his windscreen. He noticed it was some 35 feet long 'at the base', and that it might have had metallic components, although it was originally described as an 'orb' by Arthur Shuttleworth. Pell then had a car stop experience, with his engine beginning to seize up. But within minutes of his halting, the object flew away, 'gleaming pale gold', and could still be seen hovering nearby.[5]

The car stop phenomenon was most pronounced in Wales's most notorious Ufo event, as it encompasses so many other aspects of the paranormal. Pauline Coombs was driving her family of three children back to Haverfordwest in January 1977 when they saw an orange phosphorous light hovering in the sky at treetop height, which then began pursuing them – pulsating and filling the car with orange light. As Pauline desperately tried to outrun the Ufo, her engine faltered almost to a stop, and the headlights dimmed. But she finally made the car creep the last hundred yards back to their home with the Ufo now right ahead of them, even when they reached the garage driveway.

Later Pauline concluded that the engine failure, and the Ufo event, was part of the poltergeist activity recently witnessed in the family home, with electrical appliances fusing and blowing out. Later on, the cars her husband, Billy, bought unaccountably had engine blow-outs and electrical failures, and the family became victims of alien spacemen in spacesuits harassing them, with yet more car-chasing Ufo sightings. In addition they saw silvery-looking cars crewed by humanoid aliens actually parked outside their home.[6]

The 'Aveley abduction', in Essex, 1974, has also become notorious in British Ufo folklore. A family were travelling in the Aveley area when their car seemed to be paced by a 'big star' which behaved erratically. It was 10.10 p.m., and the road was remarkably deserted for that time of night. The light began to appear oval-shaped, with a blue iridescence. John, the driver, turned a bend and could no longer hear the sound of the car's engine or tyres – just the car radio. Then, ahead, the family could see the road covered with a kind of thick green fog, as high as a wall, virtually semi-solid. It was curved at the rear and flat at the bottom. As they got near, the car radio started crackling and appeared to overheat. Still travelling at 30 mph, the car's lights went out and the fog engulfed them, making the car jerk violently. The children in the back of the car all felt cold and tingling. Within seconds the fog lifted, the car jolted once more, and everything was back to normal.[7]

There were reports of other lorry drivers seeing a saucer-shaped object soar into the sky in the direction of the Cherwell Heights, Oxfordshire.[8] And Wiltshire was often plagued with road Ufos. The B3095 near Warminster was a hotspot for sightings in the 1970s, as well as crop circles. The Holbrook family were heading home near Brixton Deverill, Wiltshire, on the B3095 some time in 1970 or 1971. Amanda, ten at the time, recalls a number of paranormal events happening at once, with the cars vibrating and coming to an untimely stop, a bright light beaming down on them, and something unknown sitting beside her. Soon the bright light moved away and the car restarted, but her parents were 'shaking'. When they got home later than they should have they realised an hour of time had gone missing. The mother, in later life, said the illuminated object they saw was triangular in shape. Amanda said her family were perhaps psychic, and she herself had premonitions of road accidents, and her own little son had invisible 'friends'.[9]

Building contractor Peter Taylor was driving through Daresbury, Cheshire, in January 1973 when his new car broke down outside a pub before inexplicably starting up again when it passed the building. This happened twice. The second time was 7.30 at night, and he found himself across the border in Lancashire when he rang a garage about the incident from a local telephone box which had a Preston phone number. Not only that but he had lost two hours, because his watch said it was 9.30 p.m.[10]

Mrs Joyce Bowles in September 1976 was driving with a friend down a lane leading to Chilcomb, near Winchester, at 8.45 p.m. when she saw two reddish-orange lights in nearby scrubland. Her car then began to experience ignition and engine trouble, and the steering wheel locked. Mrs Bowles managed to bring the car to a halt by mounting the grass verge. Then the two in the car saw a bulky cigar-shaped Ufo only a few yards ahead of them, about 110 feet long and 5 feet high, just a foot and a half off the road, and supported by four jets of gas. The craft had illuminated bow-shaped windows through which they could see figures, seated as if they were passengers. There was a whirring sound. They then saw a tall figure emerge out of the object. It approached the car, puts its hand on the car roof and looked through the window, and the engine sprang into life.[11]

Mrs Bowles later reported that her car suddenly seemed to lift itself off the road momentarily before it stopped completely. Then she screamed as she saw a creature peering at them through the windscreen. Its eyes were pink, and actually illuminated, and the entity seemed to be covered in baking foil. It then returned to a glowing cigar-shaped craft hovering in a nearby field, and which Mrs Bowles could see had occupants. It then took off. On 7 March 1977 the same Ufo event happened, with the car faltering in a country lane, and the same encounter with a spaceman with long hair and with beings advancing towards the car, and speaking to the two women in broken English.[12]

Many people had seen a light in the sky on 8 March 1977 over Nelson, Lancashire. Just a day later Jeff Farmer and Brian Grimshaw, in the small hours, were driving to their workplace for a night shift when they saw a light descend from clouds that swirled around Pendle Hill, near Burnley. They slowed down to watch a saucer or egg-shaped object which had a very bright orange glow, with possibly a misty cloud surrounding it, yet not dense enough to conceal multiple lights rotating around its edges. The object moved closer to their car, pacing it. Then the car stop routine happened, but not until Jeff and Brian had got out. The lights dimmed but didn't fail completely. In the ensuing silence they could hear a low humming noise as the Ufo, the size of a double-decker bus, hovered overhead. Its lights were all different, mainly orange and reddish, but had a distinct electrostatic effect, with the men complaining of a tingling sensation on their heads. Jeff started to panic, saying, 'Let's get away now.' Brian said later: 'Then I got into the car and tried to start it. Even the ignition light wouldn't come on ... I put the key in and nothing happened. It didn't turn over. It was dead.' Then within minutes, when the object moved off towards Manchester, everything – lights and engine – were back to normal.[13]

The small village of Daresbury in Cheshire is regarded as a 'window area' for an assortment of car engine failures, apparitions and alien contact, and unaccountable losses of time by motorists.

A Peter Taylor suffered three days of car engine failures in 1973, and time losses.[14] And unaccountable losses do seem to be connected with Ufo occurrences. For example, Ann, aged 58, travelling with her daughter and grandchildren, saw a Ufo while passing through the town of High Bentham, North Yorkshire, early in the evening of Sunday 16 January 2005. The family had just visited a restaurant, leaving at about 5.20 p.m., and the journey home to Ingleton, about three miles, should have taken no more than twenty minutes. But, turning on the TV to see the start of the 7 o'clock news, they realised an additional hour of time had elapsed by the time they arrived home. When Ann contacted the local radio station the next day, it appeared that the broadcasting staff knew of the Ufo sighting from other people in the area.[15]

Motorcyclist Paul Green was heading home on 14 September 1965 in the early hours to West Mersea in Essex, and had reached the Langenhoe Marsh when he heard a high-pitched humming through his helmet, and saw a blue light shining from the east. But the light, even though some distance away, seemed to make his engine and lights falter and then cut out. Then, while halted, a large domed object with flashing blue lights appeared overhead. There was an alarming pulsating rhythm from the lights on the craft which seemed to impact on his chest and his head. After a struggle he manage to start up his bike and speed away from the scene, but arrived home later than he should have, given that he only had to go another three miles, so there was some missing time involved.[16]

A Mr W. Collet had been driving a lorry towards Reading, Berkshire, at 4.30 in the morning of 26 October 1967, but his vehicle was stopped near Hook, Hampshire, when his lights, engine and radio failed. He felt his ears popping and had the sense of oppression that you get before a storm, and there was a strange electrical smell. He saw a dark disc-shaped Ufo, domed at the top and conical at the base – about as wide as it was deep – some 60 feet.

When it flew off the truck started up again, but Collett experienced a strange time warp because, in spite of the road delay and halting, which he reckoned lasted about 20 minutes, he arrived at his destination 15 minutes early. And the return journey was just as weird, because his gearshift and accelerator wouldn't work properly, and the return trip required three gallons more petrol than going there.[17]

## Other Extraordinary Car Stop Events

- Major William Hill, retired, of Warminster, Wiltshire, was headed for the weekly parade of the territorial army at 8.20 p.m. some time in the 1960s. His car abruptly ground to a halt. The problem seemed to be with the car's electrics as the lights and ignition wouldn't work. Stepping out to check what was wrong, he was stunned by an invisible force, and the air around him seemed to be vibrating. There was a loud and sinister whining and crackling. He later said he felt something pressing down on him.[18]

- Carl Farlow was driving his diesel lorry with a load of cookers at about 1.30 a.m. on 6 November 1967 on the A338 between Avon and Sopley, Hampshire. As he approached a crossroads near a bridge his lights went out. He pulled up with the engine still running, and saw an egg-shaped object slowly moving across the road, but about 50 feet above it. He reckoned it was enormous – some 75 feet long. It was magenta coloured, with a whitish area at the base, humming like a refrigerator. Strangely it had a woody smell about it.

After a while the object drifted slowly to the left, gained speed, and zoomed off into space.[19]

- A clergyman complained that his car engine mysteriously switched itself on and off while travelling on Devon roads in 1969, as if his ignition system was being interfered with. Further, in that particular region of the county near Moretonhampstead, other drivers had reported mysterious car lights approaching them and then disappearing. Other drivers in the Penhill Beacon region of Yorkshire had experienced similar events in the late 1990s.[20]

- An anonymous woman, aged 43, was driving along a road in Langsford Badville, Somerset, on 16 October 1973 when she had a car stop at 11 p.m. She got out and fainted with shock when something touched her and she turned to see a robot-like entity about 6ft 5in tall, standing behind her. She was then abducted, and awoke to find herself inside a spaceship, naked on a metal table. She suffered a sexual assault and a physical examination by three small humanoid creatures. When she regained consciousness she found that she had been returned to her car, and noted that three hours had elapsed. Her car started, and she was able to drive home to tell her husband and inform the police.[21]

- Lucy Brown, of Pilton, Somerset, wrote of a time alteration experience when she had an accident on the road involving tethered horses that had bolted across a busy main road. 'Myself and a tree surgeon with others on the verge had the distinct impression of time slowing, and thus being able to contain the animals and prevent carnage.'[22]

- A young couple had parked their car on a lonely road near Poole, Dorset, on the night of 21 May 1977. They saw a large silvery flying saucer hovering over a field, with a silvery-green cone of light beaming down from its centre. It remained there for some considerable time before veering off and disappearing behind some trees. Pauline Fall, 31, saw the same thing only miles away in a country lane near the village of Longham. A beam of light – turning itself on and off – fell across the bonnet of her car, 'as if something was tracking us', she said. Indeed the beam pursued her as she drove swiftly home, before it disappeared. After that strange event the family car started playing tricks – like the engine cutting out every time she drove it, but not when her husband did.[23]

- At 11.30 p.m. on 6 June 1977 an agricultural worker was riding his motorbike home when he saw two purple lights at Lartington, County Durham. They were above the road, and to his side, but as he ascended a small hill he noticed his bike was losing power. A car that was about to overtake him also seemed to be struggling to do this. Suddenly the situation was dramatically reversed, as both bike and car were enveloped in a fuzzy ultraviolet light which actually seemed to propel them further up the hill, gaining the momentum they had both lost. Fearing he was losing control of his machine the biker struggled to bring himself to a halt, as did the car driver in his car. The rider then noticed steam pouring off his leathers, and he felt that his body had got hotter as a result of the UV radiation coming from the Ufo, or whatever it was. His motorbike had also become hot to the touch, and his brakes had worn out. The motorcyclist and car driver spoke to one another in shock.[24]

- Kerry Philpott was driving near Ebbw Vale on the evening of 27 January 1997 when he saw something large and bright approaching his car from the east. Startled, he braked to a halt and switched off his lights, but the bright orb circled his car for five minutes. He got out and actually walked through the brilliant light, and noted the total lack of sound. Frightened, he got back into the car but the car lights wouldn't come back on, nor the car radio. He began to feel unwell. The following morning he contacted his local RAF base to report the sighting.[25]

- Peter Rainbow, 41, was rounding a bend on his motorbike on the A428 at Great Houghton, Northamptonshire, in February 1983, when his engine and lights cut out. He dismounted and noticed a white glow in an adjacent field which wobbled before disappearing. His engine now started normally, and he drove on and reached Little Houghton, where the church clock gave the time as 8.30 p.m. So he had lost 90 minues.[26]

- At Paignton, Devon, a Ufo was seen on 23 September 2007, after midnight. An estimated 100 lights – mainly orange, green and red – were moving about the object.

- What could now be described as a Ufo ('a strange ship complete with rigging') was seen as long ago as the early 17th century at Portland, Dorset. The date given in the archives was 23 April 1661, and the time was 3 p.m.

- At Ormskirk, Lancashire, on the Southport Road in 1979 and 1980, orange BOLs were seen, on both times occasioned by car stopping events. At Sale, on the Drayton Road exit from the motorway, a Ufo was seen on 17 March 1978. It must have landed because the database records that a tall entity made its way to the road. The being emanated thin beams of light from its large eye sockets. The sighting lasted for one hour.

- At Digby Fen, Lincolnshire, along a country road circa 1950, glowing lights were seen. It was speculated – and highlights the overlapping nature of paranormal road experiences – that the lights were from the rear end of a phantom coach.

- At Coddington, Nottinghamshire, between Bilderton and Coddington during the 2000s, Ufos were seen in the late evening. A woman driver saw two clusters of misty spheres some 600 feet in front of her car. They floated away, gaining altitude.

- At Langford Budville, Shropshire, in October 1978, a woman driver was apparently abducted by a large 'robot' after her car broke down. Three creatures in a Ufo experimented on her.

- At Newcastle-Under-Lyme, Staffordshire, a policeman, either on foot patrol or in a police car, reported an orange sphere which passed overhead on 3 February 1985. There were three other witnesses to this.

- At Aberdeen, in July 2006, a Ufo with orange lights was seen by car drivers.

- At Spean Bridge, Fort William, Highlands, a Ufo hovered over the road on 5 April 2016, before vanishing into a hedge. The incident was timed at 10.15 p.m.

- Alan Cave, 45, was driving one October morning in 1981 from Bath to Stroud, when his car passed directly beneath an orange cloud-like Ufo. But then he seemed to have a time warp; his car radio announced it was 11 o'clock, but his watch told him it was 8 o'clock. Then his mileage counter started going back, making his car lose a theoretical 300 miles.[27]

- Paul, 21, was driving through Little Houghton in Northamptonshire one night in September 1973. He noticed a church clock tower that said the time was 2 a.m. Then something very strange happened as he found himself without his car, and wandering through a village he recognised as Bromham, but it was sixteen miles further away, and it was now 7 o'clock! He had no memory of getting there. As luck would have it he knew a friend in the village who, alarmed at Paul's story, immediately drove him along the A428 to Houghton. They found his car in a muddy field, but with no sign of tyre tracks, and the gate was closed. Some years later Paul had a recovered memory of seeing a white fuzzy glow approaching his windscreen before he blacked out.[28]

- At Church Stowe, Northamptonshire, Elsie Okensen's car travelled underneath a Ufo which she could see moving above the road. The date was 22 January 1978. The car lost power, and she lost fifteen minutes of time.

- In the mid 20th century, mysterious lights could be seen near a rectory after dusk by motorists travelling through Foxton, Northamptonshire.

- A Patrick Forsyth was travelling on the A872 towards Denny in Scotland on 27 September 1992 when he encountered a Ufo hovering over the road. It was circular and two-tiered and had a row of green lights. He then seemed to enter a 12-foot-high 'fog bank', as did the car in front. The Ufo then vanished.[29]

- Gary Wood was driving with his friend Colin Wright on the A70 in a rural area of West Lothian one night in August 1992. They suddenly saw a two-tiered disc hovering over the road. Gary accelerated sharply and, like so many other frightened drivers who see Ufos, hoped to simply pass under it and flee from the horror. But the Ufo caught up with him, emitting a kind of mist which enveloped the car, with the mist increasing its density and becoming almost black in the process. Gary struggled to regain control of the vehicle, which had now veered into the opposite lane. When Gary and Colin reached their destination, which should have been no later than 10 p.m., they found the time was now nearly a quarter to one in the morning.[30]

- William Barrett, 55, was driving towards Todmorden on the A646 on 14 January 1980, very early in the morning while it was still dark. He thought he heard an electricity generator somewhere, and his headlights illuminated a dark metallic shape in a lay-by ahead.[31]

- Billy Lowry was travelling north on the A49 on his motorbike on the night of 1 September 1983. When he reached Weaverham, Cheshire, he saw strange lights in the sky. He stopped and dismounted to get a better look. He saw that the lights were attached to a dark shape, which now loomed slowly above him. He eventually drove on, nonplussed, but saw a signpost telling him that he was no longer on his correct route, and apparently heading for a different town. In fact he was now on the A56, actually heading the wrong way. Further, checking his watch, some one and a half hours had gone missing.[32]

• On 19 September 1987 Larry Mayer was driving back home from Stocksbridge across the moors, when he had a 'strange feeling' that advised him to slow down on a deserted road. Then he glimpsed something odd in a small clearing in a roadside copse: thin strands of lights, perhaps put in a circle. The entire area seemed eerily quiet, but he drove on to the Woodhead area, just four miles further on, where he approached the aftermath of an obvious road accident, with emergency service vehicles speeding to the scene. When he arrived in Manchester he was an hour later than he should have been. The lights that he saw in the woods and the flashing lights of the emergency crews were all confusingly interrelated in his mind.[33]

• The Smith family, on the morning of 8 August 1992, were near Hockliffe, Bedfordshire, when their car became enveloped in mist and an uncanny silence descended on them. Mr Smith was at the wheel and his vision was momentarily obscured, but within seconds the mist lifted. But there was a time and space translocation, because Mr Smith realised he was eight miles further away than he should have been – way ahead at Woburn Sands.[34]

• On 15 June 2007 two sisters were driving from Leicester to visit their parents in Braintree, Essex. Getting towards midnight on the approach to Stansted Airport on the M11 they noticed a vertical bright beam of green light, 'like a stage spotlight', about 20 feet in front of them. It seemed to be coming straight down from the sky. They drove through it and it was still visible behind them. It was unlikely to have been an aircraft either from Stansted Airport or from the nearby Duxford Air Museum. But the area did include local air bases, and paraphernalia connected with radar and other technical equipment. Yet it remained a mystery.[35]

• A ghostly airman had apparently been seen several times just prior to deaths and weird events on the Halsall Moss – a notorious area, as we have seen, for spooky happenings. There were other reports of flashing orbs of light and 'ghostly sightings'.[36]

# Chapter 21

## UFOs – The Police Get Involved

The police and security services often get involved in Ufo incidents. The military had direct experience of Ufos, accounts of which went into the defence files. Andy Gilbert, in his *Credible Witness: Paranormal Police Stories*, says that unexplained events on the road, via freedom of information requests, have revealed paranormal incidents reported to the police on a regular basis.[1]

A case possibly involving defence and security issues concerns the story reported by Ken Edwards, who was driving in Cheshire on 17 March 1978. He had turned off the M62 onto a slip road, which passed by the UK Atomic Energy Commission's buildings, where there were experimental and research facilities. He saw a glowing white mass slide down an embankment on the outside of the Atomic Energy Complex, and land in the middle of the road. Ken slowed his van to a halt, after which he was aware of a humanoid being with illuminated eyes. The mass then moved across the road and passed right through the security fence surrounding the complex, The local police and security guards searched the area, but the fence was undamaged. When he arrived at home that day there were 45 minutes missing from his journey, according to Jenny Randles and a colleague from the *Warrington Guardian* who interviewed him and timed his journey. They noted that Ken also showed signs of radiation burns, and he later suffered from a series of cancers that eventually took his life while he was still in his thirties. A considerable amount of local and national press publicity resulted from this sighting.[2]

Two soldiers, Mike Perrin and Titch Carwell, while on exercises with the Royal Armoured Corp in 1978 saw a dome-shaped silvery object hovering some 50 yards distant while driving their Land Rover on the Yorkshire moors. 'It was about the size of five Land-Rovers and had portholes,' said Mike, 27. 'The lights inside were flashing red and white. I tried to start our vehicle but the engine was totally dead.' After five minutes the object flew off, and the power returned to the vehicle.[3]

During the summer and autumn of 1967 Britain experienced, says David Clarke, one of its most intense Ufo flaps. In the early hours of 24 October 1967 two police officers on patrol in their car near Holsworthy in North Devon saw a light in the sky at treetop height. PC Roger Willey described it as a 'star-spangled cross radiating points of light from all angles'. PC Willey and his colleague, PC Clifford Waycott, tried to drive towards the object at speeds approaching 90 mph along narrow lanes on the edge of Dartmoor. At a later televised press conference PC Willey said the object spun round, and seemed to have landed before taking off again. Eventually the officers gave up the chase, but managed to get the driver of a parked Land Rover to confirm the existence of the light, still visible in the sky. Perhaps spurred by the publicity of the press coverage, other policemen in Hampshire, Sussex and Derbyshire also said they had seen the 'flying cross'.[4]

In a similar incident in the late 1960s two police officers chased a Ufo on a Devon highway at 90 mph.[5]

A police sergeant drove to Barr Beacon, near Aldridge in the West Midlands, to check out a Ufo sighting in August 1971. He soon had a good view of the object and actually managed to take photos of it. He returned to Aldridge police station with his film, and the chief had the pictures developed. Then an element of censorship occurred because five of the fifteen pictures clearly showed what could only be described as a flying craft, with apertures along the side. The chief said that the pictures would have to be examined in detail by 'others', but the sergeant was not told who these 'others' were. He did some TV interviews about the sighting, and soon an American 'expert' flew over specially to meet him, and concluded that he had merely filmed a 'bright planet'.[6]

The British ambassador to Switzerland, A. K. Rothie, had a Ufo experience while driving at 6.45 p.m. on 15 October 1977 near Rolvenden in Kent. He said later he saw an object 'travelling fast from south to north and shaped somewhat like a flattened avocado pear'. The blunt leading end was made of some sort of brilliant bronze-like metal, and might even have been glowing. The rest of its body was emitting a bluish light, and from the tapering end there was a stream of 'golden sparks'. Rothie later reported his sighting to the MoD and to his local newspaper. DI55 scientists used a computer to check a range of possible explanations, and said to Rothie in a letter that, because of his status as a diplomat, they had investigated the matter 'more fully than usual, and it has been established that debris from a Soviet space satellite entered the earth's atmosphere on 15 October'.[7]

In the select residential district of Rickmansworth, Hertfordshire, an aerial object was seen hovering a mere 500 feet above the street. The date was 29 November 1979, the time 3.25 in the morning. The object was less like a Ufo than a light show – brilliantly lit along its length and with red lights above and below it. But it was seen by a woman police officer, WPC Anne Louise Brown, 21, and a male colleague who happened to be cruising in their patrol car. WPC Brown admitted later, 'I was scared stiff when it was above our car. I don't know what it was, but it was definitely too big and too bright to be a plane or a star. I told my colleague he must be crackers to report it back.' Minutes later, two other officers in their panda car saw the same shape above nearby Chorley Wood, and gave chase after alerting their HQ. But it eluded them, only to reappear two hours later. Hertfordshire police checked with West Drayton traffic control, who confirmed there were no planes in the area. Inspector George Freakes said: 'This is being treated seriously. We are convinced the officers saw something – they were very genuine types – yet no one can explain exactly what it was.'[8]

Policemen in Scotland were called in after a flood of calls reporting a huge shape, late in the evening, that could be seen for 20 minutes before it streaked away over nearby hills. Five policemen confirmed the sighting in Dumfries in late 1979 and two of them described the incident at a press conference. Sergeant Bill McDavid, 39, said he drove within a mile of the huge thing, which was 500 feet up. It was virtually an airship with six lights shining from several compartments. PC James Smith confirmed this. The Glasgow weather centre said the sighting could have been lights reflecting off low clouds, but someone from the centre had the courage to countermand this by saying that reflected light is usually just a yellow glare, which wouldn't account for a cluster of coloured lights. 'I have no explanation as to what these people really saw.'[9]

Two patrol officers, possibly in 1988, had stopped near a housing estate on the outskirts of Birmingham. At about 3 a.m. they experienced an intense white light which lit up the inside of their vehicle. They then saw a faintly illuminated white object, deadly silent, fly straight past them. They watched it zoom away, and then do a sharp 90-degree movement to the left, apparently turning up a road junction, and then disappear from view. They started up their car and drove quickly to the junction only to find it was a narrow pathway.[10]

## PC Tony Dodd – Ufo Investigator

The late Tony Dodd was an important Ufo researcher, who took up full-time investigations shortly after resigning from the police force. As a sergeant based at Skipton, Tony Dodd often did night patrols in his police car along the roads and lanes of North Yorkshire. He was spurred to take the subject seriously when his duties often led him to investigate Ufo sightings by motorists, householders and various others in the northern counties.

But it was his own sighting of Ufos that finally obliged him to dismiss conventional police ideas that these objects were the misidentification of normal phenomena or optical illusions, or the imaginations of tired drivers at night, and so on. With a colleague, travelling at 2.30 a.m. on a bitterly cold night in January 1978 in response to a missing person report, they both noticed a flying saucer some 200 feet in front of them – a huge bright disc with the familiar dome shape on top, with small dark portholes round the side, and with coloured lights of all shades pulsating on and off round the rim. The object was 100 feet off the road and slowly moved away at first, causing the car radio to crackle, before accelerating away into the night sky. Another police car pulled up alongside Dodd's car and the crew said they had also seen the Ufo.[11] Soon more and more strange reports were coming into his police station – from postmen, milkmen, farm labourers and others who were out at night, and often he had to personally investigate them. His police colleagues had also reported Ufos.

Dodd wrote later that the most common sighting was a large orange ball of light, which had small pulsating red lights inside. He said they would not only fly past his police car, but do return visits! Over the years, in many cases 'the cloud-base was no more than 200 metres (660 feet) above my head, with these strange machines appearing beneath it'.[12]

He tells how, in 1982, a young woman came into his station to complain about her car being buzzed by a low-flying helicopter, which Dodd knew could not actually have been a normal flying craft of any sort. But it was the only explanation the woman could give. It was a wintry March, and she had set off to see her mother at 9.30 p.m. She was on a lonely stretch of road that cuts across the moorland. She noticed a red and blue light in her offside mirror, although not belonging to any car that she could see. The lights were strangely soft and diffuse, but able to light up the whole of the offside of her car in a blue light. Then the lights seemed to rise into the air, before another bright cone of light beamed down from the sky. This was largely focused on the adjacent field she was passing. She told Dodd that she had returned home from her trip an hour later than she should have done – she had experienced a time warp.[13]

Dodd begins his book, *Alien Investigator*, by highlighting the rather sinister human involvement in Ufo investigation, and attempts at disinformation and suppression of the subject, with possible intelligence and security issues being involved. The 'Men in Black' phrase is the reference to a well-known phenomenon where strange men in dark suits approach Ufo witnesses by going to their homes and asking them intrusive questions about what they have seen. But there does appear to be an element of truth attached to this legend because witnesses who are unknown to each other often say that men 'turn up' to ask them questions, even though they have not made their sightings of Ufos public, such as notifying the local press.

The Men in Black syndrome is a major theme running through American Ufo books. It is often associated with large, dark cars, often (surprisingly) British (and often a Jaguar). Jenny Randles says the MIB, as they are abbreviated to, ask Ufo witnesses probing and surprisingly knowledgeable questions about their experiences. One witness said he was visited by two MoD investigators who were parked outside his address in a black Jaguar after he had briefed a Ufo group on his sighting. Clearly, defence personnel somehow got to hear of this meeting. But Jenny Randles said it was absurd that the MoD would be checking out such an innocuous event, although it does indicate the seriousness with which defence issues were, or are, taken into account.

Ms Randles herself in January 1997 was writing a book on MIB cases when she saw a dark, old-fashioned Jaguar with a 1962 number plate ('straight out of one of my older cases') as she visited a bank in Buxton, Derbyshire, where she lived. A smartly dressed man in a dark suit was standing next to the old car, and was unnervingly staring at her as she made her exit from the bank.

She also heard odd clicking noises on her phone at the time she was investigating the Rendlesham Forest affair (see Internet discussions about this well-known Ufo event). She saw a telephone van parked not far away from her home, with men staring in her direction. She went back inside, and the men were apparently aware of her contacting the phone company to make an enquiry about work on the line, as they promptly disappeared.[14]

Tony Dodd was not himself immune to MIB probing. Some weeks after he and his wife had returned from America – where they met various Ufologists and attended conferences – they seemed to have attracted the attention of strangers. One man with an American accent seemed to have found out where Dodd lived in Grassington, and began to pester him with the usual type of Ufo-related questions. Dodd was aware that he was being pursued stealthily in his car, even around the Yorkshire moors. Dodd found this rather fun, because, knowing the area and its villages well, he could easily enough lose his pursuers, who were often left stranded in narrow little lanes and cul-de-sacs.[15]

Dodd mentioned a curious incident involving a diplomat who got out of his car and handed a 'bully brown envelope' to the driver of a Ford Escort that had pulled up beside him, a small man in his early forties. The unidentified diplomat, from an unknown country, nodded towards another car – a dark blue Rover – parked on the other side of the road, hinting that the pair were being watched. When the driver of the Escort drove off, the crew in the Rover – four of them – chased after him and his package. But, through his superior knowledge of London's streets, the Escort driver managed to throw them off his tail.

What was worrying him was the fact that while he was being pursued he could identify, in his rear-view mirror, one of the men in the car as the same one who had appeared on his doorstep a few weeks earlier, with a female colleague, warning him that he was under surveillance. He stopped briefly on his circuitous cat-and-mouse journey to post the package to Tony Dodd, whom he knew and of whose Ufo-hunting activities he was aware.

But the package never arrived. Dodd later discovered that it contained sensational photos of aliens on board an American warship in the North Atlantic, and other Ufos at certain American Air Force bases.

## Dodd Gets Colleagues Involved

Dodd managed to get some of his police colleagues involved in Ufo investigations. But he soon realised, as did the others, that discussions about seeing Ufos had to be kept fairly secret at work to avoid being thought of as a 'nutcase', or being gullible – 'not a good trait for a policeman'. Dodd began to see other Ufos in the sky on his trips over the moors, especially around Carleton Moor, where other reports filed away in cabinets indicated this was a familiar area for them. He took to observing the area at night when he was off duty, often with friends or police colleagues, who could act as witnesses.

On the night of 7 November 1983 he and his wife were in his own car driving along a quiet country lane near Addingham when they both saw a large 'spinning top' festooned with 'hundreds' of tiny pulsating red lights. It zoomed over the roof of their car. This time Dodd had his camera with him, and managed to take some pictures. He sent them to a Ufo research group based in Arizona who had the negatives professionally examined. They found no evidence of hoaxing or airbrushing, and said in a report that they were the best unfaked Ufo pictures they had seen. Inevitably they lacked definition (they were taken in darkness), but they could still reveal that the object was near spherical in shape and about 30 feet in diameter, and had a vapour trail.[16]

Dodd's team would sometimes wait in their patrol car at night to see whether the Ufos were prone to make regular returns. One night, after a boring wait of three hours with nothing appearing, Dodd got out of the car to stretch his legs only to become aware of a large object hovering overhead. Like the earlier one he saw, it was colourfully illuminated with what looked like fairy lights. Despite the coppers keeping watch on all sides they never saw the object arrive.

On one occasion he saw a cylindrical object, hovering, some 15 yards in length with a line of illuminated 'windows'. As he approached the object it turned on a bright light at its rear which, as the craft increased its speed as it flew away, grew brighter, soon enveloping the object in a weird white shape.

Once the Dodd team were travelling in a squad car along the A65 from Skipton towards Gargrave in the early hours of a cold snowbound morning to meet up with other police officers to exchange mail with them. Dodd and his patrol colleagues saw a large light in a vale below the crest of a hill they had reached. They thought it was a house or a bungalow with its lights left on. But the light was in an empty field and started to move. The driver stopped and they all watched in fascinated silence as it glided across the field. It was now clearly dome shaped, with white light streaming from 'windows'. After the assignment the patrolmen decided to return to the field where they had seen the mysterious object. They got out of the car and walked across the field. There was no trace in the virgin layer of snow – it was untouched, without even an animal's pawprint. Whatever it was, the object had not been in contact with the ground.

Dodd said he instinctively believed the Ufos or aliens were friendly – usually. But the one time he thought otherwise was when he and some friends saw bright lights dancing about and 'doing aerobatics' at quite a low altitude over some nearby hills, and then turning into a huge ball of dazzling orange light when the smaller lights had reached road level. Indeed the car's headlights seemed to provoke the new enlarged light. 'I was scared, and rammed the car into reverse, killing the lights. I drove backwards down the hill in darkness, and the orange light shot upwards at great speed. I had a distinct feeling that our presence was not wanted there that night ...'[17]

The other time he thought they were menacing was when he tried to connect them with another famous road Ufo case, and an apparent murder. This was the Zygmund Adamski case, where a Polish miner was mysteriously found dead on a coal heap in July 1980, which Dodd was called out to attend to. The victim had strange burn marks on his neck, and his body was miles away from where he lived.[18]

Dodd was also connected with the weird Ufo sighting in a Yorkshire lane in November of the same year. Constable Alan Godfrey, whom Dodd knew, was on car patrol near the small town of Todmorden on 29 November 1980 when he saw a luminous saucer in the air, and later saw a brilliantly lit Ufo spread right across the road, causing him to stop. Then there was an abduction experience. This event is one of the most important cases in British Ufo history, and is often cited in the Ufo literature.[19]

# Epilogue

What are we to make of all these stories? So much ground (with its many roads!) has been covered that it is difficult to sum it all up. But there are many books, features and magazine articles on the subject of haunted roads to help us in order to get a useful perspective on this puzzling phenomenon.

Michael Goss maintains that the hitchhiker legends remain 'classic fabrication – a supernatural tale told as a matter of truth because that is part of the narrative convention'. They have, he says, 'been around too long for us to take the implications of individual components … seriously'. Such hitching stories 'touch some deep core within the narrators' (the witness story-tellers), or they are spawned by TV or 'disaster-horror films'.[1]

This leads to issues of veracity and verification: how can we know that the hitchhiker accounts of journalists are actually true? The stories do turn up in local and national press accounts (but not as frequently as Goss makes out), and might even be the most common type of road ghost story. And that might be because all the hitchhiker legends are very similar to poltergeist and haunting manifestations, which indicate that the phenomenon, behaving the same everywhere, is in a class of psychic activity aiding credibility in its own way, with similar haunting cases with believable details happening in adjacent districts.

Yet there remain problems of perception on dark nights by tired drivers, and other observational or interpretation issues. Hallucination or auto-suggestion must also be considered. And there is always the danger of a hoax, or personal aggrandisement. Reports of vanishing hitchhikers made to the police could all be spurred by a memorable but disturbing press article describing how something odd happened to another driver. The events themselves are often assumed to be unreal, or vividly embellished, or the product of subjective thinking and illusions by a driver simply seeing dark shadows in the back of his car while simultaneously spotting a pedestrian outside seemingly about to enter his vehicle, or having just got out of another one. People are believed, and look sincere, when they step forward to tell their ghost stories, but it is always what the witness perceives to be true. The person may actually be a real hitchhiker, and there may be perfectly plausible reasons why she seems to disappear from the car. Dates and exact locations and addresses can be verified, precise details of where the woman was picked up, and so on.

Let us take my title, *Haunted Cars and Highways*. I have already illustrated that cars can be part of the paranormal. Before I venture into the unlikely physics of this, let us first look at machinery, devices and artefacts in general. What, we might ask, is real? Is anything that looks solid actually so, or just a hologram of the real thing arising from the mysteries of quantum mechanics?

Ghostly activity has an affinity with electrical devices and can cause car engines to stop, as we have seen, which is emblematic of the poltergeist theory, where electrical appliances and light bulbs can be unaccountably switched on and off in people's homes. But even more extraordinary is the way the car of the driver who sees a Ufo virtually grinds to a halt. Time, distances, shapes, familiar mechanical functions, and other normal human measurements and understandings, seem to be affected by Ufo sightings. Nothing seems to be right, or goes right later.

There are several examples of malevolent machines. A milking machine in post-war New South Wales, Australia, regularly sent its metal pulsator plates inexplicably flying off and landing up to 250 yards distant from the milking shed. In 1949, for nearly the entire year, the local press were reporting that some mysterious force had caused them to fly out of the shed so fast that they looked as if they had suddenly become invisible, before reappearing further away, usually on a stony plateau to the north of the farm. These discs were made of brass and kaelite, weighing 13 ounces and three inches in circumference. But it would not have been easy for the discs to reach the area where they landed, as there were various building structures and roof angles in the way. And it happened when the machines were not actually working, and they would have been difficult to remove manually. Boffins from Australia's CSIRO, its leading science body, suggested a 60,000-volt power line passing close to the property may have been responsible. This was dismissed by Alexander Portors, an engineer of 30 years' experience, who was very familiar with the machine in question. He did not accept any poltergeist connection, suggesting instead that some power had somehow built up inside the machine.[2]

In a time slip the living ghost, an interactive ghost, can be displaced from its proper time, being partly in and partly out of its surroundings. An example of this is the story of an old bakery that was being converted into a pub, and in the top room there was an old derelict mill wheel. Peter, a plumber and gas fitter, who was working on the conversion, often chatted with an elderly man gazing at the old mill wheel. This was in fact the ghost of Mr Thomas, an engineering inspector who died years earlier. But the old inspector could have been made to materialise to Peter through some manifestation of the occult. The ancient mill, its machinery, Peter himself and the deceased Mr Thomas were spookily linked in some way. The mill wheel had not been modified or repaired, and thus remained in its 100-year time zone, as did the old man. Peter simply saw the mill as it was in the 1890s.[3]

Navvies – road builders and labourers – worked near the Yarwell Tunnel in Cambridgeshire, not far from Peterborough. During its construction in the 1840s special brick kilns were established locally. Several navvies, mainly Irish, met their deaths in the Yarwell area, either from drunkenness or from falling to the ground from scaffolding inside the tunnel. Subsequent maintenance work in the tunnel had brought about mysterious noises and agonising cries and 'sounds of men fighting'. Poltergeists made vital tools disappear, and even caused ghostly sabotage. A freight train once went suddenly through the tunnel unannounced, and someone received a blow to the head which never left a mark on him. At nearby Wansford station a white cat called Snowy, belonging to the stationmaster, one day failed to turn up for his meal. So the stationmaster – who was somewhat deaf – went looking for him, failed to hear the oncoming train and was killed. Snowy was never seen again, but on occasion his ghost can be seen crying piteously when entering the tunnel never to reappear.[4]

Often motorists and police are quite aware of the reality of our haunted highways – they know they, and others, have encountered phantoms of sorts. A Yorkshire family, Jack and June Cartwright and their two children, returning by car from a camping holiday in the West Country one summer, were caught in a rainstorm and the car's electrics and car lights began to fail. They were lost, and decided to spend the night in an old parcels office of a disused and derelict railway station they came across. Nearby, an old booking or staff office in a separated shed-like building – which they had checked out earlier – now seemed to have a light on inside. Jack thought he could hear voices and decided to investigate. He managed to enter the building through the main door, which was previous locked. He was surprised to see a figure sitting at a desk. There was an incandescent glow. And the room seemed to be tidier than it was before, as if it was still in use – like a time warp of an earlier age. The figure suddenly noticed Jack, advanced towards him and challenged him before abruptly disappearing. The following day the booking office was as it had been earlier – derelict, dusty and disused, festooned with cobwebs, and with a locked and barred front door. Stopping off at a garage for a minor repair the following day, Jack learned from the proprietor that the old station was haunted by a deceased porter – probably the one Jack saw saw.[5]

Glynnis and Ron Bush, and their young family and their own parents, some time in the summer in the late 1970s, had booked a holiday cottage in Snowdonia. When they arrived after a long trek by car, they were struck to note how old-fashioned and Victorian it looked inside, with no mod cons, and hints of spookiness when the grandfather clock in the hall stopped ticking only minutes after they started to bring in their luggage. Nevertheless, they had an enjoyable holiday cruising around Wales, until one of the children saw the ghost of an elderly woman on the stairs, and until Ron's car engine packed up, for no reason. An AA mechanic turned up but could find nothing wrong. When the mechanic was invited into the cottage for a cup of tea, Glynnis noticed that the house had suddenly become 'bone-chillingly cold'. The mechanic soon departed. Ron, aware that the failed ignition and electrics in the car was the cause of his car's problems, resignedly went out to try to start the car once more, and it jumped into life. Glynnis and Ron then handed the cottage keys back to the agent in the village, deciding to call off the rest of their holiday. It was then that the agent told Glynnis and Ron that the old lady who owned the cottage had died only a few months back.[6]

Jenny Randles, writing thirty years ago, said that the car stop syndrome was now so prevalent that two detailed catalogues were already available, recording hundreds of examples.[7] In 1954, reports from all over the world showed that strange objects in the sky could interfere with electronic gear, and could outfly jets with tantalising ease. Frank Edwards recalled how in Brazil, in the 1950s, a small automobile was flipped into a ditch by an approaching Ufo.[8]

Possibly the physical explanation can be combined with parapsychological and ionisation theories and others relating to geomagnetic anomalies, and other scientific explanations that can create certain 'window areas' where this kind of thing is likely to happen.

An electrical engineer and spirit investigator, Vic Tandy (1955–2005), heard rumours that his laboratory was haunted with poltergeists, but noises were attributed to the vibrations of various electrical devices. A cleaner told him that she had seen something, possibly, thought Tandy, due to cooling or heating pipes in the building. He himself experienced weird sensations and apparitions. He had used electrical equipment to check out reports of hauntings at certain locations where he was convinced there was a scientific explanation. Making a 'reading' at a ticket hall at a London Tube station, he said that sounds from the street outside the ticket hall could penetrate downwards, and could be mistaken for crying or wailing. But he worked out that some of them were coming from infrasound waves generated by a fan in the extraction system.

Indeed his experiments failed to reproduce genuine haunting sounds or visions.[9]

Steve Parsons founded a paranormal investigation society in 1993 to beef up the science of various theories, and to clear up some confusions. He carried on with Tandy's techniques, and the implications of infrasound from previous medical syndromes, such as cot deaths and brain tumours. The sound detectable by humans ranges from 20 Hz to 20,000 Hz. But infrasound cannot properly be heard but sensed, in the same way a dog whistle cannot be directly heard. Infrasound at 19 Hz can bend round objects rather than be reflected, because its wavelength is longer.

Alan Murdie, a regular ghost commentator on *Fortean Times* magazine, was rather sceptical about Internet videos showing ghosts from CCTV or videos. Often it is mistaken light and shade, and the videos appear many months, sometimes years, afterwards, when the precise camera positions and exact levels of illumination could not be recalled. He dismisses most 'ghost hunts', with investigators preconditioning themselves to see phenomena; and most apparition reports, he writes, come from people who expect something to happen.[10]

Nevertheless, ghosts, it seems, *are* attracted to all forms of transport. Paul Fisher was a London Tube station manager at Stockwell station, and would occasionally do an inspection by walking along the tracks at night. He came across a railman in an old-fashioned tunic, carrying a Tilley Lamp, which had not been in use by rail engineers for years. He spoke to him, and the man replied with desultory answers. On returning to his office he contacted seniors at the station who knew nothing about 'any other guy', and no one had been booked to work in the tunnel that night. Nevertheless, an emergency alert had to be sent out, and trains halted while a search of the tunnel was carried out. Inevitably nothing was found. It was later revealed that in the 1950s a maintenance worker was killed by a Tube train on the Northern Line.[11]

A bereaved mother of a soldier killed in the First World War, a Mrs Aysclough, began to make regular daily journeys to the station where she had first bid him a tearful farewell as he went to war. She did this for forty years until 1958, when she died at the age of 80. Two years later the railway station was closed, and eventually converted into a house. The subsequent owners of the house, the Parkers, one snowy Christmas in 1981, heard a woman's voice, apparently outside. She was calling for a 'Bob', and another voice seemed to reply 'Mother'.

Puzzled and alarmed, John Parker looked out of the window and could see nothing. But looking further afield, to what would have been the old platform, now grassed over, he could vaguely perceive an old lady staring at what would have been the railway track. Then he saw another figure, obviously a soldier complete with peaked cap and rifle, advancing towards the old lady. Then the two figures abruptly disappeared. John donned his boots and overcoat and quickly made his way out of the house. There was nothing – and no footprints in the snow. When he returned to the house and took off his boots, John found an old and dirty envelope attached to the boot's sole, with the initials OHMS stamped on it. There was a letter inside, just two lines long, that began: 'Dear Mrs Aysclough, I regret to inform you …'[12]

A Mr Gordon Ash, a building surveyor, wrote of an experience he had in January 1983. Travelling on the Tube to Victoria, his attention was drawn to a sad-looking young woman, with dark hair tied back and wearing a full length dark blue coat buttoned up to the neck. But he noticed that her complexion was deathly pale, and she had dark rings round her eyes. She could in fact have been desperately ill, he surmised. He stood up to stand by the automatic doors ready to disembark. He then gave one last look at the woman, but she had vanished. She was not waiting at any of the exits, and she would have had to pass in front of him in order to make her way to another carriage. To make sure, he looked up and down the platform. There was no sign of her.[13]

Peter McCue points to the ghostly nature of hitchhikers actually speaking during their rides. 'Phantom figures', as he puts it, 'are seldom talkative.' But sometimes you can actually speak to a ghost, who replies. In several cases in this book we have seen hitchhiking ghosts do this, but in most cases in a desultory way. There has never been any report of a lengthy conversation on any subject, or even general chit-chat. Several ghosts, when asked where they want to go to, simply pointed ahead. I mentioned earlier in the book what psychic investigator Phil Whyman refers to 'interactive ghosts'. These are the most widely reported type of ghost, but have in common the fact that they interact in some way with their surroundings and with their observers. The interactive ghost is a 'full bodied manifestation', as Whyman describes it: an entire person that looks real and ordinary until it disappears, even passing through solid barriers such as walls. The partial manifestation is only when you see, say, the torso, or the legs walking towards you! Both these categories are in the minority of experiences. Phil Whyman says that the aural phenomena are the most common, such as voices, footsteps and sounds.[14]

In his book *Apparitions*, G. N. M. Tyrrell focuses on how ghosts appear and behave like material persons. 'They adapt themselves almost miraculously to the physical conditions … For instance, they can cast shadows, even though they cannot be touched (they tend to back off if you do this, or your hand passes right through them).

They can walk through walls and locked doors, and can be seen reflected in mirrors.'[15] Aniela Jaffe, in her book *Apparitions and Precognition,* wrote about:

> ghosts who cannot be distinguished from the living, and who adopt the mannerisms and gestures of the living. They can vanish through closed doors or walls, but can reveal their presence via unexplained perfume or tobacco smells. They can appear out of nowhere, but seem connected with your life, or are aware of who you are and what you are doing.[16]

Ron Halliday, a psychoanalyst concerned with people's experiences, confirms that his patients' descriptions of Ufos are like ghostly encounters, and says that phantom beasts and Ufos are connected and related. But they can appear solid, which poses obvious problems for Halliday. Halliday is also puzzled by 'phantoms' that appear solid and then 'dematerialise'. Peter McCue says that other studies of a psychological nature could find no significant emotional intelligence differences, or fantasy-proneness.[17] Other sceptics talk of 'auto-suggestion', and of motorists themselves being aware of road ghost legends, and then having a mixed personal reaction when they think they have struck a person in the road, halt and then look under the car for the body. Then there are the Jungian theorists who allude to the old hag theories and gender roles of male drivers and female hitchhikers.

Perhaps road ghosts are enacting mythological archetypes from the past, as messengers either of hope or of doom. They also represent in effect all of the victims of tragic deaths – male and female – and none at the same time, because they are archetypes, and in a sense metaphors or holograms. This might explain the difference between natural and violent deaths. Somebody who dies peacefully leaves the body for another place. Someone who dies violently may not be able to do so, and the sudden transition makes him or her bewildered, and they remain earthbound.[18] Spirits themselves could be confused, repeating the mundane performances that ghosts often give in haunted houses, appearing in the same rooms and doing the same things. Vehicle ghosts affect people doing familiar repetitive things like journeying to and from their workplace or to the local shopping centre. The ghosts themselves seem to want to join in the routines.

The hitchhiker story is the modern version of an old folklore, where ghosts hitch rides on old-time horse-drawn carts that were heading for town. Almost as if aiming for continuity, hitchhiking ghosts have to carry on to the present day. Ghosts tend to appear in familiar surroundings, and it could be assumed that the moving car or cab is itself a kind of mobile haunting place. In many cases the ghosts of tragedies and accidents are simply telling witnesses that they have died there, but their perambulations seem to have been added on.[19]

In their book *Haunted Objects*, Chris Balzano and Tim Weisberg say a spirit is the essence of a person's life. It might be a 'residual' haunting in an ornament or a doll – the essence is trapped and acts like a recording of a moment or a person. This could be the same with cars and the visions of figures along the high road. The authors go on to discuss a ghost that has a mind that is still active, and a 'body' that can interact with its surroundings, a point made earlier. This also can be the haunted highway phenomenon. The authors say the easiest way ghosts can communicate is through electrical devices, and they quote several examples when radios started to turn themselves on in a house in Lakewood, Washington, and tools had been thrown around in a house that had poltergeist activity. Ghosts may want to hang on to something familiar in their earthly life, 'and will not rest until cherished items are in the hands of the people who deserve them'. This also applies to haunted dolls.[20]

In regard to cars, Balzano and Weisberg cite the death of James Dean. He died in a car crash, but parts of the car were retrieved and cannibalised, only for tragedies and accidents to affect those people and motorists who re-used the parts. This also happened in the case of the car that drove Archduke Franz Ferdinand of Austria round the streets of Sarajevo in 1914, when he was killed by a sniper. When the car was repainted and sold on to others, they also suffered tragedies of various sorts.[21]

But it is odd that ghosts whose original person did not die in a road accident should want to pester car drivers. Earlier in this book we came across spiritual road ghosts resenting the fact that they had been killed on the road. Yet a woman driver once complained that her sat-nav once took her past a cemetery where her friend was buried, yet it wasn't on her route. She wrote to Derek Acorah, a regular spook adviser on *Chat It's Fate* magazine, who surprisingly said the same thing had happened to him on his way to help a lady with an unwanted spirit in her home at Southport. His sat-nav played up several times, even after he had reset it. Acorah's own spirit guide hinted that this was the woman's late husband, Sam, trying to 'come through'. Sam's spirit even retuned Acorah's car radio to a station playing his favourite country and western song. He wrote that 'spirits will try all sorts of ways to let us know they are still with us'.[22]

The liminal theories, however, are vaguely paranormal, and not capable of being integrated into any parapsychological or physical explanation. There can be massive and disturbing earth-moving programmes, changes in road layouts, the digging up of sacred turf, and major refurbishments, all of which, apparently, result in hauntings or vanishing cars, or non-existent slip roads.

Actual interactions with hitchhikers tend to divide the road ghost analysts. If they are not real people it is difficult to explain how they can leave a warm impression in the car seat. In his book Michael Goss says many cases involved definitive interactions between the phantom and the witness, like conversations. But Rob Gandy says the Moss, Lancashire, episodes of hauntings and spooky road lights were rather different, with no interaction, and were not in the usual ghostly tradition involving deaths.

The driver in his car is the example of a ghostly relationship, as we have seen throughout this book. The 'vehicle at night', or 'the 'haunted car' syndrome, has become worthy of serious research – the car is an extension of one's own body and senses. The headlights are the eyes, and the wheels are in effect the legs and feet of the driver. His metabolism and nerves become the electrical wiring and ignition of his car, and the steering wheel and brakes are the awareness or consciousness of the driver.[23]

The fact that mature motorists should see fairies by the side of the road while they are actually driving is surprising, if we are to go along with the legend that they are normally seen by children exploring local woods or romping in fields, and that fairies are rather delightful little winged creatures. But Simon Young, who has investigated British and Irish fairy legends, highlights a rather neglected and malign aspect of fairy lore, and I have referred to this concept in earlier chapters. They are more often pixies, or even mutations of leprechauns. When innocent travellers and explorers get lost in the woods or countryside it could be the work of these mischievous pixies, a legend that has echoes in the folklore of other countries.[24] Throughout this book we have seen how motorists have indeed been led astray, compelled to turn off at the wrong junction, or even led to believe that a junction or a road exists when it doesn't. Again, we note the stories of small goblin-like entities that approach and frighten the occupants of parked cars. Some curious foreign investigators of the antics of fairies, like Mirjam Mencej, associate orbs of light with their appearances, and I have tried to illustrate in this book the interrelated aspects of the paranormal, from Ufos, black cats and large wolf-like phantoms, as well as fairies.

Indeed, are the black cats seen near, or from, the road just large domestic pets, escaped panthers from zoos, or another alarming variety of alien entities? These ABCs are, in most cases, regarded as real animals, with evidence of killed livestock found with the paw marks characteristic of big cat attacks. This applies to the alarming wolf-like shucks. But seldom are the carcases of these creatures seen on roads, which is odd if they are supposed to have been run over by passing cars. Although they may have been struck – like the famed jaywalkers – they have mysteriously disappeared afterwards. It is also doubtful that such creatures, if they existed, would not be known about by academics or countryside authorities.

There is also the matter of coincidences and the more scientific equivalent – *synchronicity*. Why do different (and sometimes the same) drivers see the same apparition, the same phantom jaywalker, on the same stretch of road, even at the same time of day or night? Clearly, once again, these apparitions are evidence of the paranormal. And yet in science two events coinciding inexplicably with each other is known as synchronicity when there is an event or phenomenon that is in an exact, or simultaneous, harmony with another similar event. Scientists adopted synchronicity as a fundamental constant that could be explained mathematically or with calculus. Marie-Louise von Franz, a Jungian supporter and mathematician, believed that synchronicity is a manifestation of a much wider principle of 'acausal orderedness'. Most strange occurrences in life are, then, merely *acausal,* without a known cause.

But when psychologists linked up with scientists it didn't really help matters. You could look at coincidences from a psychological point of view – 'isn't that strange?' – but it is undermined by examples of sudden moves – like the driver forced to swerve round a phantom jaywalker, which other drivers have done – which make the synchronicity look like a spooky force at work. Brian Inglis wrote that 'there are influences at work which, in human terms, are consciously guiding our actions at critical moments ...'[25]

Synchronicity might, then, be a link between two parallel worlds, with slight variations in those worlds, with one motorist seeing the road phantom from a slightly different angle to that of another. Or the link could actually be between the physical world and the *paraphysical* world. Synchronicity, as well as road hauntings, suggests that hologram theory is involved – a point I will address below – as does 'virtual reality' – a potential reality and a real reality where a repetition of something takes place when two coincident events come together. If people suspect there is an element of mystery attached to coincidences then a new alignment of forces within the human personality can have a spiritual dimension that soon dawns on the experiencers.

## How Can Cars Not Be Solid?

Let us get to the fundamental scientific conundrum. How can large metallic objects like cars, weighing several hundredweight – that can actually collide with your own car – NOT be solid? How can cars and trucks actually be ghostly? Are they real cars or simply holographic projections of cars, a kind of 3D image of the real thing?

Matter – the steel, glass and rubber of the car – is solid, surely. Why do motorists report stories to the police of onrushing cars 'passing through them'?

If they are actually real cars, then where is the extra material coming from to make them? Recent discussions about parallel universes suggest that extra teravolt energy could come from a neighbouring cosmic bubble. A lot of *potential* matter exists inside atoms, a peculiar conclusion derived from speculation about the amount of energy that is hidden in the cosmos, and even in the atom itself. Cosmic energies are denoted in electron volts (eVs), gigaelectronvolts (GeVs), or teraelectronvolts with one teraelectron volt (TeV) being equal to $10^{-12}$ electron volts. Something could be happening to produce extra teraelectronvolt energy from which new matter could be created.

The atoms of the car, remember – *before they become part of a car* – are in some kind of transitional, or probabilistic, state. In a laboratory, once a scientist has observed an atom in one state, it is no longer in this probabilistic state – it has 'decohered'. The atoms, the particles, don't really exist until they are observed by the experimenter. The trillions of particles that make up matter destroy the overlap of probability. If this overlap is not destroyed the person or object remains as some kind of image, a kind of vagueness, waiting to be 'decohered'. But of course the atoms become aggregated into solid matter – matter becomes definite and real, and is no longer subject to quantum effects. Similarly the solid person or object materialises as a kind of 'decoherence'.

However, there is a snag: sometimes in the laboratory the decoherence of the particle is only partly successful, and this could well apply to matter itself. Matter must have only a *potential* existence if *atoms* have only a potential existence; standard physics is never clear about this. Scientists deny this lack of clarity: large macro objects and the universe are ruled by two different sets of laws dealing with the very small (atoms) and the very large (the universe itself), where the very large objects don't behave like the very small. I was surprised to read a recent *New Scientist* article which actually reinforced the confusion on this point.[26] Yet with the emergence of 'multiverse' theories, often discussed in the same journal, even solid objects can theoretically be in two different worlds at the same time, with only minor variations of the same object or person in each one.

Howard Wiseman of Griffith University in Queensland, Australia, said we should think of universes coexisting in the same space as ours, like ghosts. Our universe shares space with other universes which may not have the same Newtonian laws of physics as ours does. And we can either assume or not – as the case may be – that these other universes share the same quantum weirdness as a result of these worlds and universes somehow interacting with each other. We would only know about them when they interact with our world, but if they utilise entirely different physical principles they will perforce be *paraphysical* – physics beyond the normal – and could account for paranormal events happening on earth. Psychic researcher James Cranshaw says that subatomic particles can produce wave patterns in tones and overtones and produce characteristic sights and sounds. Matter seems to be emergent and transitory, appearing like ordinary matter but having no permanent existence itself.[27]

In any event, every object, even a person, has its contours, rather than its substance or mass, determined by the number of Planck squares covering its surface. Everything solid you see is really only the cross-section of the real thing. It exists in the fourth dimension, which means it has duration, and the continued visible existence of anything is proof of its duration, until it disappears. In the case of animate objects like people and cars, we can see them moving in time. The subatomic particle, when observed, is in two places (or positions or configurations) at once, so one could assume that the car that suddenly vanishes at the crossroads could also have another version of itself going somewhere else, and I have mentioned cases in this book where the onrushing and vanishing car is still seen as a solid car receding in the driver's rear-view mirror.

In an earlier book I gave many examples where people experience time warps and apparitions when physics says they shouldn't. I mentioned the case of a Mrs Marshall who noticed that a familiar street clock, one that she had consulted virtually every day, had suddenly disappeared. Perturbed, she went into a nearby shop only to be told that the clock had been taken down about a year earlier.[28] In other words the entirety of the solid object that we see – the complete human car driver or the complete road vehicle that we see disappearing – could reasonably be its hologram, its projection, or even its potential.

Neither is science very clear on the subject of *time* and its relation to reality. We see the car on the highway because trillions of photons in the air create light, and the light gives us the visibility. But light functions, like matter and radiation in the universe, only in time. This time factor alone can affect visibility and invisibility. Photons have no mass, because if they did they would not be able to reach light speed: they would become so dense that they would stop in their tracks. On the other hand if a photon has no mass it has no weight or displacement, so it does not, in a sense, exist. Particles can zoom backwards and forwards in space, but also backwards and forwards in time. The many strange 'time warp' experiences that drivers have – where a journey seems to take hours longer than it should have done – could be proof of the strangeness of physics that we do not understand. This is why paranormal events seem to happen, because they are more normal than we think: they are a manifestation of reality that we haven't understood. Yet surely if a driver says he sees a car that vanishes, or says that his trip has taken hours longer than it should have done when he checks the watch strapped to his wrist, he is telling us not what he *thinks* is the truth, but the actual truth that can, in many cases, be verified. Something, then, is not quite right with reality.

Peter McCue is surprisingly ambivalent and contradictory in his own book on paranormal events on Britain's roads, saying that Ufos may well be apparitional events, but at the same time, as a parapsychologist himself, he plumps for the hallucinatory or false memory explanation. He even suggests that interior car lights coming on when the hitchhiker enters the car, or the driver hearing the seat belt being clicked into place, are part of the same hallucinatory experience. But on virtually the same page he says Ufo memories could well be implanted by 'tricksterish high intelligences'.[29]

He wrote that he didn't think that roads acted like 'psychic cobwebs', trapping the souls of the dead, nor could he explain why jaywalkers act like 'suicidal maniacs,' citing the comment by Sean Tudor in his book on the Blue Bell Hill ghosts.[30] But it is also odd that McCue believes that 'intelligent direction' or 'orchestration' is involved, even in cases of 'translocations', which also involve poltergeist activity.

But what about phantom cars, coaches and horses that are assumed to be materialisations from the past? It strains credibility to imagine a ghost, while beaming an image of itself to the percipient, and while able to project a picture of himself in period clothes, is also able to transmit the image of himself in a car. A Swedish psychiatrist once reported that a patient called Jakob, while driving, momentarily thought of a friend called Eva. He was then 'transported astrally' to his friend's home, and right into the room where she was sitting. Eva herself had the remarkable experience, if true, that she actually saw Jakob 'sitting in front of me in the car ... I also saw the clock in the car. I think it was a couple of minutes before six.' Yet a Dr Alan Gould, a senior member of the Council of the Society for Psychical Research, said that while 'animism' (where a body appears physical but is not) could account for ghosts being seen in solid form complete with their clothes, he felt doubtful about including parts of cars. It is extremely odd, he mused, about the girl being able to see the correct time on the car's clock.[31]

It is worth at this stage considering the extraordinary 'Philadephia Experiment' which caused controversy when a popular book of that title about it appeared in the late 1970s, authored by Charles Berlitz and William Moore. An alleged military experiment was carried out by the US Navy in a Pennsylvania shipyard which made a ship suddenly disappear from the yard to reappear at another naval site in Virginia, and then return to Philadelphia, on 28 October 1943, although other commentators say the incident happened at sea rather than in dockyards.[32]

Critics of this event deny this actually happened, and say there was a misunderstanding about the 'experiment' which was an attempt to deflect radar or electromagnetic signals with a form of degaussing to 'cloak' the ship, or ships, to make them in effect 'invisible' to enemy radar. The word 'invisible' was played up by popularisers of the naval experiment, and involved partly understood theories of Einstein's attempt at a 'unified field' involving gravity and electromagnetism. Other important theories and actual experiments by physicists such as Robert Harrington Kent, during and after the Second World War, and those of Dr Thomas Townsend Brown, also added to the confusion. Both of them suggested that types of degaussing could not only bend radar waves but also light waves. Brown is interesting in that he was also involved in Ufo research, trying to understand their motive power, and actually performed experiments in which he made 'dielectric' discs (a kind of electrical insulator) fly under certain laboratory conditions.[33]

A 'Dr Rinehart' suggested that one result of the Philadelphia Experiment was the 'Zeemanising' of atoms, which makes a split in the excitation states of atomic particles. This would fundamentally alter our understanding of quantum physics. There were also, he said, 'interdimensional' and unanticipated mass displacement side-effects of the Philadelphia Experiment. This caused, or could have done depending on what people at the time say they observed, actual antigravity or teleportation effects.[34]

The Philadelphia Experiment should be looked at in regard to other transport mysteries that seem to distort conventional physics. Other impossible allegations have been made. At Longdendale Valley, Derbyshire, in the spring of 1997, there was a phantom aircraft crash, identified in the archives as a B29, an aircraft in service in the immediate post-war years. Some reports said it was the 'ghost' of a Skytrain F13 which crashed in 1946. Also at Longdendale Valley, Blacklow Hill, in May 2003, wartime bomber droning sounds were heard. At Rawsley on 3 August 2015 a phantom Lancaster bomber flew over Richard and Helen Jephson, but there was no crash as expected. In Norfolk there are phantom wartime planes and haunted airfields. At Portland, Dorset, in May 1976, there was an apparition of tanks, jeeps and US soldiers, which some thought might have been part of a movie production. In my book *Our Holographic World* I mention several other examples of phantom wartime planes seen in British skies.[35]

There are several accounts of 'ghost trains' in occultic literature. A ghost train can gain its reputation if it is run infrequently, and often without passengers, raising issues about why it exists at all, and whether it is a real train. It looms out of the mist and is seldom seen again, at least not for several hours after. Further, the train is not entirely whole and often seems to traverse depopulated countryside routes, with hardly any houses or buildings to be seen for miles. And only a few people seem to know about it. It becomes a ghost hunter's hobby, for people who like to put up with infrequent or unknown travel schedules across lonely landscapes, and often without a return ticket. Only later, or before its passing or disappearance, does the ghost train become 'real'. It is in its surroundings at the time it appears to the observer, but instantly out of its surroundings seconds later.

There is a stunning example of this happening, which I referred to in my earlier book. It involves the most peculiar and disturbing story of the skull of Nikolai V. Gogol (1809–1852). A theatre aficionado stole the skull from his tomb and put it into a casket, which was later stolen by students who took it on a train ride across the Russian countryside in the spring of 1911. The train entered a tunnel and a thick white cloud enveloped it, and the train was never seen again, all 106 passengers vanishing.[36] The train from then on was said to become apparitional, passing through or seen in many cities and regions of Russia.

But not all phantom trains could have been the Gogol Skull train, which had many carriages. For example in 1955 in the area of Balaklava in the Crimea, a phantom pre-World War I train was seen, but only had three cars, and had closed window blinds (which would be unusual in a passenger train) and had an empty driver's cabin. It passed over an old railway embankment from which the rails had been removed years before. Another similar historic train was seen in the Poltava region of Ukraine in September 1991, and was reported in two newspapers, *Pravda Ukrainy* and *Slava Sevastopolya*. In that year a scientist, a V. P. Leschatiy from the Ukrainian Academy of Sciences, and chairman of its anomalous research group, was seen to actually jump onto a phantom train as it passed by a level crossing. The man was never heard from again.[37]

In 2002 a TV station technician named Vyacheslav Fomenko was on a railway platform in Zaporozhye, in the Ukraine, when he was stunned to witness an imminent head-on crash between a modern train and an antiquated one that was travelling on the wrong line, and which had appeared out of nowhere. But the phantom train vanished just seconds before a collision would have taken place.[38]

Albert Budden gives a psychological explanation for this and similar events, attributing them to ambient electrical fields and 'electrical fogs', charged-up inert gases like neon, krypton, argon and xenon, causing them to fluoresce. There is a 'frozen' aspect to car stops, and motorists feel paralysed, which Budden calls 'akinesia'.[39] But 'electric fogs' introduces another angle that has been used to explain the 'Bermuda Triangle', where hundreds of ships and planes have unaccountably disappeared since the Second World War. A commercial pilot and coastguard, Bruce Gernon, writes about how, on his several trips through the 'Triangle' in the Bahamas, the electronic fog is related to cloudy and normal foggy weather, but it seems to cling to the aircraft and travels with it, causing electronic failures of its navigational equipment.[40]

Palls of mist and fog have long been part of supernatural experiences, and several have been mentioned in this book as appearing on roads and highways. Some boys, barely in their teens, in a Glasgow public park, dared to try to enter a boarded-up ancient tower at night. The tower was said to be the menacing haunt of 'black magic devil worshippers'. At the end of a sloping path there was an arched doorway with a stout wooden door with ornate metal hinges. The boys had a distinct sense of foreboding, and hesitated, fearful of even touching the doors. At that point a friend at the bottom of the path shouted a warning of 'an almost solid wall of dense fog coming down the slope of the glen through the trees … We fled in terror.' The following day the gang went to visit the tower again, and were astonished to see that the doorway was sealed completely by stones of irregular shapes and sizes. 'They were unlikely', wrote Scott Wilson, one of the youths, 'to be easily mistaken in the gloom for the regular stout planks and hinges we had seen the other night …'[41]

# Notes

There are often several Internet sources for the events covered and so I have just suggested relevant search parameters where appropriate.

## Chapter 1: Britain's Haunted Roads

1. Yorkshire paranormal database.
2. Leo Ruickbie, *The Supernatural*, Constable and Robinson, 2012. p. 13.
3. *Fate and Fortune* magazine, April 2018, p. 41.
4. Richard Newman, *Haunted Bridges*, Llewellyn Publications, 2016, p. 88.
5. *Fate and Fortune* magazine, January 2015, p. 22.
6. Michael Clarkson, *The Poltergeist Phenomenon*, New Page Books, 2011, p. 93.
7. Ruickbie, op. cit., p. 13.
8. *Fate and Fortune* magazine, November 2017, pp. 6–7.
9. *Chat It's Fate* magazine, March 2015, p. 14.
10. Wikipedia: 'Reported Road Casualties in GB'.
11. John Harries, *The Ghost Hunter's Road Book*, Letts & Co, 1974, p. 21.

12. Theresa Cheung, *An Angel Called My Name*, Harper Element, 2008, pp. 39–45.
13. David Clarke, 'Road Ghost' website, https://drdavidclarke.co.uk/urban-legendary/road-ghosts/.
14. *East Anglia* magazine, vol 34, pp. 224–225.
15. Roger Boar and Nigel Blundell, *World's Greatest Ghost Stories*, Octopus Books, 1983, p. 113.
16. Internet: 'Hairy Hands', Wikipedia.
17. Hereford paranormal database.
18. Devon paranormal database.
19. http://ghost-investigators.blogspot.com/2009/12/pretoria-pit.html.
20. Harries, op. cit., p. 46.
21. Brian Inglis, *Coincidence*, Hutchinson, 1990, p. 123.
22. 'Mysteries of the Unexplained', *Reader's Digest*, 1989, pp. 173–174.
23. Lanarkshire paranormal database.
24. *Fortean Times* magazine, March 2016, p. 71.

# Chapter 2: Liminal Places and Sacred Borders

1. Jenny Randles, 'The Cursed Crossroads', *Truly Weird*, Collins and Brown, 1998.
2. *Daily Telegraph*, 19 May 2008.
3. 'Haunted Roads', *The Ley Journal*, 121, 1994, pp. 1–7.
4. Sean Tudor, *The Ghosts of Blue Bell Hill*, White Ladies Press, 2017, p. 283.

5.  Ibid., p. 331.

6.  *Kent Messenger*, 31 July 1970, p. 18.

7.  *Fate and Fortune* magazine, August 2014, p. 49.

8.  Peter Moss, *Ghosts Over Britain*, Elm Tree Books, 1977, p. 109.

9.  W. B. Herbert, *Railway Ghosts and Phantoms*, BCA Books, 1992, pp. 41–42.

10. Arthur Shuttle, *The Warminster Mysteries*, The Book Service Ltd, 1973, p. 134.

11. *Sunday Express*, 1 April 1979.

12. Bob Ricard and John Michell, *Rough Guide to the Unexplained*, Rough Guides Ltd., 2017, p. 209.

13. Anthony North, *The Paranormal: a Guide to the Unexplained*, Blandford Press, 1996, p. 74.

14. Ricard and Michell, op. cit., p. 209.

15. *Chat It's Fate* magazine, August 2016, p. 49.

16. Brad Steiger, *Real Ghosts, Restless Spirits and Haunted Places*, Visible Ink Press, 2003, p. 324.

17. Herbert, op. cit., pp. 236–237.

18. Joan Forman, *The Mask of Time*, McDonald's and Janes, 1978, p. 146.

19. Anthony Peake, *The Labyrinth of Time*, Arcturus, 2012, p. 231.

20. Yorkshire paranormal database.

21. Suffolk paranormal database.

22. Aberdeenshire paranormal database.

23. *Chat It's Fate* magazine, February 2018, p. 34.

24. Forman, op. cit., p. 62.

25. Essex paranormal database

26. Norfolk paranormal database.
27. Colin Wilson, *Beyond the Occult*, Watkins Publishing, 2008, pp. 140–141.
28. T. Swanz, http://uforeview.tripod.com/timeslips.html.
29. Forman, op. cit., pp. 54–55
30. *Chat It's Fate* magazine, February 2017, p. 34.
31. Forman, op. cit., p. 152.
32. J. Bernard Hutton, *On the Other Side of Reality*, Award Books, 1969, pp. 171–175.
33. Jenny Randles, *Time Storms*, Piatkus Books, 2001, p. 81.

# Chapter 3: The Legacy of Haunted Landscapes

1. Buckinghamshire paranormal database.
2. Herefordshire and Worcestershire paranormal database.
3. Buckinghamshire paranormal database.
4. Warwickshire paranormal database.
5. Anthony North, *The Paranormal: a Guide to the Unexplained*, Blandford, 1996, p. 72.
6. See Internet: 'Cambridge ghosts and other paranormal events'.
7. John Harries, *The Ghost Hunter's Road Book*, Letts & Co, 1974, p. 45.
8. Derbyshire paranormal database.
9. Herefordshire paranormal database.
10. Colin Wilson, *The Occult*, Watkins Publishing, 2006, pp. 212–213.
11. *Chat It's Fate* magazine, September 2017, p. 45.

12. Harries, op. cit., p. 50.

13. *Fortean Times* magazine, September 2018, p. 45.

14. Essex paranormal database.

15. Bedfordshire paranormal database.

16. Harries, op. cit., pp. 15, 25–27.

17. Roy Bainton, *The Mammoth Book of the Unexplained*, Little Brown Book Group, 2013, p. 208.

18. *Fortean Times* magazine, October 2017, p. 35.

19. www.fairyist.com/fairy-places/welsh-fairies.

20. *Fate and Fortune* magazine, February 2017, p. 27.

21. *Mail on Sunday*, 23 September 2018; *Chat It's Fate* magazine, December 2018, p. 8.

22. A75, Scotland's most haunted, http://www.trucknetuk.com/phpBB/viewtopic.php?t=150809&p=2391423; see also *BBC News*, 'The A75 Kinmount Straight – Trip on "most haunted road"'.

23. *Daily Express*, 28 October 2010.

24. https://www.theguardian.com/uk/2006/oct/31/britishidentity.martinwainwright .

25. Andy Gilbert, *Credible Witness*, ISBN: 978-11-326-92772-1, 2017, p.28. Self-published, royalties to Burntwood Memorial Community Association.

26. Paranormal England – Greater Manchester.

27. Cumbria paranormal database.

28. Sean Tudor, *The Ghost of Blue Bell Hill*, White Ladies Press, 2017, p. 336.

## Chapter 4: Landscape Ghosts

1. Internet: 'Eerie Place – Haunted: Hollingbourne Manor House, Kent'; John Harries, *The Ghost Hunter's Road Book*, Letts & Co, 1974, p.45.

2. www.bbc.co.uk/norfolk/content/articles/2005/04/02/asop_blickling_hall_ghost_feature.shtml: 'The ghost of Anne Boleyn'.

3. Internet: 'Haunted History: The great King Rufos and the Rufoses'.

4. Shropshire database: '17th Century Boy'.

5. Morgen Redritch (ed.), *Ghosts, Gedden and Grossett*, 2010, pp. 50–51.

6. www.bbc.co.uk/blackcountry/content/articles/2007/10/30/a456_ghost_feature.shtml.

7. Saddleworth White Rose Society, newsletter, autumn, no. 16.

8. John Harries, op. cit., p. 40.

9. Andy Gilbert, *Credible Witness*, ISBN: 978-11-326-92772-1, 2017, pp. 28–29. Self-published, royalties to Burntwood memorial Community Association.

10. Surrey paranormal database.

11. Harries, op. cit., p. 103.

12. Hampshire paranormal database.

13. Peter Moss, *Ghosts Over Britain: True Accounts of Modern Hauntings*, David & Charles, 1978, pp. 69–70.

14. Yorkshire paranormal database.

# Chapter 5: Phantom Stagecoaches and Horsemen

1.  Colin Wilson and Christopher Evans, *Strange but True*, Pergamon Books, 1995, p. 104; John Harries, *The Ghost Hunter's Road Book*, Letts & Co, 1974, p. 104.

2.  Internet: 'Ghosts and hauntings of the Highways and Byways'.

3.  Harries, op. cit., p. 44.

4.  Guide quote, Castleshaw Roman Fort, 2012, and email 28 August 2017.

5.  *Fate and Fortune* magazine, January 2018, pp. 20–21.

6.  Leo Ruickbie, *The Supernatural*, Constable and Robinson, 2012, p. 14.

7.  Internet: 'Haunted in the spirit of Sir Francis Drake'.

8.  'The Haunted Bypass', *Strange but True,* ITV programme, 2 December 1994.

9.  Internet: 'Road ghosts: haunted highways', Dr David Clarke; David Clark, *The Supernatural Peak District*, Robert Hale, 2000, pp. 33–34.

10. *Phenomena Magazine* (US), November 2011, p. 48.

11. *Annandale Observer*, 29 October 2010, p. 53.

12. Harries, op. cit., p. 127.

13. *Hampstead and Local Advertiser*, 17 October 1985.

14. Internet: 'Welcome to roadghosts.com!' Road ghosts 'index page'.

15. Bedfordshire paranormal database.

16. Gloucestershire paranormal database.

17. Harries, op. cit., p. 99.

18. *Fortean Times* magazine, April 2018, p. 17.

19. See Facebook public group: :Mysterious Britain and Ireland, October 2016.

20. *Chat It's Fate* magazine, midsummer 2017, p. 62.

21. *Fortean Times* magazine, June 2015, p. 39.

22. Harries op. cit., p. 63.

23. Ibid., p. 32.

24. Ibid., p. 36.

25. *Phenomena* magazine, November 2011, pp. 12–13.

26. *Fate and Fortune* magazine, September 2018, pp. 36–37.

27. Internet: 'Ghosts of Bury St Edmunds, and other paranormal reports'.

28. Internet: David Farrent, 'The Spectral Coach of Enfield'.

29. *It Happened to Me: Real-life Tales of the Paranormal*, vol. 1, Dennis Publishing, p. 24.

30. *Fortean Times* magazine, September 2015, p. 37.

31. *Fortean Times* magazine, April 2016, p. 36.

32. Brad Steiger, *Real Ghosts, Reckless Spirits and Haunted Places*, Visible Ink, 2003, p. 402.

## Chapter 6: The Reality of Spooky Cars

1. Jenny Randles, *Time Storms*, Piatkus, 2001, p. 84.

2. *Fortean Times* magazine, January 2013, p. 74.

3. Alasdair Wickham, *The Black Book of Modern Myths*, Arrow Books, 2012, p. 26.

4. *Fate and Fortune* magazine, February 2017, p. 27; Peter Haining (ed.), *The Mammoth Book of True Hauntings*, Constable and Robinson, 2008, p. 272.

5. 'Mysteries of the Unexplained', *Readers Digest*, 1988, p. 174.

6. Warwickshire paranormal database.

7. Alan Radnor, *Paranormal or Normal?*, Headline Publishing, 1989, p. 149.

8. Wickham, op. cit., p. 26.

9. John A. Keel, *Our Haunted Planet*, Galde Press, 1971, p. 184.

10. Wickham, op. cit., p. 27.

11. Peter M McCue, *Paranormal Encounters on Britain's Roads*, The History Press, 2018, p. 38.

12. Ibid., pp. 39–40.

13. *It Happened to Me: Real-life Tales of the Paranormal*, vol. 5, Dennis Publishing, p. 12.

14. West Glamorgan paranormal database.

15. W. B. Herbert, *Railway Ghosts and Phantoms*, BCA Books, 1992, pp. 195–196.

16. *Fortean Times* magazine, January 2018, p. 77.

17. Brad Steiger, *Real Ghosts, Restless Spirits and Haunted Places*, Visible Ink, 2003, p. 507.

18. *Fortean Times* magazine, Christmas, 2017, p. 77.

19. Jackie Newcomb, *An Angel by My Side*, Harper Element, 2002, pp. 28–29.

20. *Fortean Times* magazine, June 2015, p. 15.

21. McCue, op. cit., p. 42.

22. *Daily Mail*, letter, 7 September 2017, p. 63.

23. *Fortean Times* magazine, December 2014, p. 75.

24. Ibid., p. 75.

25. *Fate and Fortune* magazine, October 2018, pp. 8–9.

26. Roger Boar and Nigel Blundell, *World's Greatest Ghost Stories*, Octopus Books, 1993, pp. 127–128.

27. Herbert op. cit., pp. 39–40.

## Chapter 7: Phantom Cars across Britain

1. Jacky Newcomb, *An Angel by My Side*, Harper Element, 2002, pp. 121–122.

2. Peter M. McCue, *Paranormal Encounters on Britain's Roads*, The History Press, 2018, pp. 46–47.

3. West Midlands paranormal database.

4. *Fortean Times* magazine, July 2015, p. 71.

5. Peter Underwood, *Gazetteer of Scottish Ghosts*, Fontana, 1974, p. 177.

6. McCue, op. cit., pp. 40–41.

7. Internet: www.castleofspirits.com.

8. 'The A21, Most Haunted in the UK', Radio programme, *Kent Live*.

9. McCue, op. cit., p. 40.

10. Roger Boar and Nigel Blundell, *World's Greatest Ufo Mysteries*, Octopus Books, 1983, p. 113.

11. Frank Smyth, *Ghosts and Poltergeists*, Aldis Books, 1976, p. 60.

12. *Fortean Times* magazine, April 2012, p. 46.

13. Paul Devereux, *Haunted Land: Investigations into Modern Mysteries*, Piatkus Books, pp. 140–142.

14. See Dr David Clarke, website.

15. *Fate and Fortune* magazine, September 2015, p. 25.

16. Jenny Randles, *Time Storms*, Piatkus Books, 2001, p. 81.

17. Boar and Blundell, op. cit., pp. 32–33.

18. *Fortean Times* magazine, June 2015, pp. 15, 33–34.

19. *Fate and Fortune* magazine, February 2016, p. 29.

20. Ibid., September 2018, pp. 34–35.

21. *Chat It's Fate* magazine, September 2018, pp. 26–27.

## Chapter 8: Premonitions and Omens

1. Dennis Bardens, *Ahead of Time*, Robert Hale, 1991, p. 46.

2. Derek Acorah, *Derek Acorah's Amazing Psychic Stories*, Harper Element, 2006, pp. 50–51.

3. *Fate and Fortune* magazine, May 2014, pp. 28–29.

4. Ibid., August 2015, p. 16.

5. Theresa Cheung, *An Angel Spoke to Me*, Simon and Schuster, 2011, p. 40.

6. *Chats It's Fate* magazine, April 2017, pp. 14–15.

7. Ibid., p. 4.

8. Ibid., January 2018, p. 67.

9. *Fate and Fortune* magazine, July 2018, p. 17.

10. Ibid., September 2018, pp. 30–31.

11. Cheung, op. cit., p. 38.
12. Theresa Cheung, *An Angel Saved Me*, Simon and Schuster, 2011, p. 36.
13. *Chat It's Fate* magazine, January 2018, p. 7.
14. Ibid., October 2018, pp. 22–23.
15. Ibid., October 2015, pp. 4–5.
16. *Fate and Fortune* magazine, November 2017, p. 40.
17. *Spirit & Destiny* magazine, November 2018, p. 46.
18. *Fate and Fortune* magazine, September 2014, p. 53.
19. Brian Inglis, *Coincidences*, Hutchinson, 1990, p. 85.
20. *Chat It's Fate* magazine, November 2014, p. 33.
21. Theresa Cheung, *An Angel Called My Name*, Harper Element, 2008, p. xv.
22. *Fate and Fortune* magazine, February 2017, p. 22.
23. Doreen Virtue, *Saved by an Angel*, Hay House, 2011, p. 163.
24. *Fate and Fortune* magazine, May 2016, p. 23.
25. *Chat It's Fate* magazine, March 2015, pp. 44–45.
26. Cheung, *An Angel Spoke to Me*, op. cit., pp. 86–87.
27. *Chat It's Fate* magazine, September 2014, pp. 14–15.
28. *Fortean Times* magazine, August 2014, p. 73.
29. Acorah, op. cit., pp. 229–230.
30. Ibid., p. 235.
31. *Fate and Fortune* magazine, April 2015, p. 27; *Chat It's Fate* magazine, April 2016, p. 15.
32. Acorah, op. cit., p. 52.

# Chapter 9: 'Saved by Angels'

1.  Glennyce S. Eckersley, *An Angel at My Shoulder*, Rider, 2007, p. 1.
2.  Glennyce S. Eckersley, *Angels and Miracles*, Rider, 1997, p. 36.
3.  *Chat Its's Fate* magazine, September 2014, pp. 4–6.
4.  Derek Acorah, *Derek Acorah's Amazing Psychic Stories*, Harper Element, 2008, p. 190.
5.  Jacky Newcomb, *An Angel Saved My Life*, Harper Element, 2006, p. 69.
6.  Ibid., p. 74.
7.  *Fate and Fortune* magazine, February 2014, p. 15.
8.  *Chat It's Fate* magazine, May 2018, p. 42.
9.  Ibid., July 2017, pp. 44–45.
10. Eckersley, *An Angel at My Shoulder*, op. cit., pp. 51–52.
11. *Fate and Fortune* magazine, November 2018, pp. 18–19.
12. Theresa Cheung, *An Angel Saved Me*, Simon and Schuster, 2011, p. 39.
13. Ibid., pp. 40–41.
14. Ibid., pp. 41–42.
15. 'Take a Break', *Fate and Fortune* magazine, July 2017, p. 15.
16. Cheung, op. cit., pp. 44–45.
17. Acorah, op. cit., pp. 36–37.
18. Theresa Cheung, *An Angel Called My Name*, Harper Element Books, 2008, pp. 143–144.
19. *Chat It's Fate* magazine, September 2014, p. 33.
20. Cheung, *An Angel Saved Me*, op. cit., pp. 42–43.
21. *Chat It's Fate* magazine, September 2018, pp. 22–23.

22. Theresa Cheung, *An Angel Spoke to Me*, Simon and Schuster, 2011, pp. 70–71.

23. 'Take a Break', *Fate and Fortune* magazine, July 2012, p. 17.

24. *Chat It's Fate* magazine, November 2018, p. 25.

25. 'Take a Break', *Fate and Fortune* magazine, September 2016, pp. 26–27.

26. Ecklersley, *Angels and Miracles*, op. cit., p. 34.

27. Cheung, *An Angel Saved Me*, op. cit., p. 49.

28. Eckersley, *An Angel at my Shoulder*, op. cit., pp. 18–19.

29. Cheung, *An Angel Saved Me*, op. cit., p. 35.

30. Cheung, *An Angel Called My Name*, op. cit., pp. 123–124.

31. Acorah, op. cit., pp. 47–48.

32. *Chat It's Fate*, June 2017, p. 7.

33. Diana Cooper, *True Angel Stories*, Findhorn Press, 2013, p. 107.

34. Cheung, *An Angel Called My Name*, op. cit., p. 98.

35. *Fate and Fortune* magazine, August 2017, p. 23.

36. Derek Acorah, op. cit., pp. 50–51.

37. Ibid., pp. 48–49.

38. Cheung, *An Angel Spoke to Me*, op. cit., pp. 195–196.

39. Cheung, *An Angel Saved Me*, op. cit., p. 50.

40. Cheung, *An Angel Spoke to Me*, op. cit., p. 98.

41. *Fate and Fortune* magazine, February 2016, p. 23.

42. See Doreen Virtue, *Angel Visions*, Hay House, 2009.

43. Jacky Newcomb, *An Angel Saved My Life*, Harper Element, 2006, p. 167.

44. Eckersley, *Angels and Miracles*, op. cit., p. 36.

45. Newcomb, op. cit., p. 175.

46. Cheung, *An Angel Called My Name*, op. cit., pp. 71–75.

47. Cheung, *An Angel Spoke to Me*, op. cit., pp. 206–207.

48. Newcomb, op. cit., p. 176.

49. Cooper, op. cit., p. 106.

50. Ibid., pp. 104–105.

51. Glennyce S. Eckersley and Gary Quinn, *Believe and Receive*, Rider, 2007, pp. 95–97.

52. *Fate and Fortune* magazine, January 2018, p. 20.

53. Newcomb, op. cit., pp. 122–123.

54. Cheung, *An Angel Saved Me*, op. cit., p. 46.

55. *Fate and Fortune* magazine, August 2014, pp. 6–7.

56. Cheung, *An Angel Saved Me*, op. cit., p. 38.

57. Ron Quinn, *Mysterious Disappearances*, BZB Publishing, 2012, p. 11.

58. Cheung, *An Angel Saved Me*, op. cit., pp. 47–48.

## Chapter 10: The Vanishing Hitchhiker Legends

1. Beardsley and Hankey, *The History of the Vanishing Hitchhiker*, California Folklore Quarterly, January 1943, p. 16.

2. Michael Goss, *The Evidence for Phantom Hitchhikers*, Coronet, 1984, p. 18.

3. Jan Harald Brunvand, *The Vanishing Hitchhiker*, Picador, 1981, pp. 27–29.

4. *Fate and Fortune* magazine, November 2018, pp. 6–7.

5. Ibid., July 2014, p. 23.

6. Goss, op. cit., p. 43.

7. Sean Tudor, *The Ghosts of Blue Bell Hill*, White Ladies Press, 2017, p. 93.

8. Jacqueline Simpson, *The Folklore of Sussex*, B.T. Batsford Ltd, 1973, pp. 50–51.

9. Tudor, op. cit., p. 133.

10. *Fortean Times* magazine, October 2017, p. 47.

11. Internet: Cy Sedgwick, 'Who is the Phantom Hitchhiker that haunts Blackwall Tunnel?'

12. *Fortean Times* magazine, October 2017, p. 42.

13. *Sunday Express*, 15 January 1956, p. 5.

14. Roger Boar and Nigel Blundell, *World's Greatest Ufo Mysteries*, Octopus Books, 1983, pp. 129–130.

15. Goss, op. cit., p. 15.

16. Derek Acorah, *Derek Acorah's Amazing Psychic Stories*, Harper Element, 2006, pp. 183–184.

17. *Strange but True*, LWTV Productions, 13 September 1996.

18. Andy Gilbert, *Credible Witness*, ISBN: 978-11-326-92772-1, 2017, pp. 55–56. Self-published, royalties to Burntwood Memorial Community Association.

19. *Fortean Times* magazine, July 2018, p. 77.

20. Ibid., June 2015, p. 35; Peter M. McCue, *Paranormal Encounters on Britain's Roads*, The History Press, 2018, pp. 77–78.

21. *Fortean Times* magazine, June 2015, p. 34.

22. Ibid., June 2015, p. 36.

23. *Chat It's Fate* magazine, September 2013, p. 49.

24. *Fortean Times* magazine, April 2015, p. 73

25. *Sunday People*, 14 July 1974, p. 9.

26. *Fortean Times* magazine, June 2015, pp. 32–39.

27. McCue, op. cit., p. 87.

28. Andy Gilbert, op. cit., p. 79.

29. Joan Forman, *The Haunted South*, Jarrold Publishers, 1989, pp. 100–101.

30. Terrence Whitaker, *England's Ghostly Heritage*, Robert Hale, 1989, pp. 129–131.

31. Wikipedia: 'Reported road casualties in Great Britain'.

32. Goss, op. cit., p. 9.

33. Ibid., p. 10.

34. Ibid., p. 75.

## Chapter 11: The Phantom Jaywalker

1. Sean Tudor, *The Ghosts of Blue Bell Hill*, White Ladies Press, 2017, pp. 246–247.

2. Michael Goss, *The Evidence for Phantom Hitchhikers*, Coronet, 1984, p. 29.

3. http://www.bbc.co.uk/news/UK-scotland-south-scotland - 24655488. 'The A75 Kinmount Straight: trip on an "almost haunted" road'.

4. Tudor, op. cit., pp. 208–209.

5. Roger Boar and Nigel Blundell, *World's Greatest Ghost Mysteries*, Octopus Books, 1983, pp. 124–125.

6. Ibid., p. 131.

7. Andy Gilbert, *Credible Witness*, ISBN: 978-11-326-92772-1, 2017, p. 21. Self-published, royalties to Burntwood Memorial Community Association; www.roadghost.com; *Birmingham Evening Mail*, 2 January 1966, p. 1; *Birmingham Post*, 3 January 1966, p. 5.

8. Internet: 'Ghosts and hauntings on the Highways and Byways'.

9. Tudor, op. cit., p. 299.

10. *Kent Messenger*, 2 July 1999, p. 51.

11. Peter Moss, *Ghosts over Britain*, Elm Tree Books, 1977, p. 66.

12. Ibid., pp. 163–165.

13. Arthur Shuttlewood, *The Flying Saucerers*, Sphere Books, 1978, pp. 13–14.

14. Janet and Colin Bord, *Modern Mysteries of Britain*, Grafton Books, 1988, pp. 36–37.

15. Derek Acorah, *Derek Acorah's Amazing Psychic Stories*, Harper Element Books, 2006, p. 186.

16. *Chat It's Fate* magazine, September 2014, p. 49.

17. Derbyshire paranormal database.

18. Nottinghamshire paranormal database.

19. www.lincolnshire.co.uk, 5 December 2016.

20. *Fortean Times* magazine, September 2018, pp. 42–43; Ibid., June 2015, pp. 38–39; see also Internet: 'Haunted roads in Southport, West Lancashire'.

21. *Fortean Times* magazine, June 2015, pp. 32–39.

22. Ibid., September 2014, pp. 43–44.

# Chapter 12: Dangerous Phantoms across Britain

1. *Annandale Observer*, 1 August 1997.

2. Ibid.

3. Andy Gilbert, *Credible Witness,* ISBN: 978-11-326-92772-1, 2017, p. 21. Self-published, royalties to Burntwood Memorial Community Association; www.roadghost.com; *Birmingham Evening Mail,* 2 January 1966, p. 1; *Birmingham Post*, 3 January 1966, p. 5.

4. *Luton Today* newspaper, 5 November 2008.

5. Colin Wilson, *The Supernatural*, Watkins Publishing, 2011, p. 430.

6. Sean Tudor, *The Ghosts of Blue Bell Hill*, White Ladies Press, 2017, p. 355.

7. Peter M. McCue, *Paranormal Encounters on Britain's Roads*, The History Press, 2018, p. 73.

8. Lee Brickley, *Ufos, Werewolves and the Pig-Man*, Yam-Yam Books, 2013, pp. 100–103.

9. Roads to the otherworld: http://www.mysteriousbritain.co.uk/england/west-midlands/hauntings.

10. Arthur Shuttlewood, *The Warminster Mystery*, Neville Spearman, 1967, p. 167.

11. Leicestershire paranormal database.

12. Yorkshire paranormal database.

13. Tudor, op. cit., p. 209.

14. *Fortean Times* magazine, August 2016, pp. 20–21.

15. *Fortean Times* magazine, October 2017, pp. 43–44.

16. Ibid.
17. Paul Devereaux, *Haunted Lands: Investigations into Modern Mysteries*, Piatkus Books, 2003, pp. 76–79
18. Sean Tudor, op. cit., p. 273.
19. Reuben Stone, *Poltergeists and the Paranormal*, Blitz Edition, 1993, p. 52.
20. See Andy Gilbert, *Credible Witness*, ISBN: 978-11-326-92772-1, 2017, pp. 22–24. Self-published, royalties to Burntwood memorial Community Association.
21. Coventry area paranormal database.
22. Lincolnshire paranormal database.
23. See Sean Tudor website.
24. Derbyshire paranormal database.
25. Dorset paranormal database.

## Chapter 13: Female Road Ghosts

1. See *Somerset Standard and Guardian*, 9 September 1999; *Bristol Evening Post*, 9 September 1999.
2. See *Brighton Evening Argus*, 2 December 1976.
3. *Kent Messenger*, 18 October 2013, p. 31.
4. Roger Boar and Nigel Blundell, *World's Greatest Ufo Mysteries*, Octopus Books, 1983, p. 130.
5. Sean Tudor, *The Ghosts of Blue Bell Hill*, White ladies Press, 2017, pp. 321–322.
6. *Fortean Times* magazine, August 2016, p. 18.
7. *Chat It's Fate* magazine, September 2018, p. 61.

8.  John Rackham, *Brighton's Ghosts, Hove Hauntings*, Latimer Publications, 2001, pp. 305–307.

9.  Somerset paranormal database.

10. Surrey paranormal database.

11. Andy Gilbert, *Credible Witness*, ISBN: 978-11-326-92772-1, 2017, pp. 24–28. Self-published, royalties to Burntwood Memorial Community Association.

12. *County Times and Express*, Mid Wales, cited by Janet and Colin Bord, *Modern Mysteries of Britain*, Grafton Books, 1988, pp. 35–36.

13. Boar and Blundell, op. cit., p. 65.

14. Ibid., p. 113

15. Ibid., p. 130.

16. *Wales on Sunday* online, 7 August 2011.

17. See W. B. Herbert, *Railway Ghosts and Phantoms*, BCA Books, 1992.

18. Internet: 'The Spooky Isles – The ghost of the wicked lady haunts Nomansland Common'.

19. Internet: 'The Leghs of Lyme'.

20. Internet: 'The UK's most haunted roads – Including the A6'.

21. John Harries, *The Ghost Hunter's Road Book*, Letts & Co, 1974, p. 38.

22. *Fate and Fortune* magazine, October 2018, p. 21.

23. Internet: 'British Legends and Mysteries, The Most Haunted House in England'.

24. Boar and Blundell, op. cit., p. 106.

25. Colin Wilson, *The Occult*, Watkins Publishing, 2006, p. 430.

26. Internet: Hauntedplaces.co.uk/northamptonshire.htm.

27. Internet: 'Essex ghost hunters, reference Canewdon Church'.

28. *Fate and Fortune* magazine, October 2014, p. 23.

29. *Chat It's Fate* magazine, June 2015, p. 34.

30. Peter Moss, *Ghosts Over Britain*, Elm Tree Books, 1977, pp. 29–30.

31. Nottinghamshire paranormal database.

32. Sean Tudor website, roadghosts.com, February 2003.

33. *Fate and Fortune*, August 2013, p. 23.

34. Moss, op. cit., p. 144.

35. *Fate and Fortune* magazine, July 2016, p. 3.

36. *Kent Messenger* newspaper, 19 December 2003, p. 35.

37. Internet: *Autotrader*, 'Most haunted roads in Britain'.

38. *Fortean Times* magazine, October 2017, p. 46.

39. BBC Scotland broadcast, 'Ghostly Ground', 4 July 2011.

40. Peter M. McCue, *Paranormal Encounters on Britain's Roads*, The History Press, 2018, p. 50.

41. Harries, op. cit., p. 41.

42. Ibid., p.60.

43. Internet: 'Ghosts and hauntings on the Highways and Byways'.

44. Internet: Fluxposure: 'Ghost roads – Britain's Most Haunted'.

45. Boar and Blundell, op. cit., p. 30.

46. *It Happened to Me: Real-life Tales of the Paranormal*, vol. 1, Dennis Publishing, p. 124.

47. Tudor, op. cit., p. 364.

48. McCue, op. cit., p. 55.

49. Internet: 'Hauntings on the Highways and Byways'.

50. Internet: Fluxposure: 'Ghost Roads – Britain's Most Haunted'.

51. Joan Forman, *The Haunted South*, Jarrold, 1989, pp. 100–101.

52. Internet: *Fortean Times* forum, 8 October 2008.

53. http://www,mysteriousbritain.co.uk/scotland/dumfries/ hauntings.dumfries/bypass.html.

54. Tudor, op. cit., pp. 335–340.

# Chapter 14: The Blue Bell Hill Legends

1. Sean Tudor, *The Ghosts of Blue Bell Hill*, White Ladies Press, 2017, p. 134.

2. Ibid., p. 175.

3. Ibid., pp. 135–137.

4. *Kent and Sussex Courier*, 31 October 2008.

5. Tudor, op. cit., pp. 348–349.

6. Ibid., p. 209

7. Ibid., pp. 225–226.

8. *Kent Messenger*, 19 December 2003, p. 35.

9. Michael Goss, *The Evidence for Phantom Hitchhikers*, Coronet, 1984, p. 3.

10. www.kenthistoryforum.co.uk, 25 April 2009.

11. *Kent Today*, 22 January 1993, p. 13.

12. Tudor, op. cit., p. 245.

13. *Reveille* magazine, 9 May 1975.

14. Broadcast by KM Extra radio, 28 October 2003.

15. Andrew Green, *Phantom Ladies*, Bailey Brothers and Swinfen Ltd, 1977, pp. 149–150.

16. *Kentish Gazette*, 16 July 1974; *Kent Messenger* 17 July 1974.

17. Ted Wright, *One Dog and Her Man*, Meresborough Books, 1992, pp. 68–69.

18. Tudor, op. cit., p. 345.

19. Radio Kent interview, 6 November 2014.

20. *Kent Messenger*, 2 July 1999, p. 51.

21. Tudor, op. cit., p. 341.

22. *Evening Post*, Kent, 30 August 1977, p. 10; *London Evening News*, 12 September 1977, p. 9.

23. www.kenthistoryforum.co.uk, 9 April 2010.

24. *Meridian Tonight*, ITV, SE News, 26 October 2000.

25. Tudor, op. cit., p. 362.

26. Internet: BBC Kent, 'Weird Kent', 9 December 2003.

27. *Kent Today* newspaper, 10 November 1992.

28. Ibid., 24 November 2002.

29. Tudor, op. cit., p. 34.

30. *Kent Today* newspaper, 23 June 1993, p. 7; *Kent Messenger*, 25 June 1993, p. 13.

31. *Fate and Fortune* magazine, April 2014, p. 23.

32. Tudor, op. cit., p. 358.

33. *Kentish Express*, 13 January 2000, p. 2.

34. Tudor, op. cit., pp. 425–428.

35. *Kent Today*, 23 June 1993; *Kent Messenger*, 23 June 1993, p. 13.

36. *Kent Today*, 22 January 1993, p. 13.

37. Tudor, op. cit., pp. 252–254, 263–264.

38. Ibid., p. 260.

39. *Chatham Standard*, 16 December 1980, p. 7; *Evening Post*, 15 December 1980, p. 11.

40. Tudor, op. cit., p. 261.

## Chapter 15: High Strangeness on the Highways

1. *It Happened to Me: Real-life Tales of the Paranormal*, vol. 1, Dennis Publishing, p. 129.

2. Michael Williams, *Supernatural Dartmoor*, Bossiney Books, 2003, pp. 18–19.

3. Sean Tudor, *The Ghosts of Blue Bell Hill*, White Ladies Press, 2017, p. 243.

4. *Fortean Times* magazine, September 2018, p. 44.

5. Ibid., January 2018, p. 35.

6. Herefordshire paranormal database.

7. *Fortean Times* magazine, letter, August 2018, p. 77.

8. See W. B. Herbert, *Railway Ghosts and Phantoms*, BCA Books, 1992.

9. Internet: 'Ghosts and hauntings of the Highways and Byways – shadow figure with no face, Longstanton, Cambridgeshire'.

10. Arthur Shuttlewood, *The Warminster Mystery*, Neville Spearman, 1967, p. 132.

11. *It Happened to Me*, op. cit., pp. 130–131.

12. Tudor, op. cit., p. 334.

13. *Fortean Times*, June 2015, p. 35.

14. Shuttlewood, op. cit., pp. 133–134.

15. *Fortean Times* magazine, May 2015, p. 47.

16. Internet: Road ghosts, Haunted Highways: http://drdavidclarke. co.uk ; LWT Productions, *Strange but True*, 1994.

17. Andy Gilbert, *Credible Witness*, ISBN: 978-11-326-92772-1, 2017, pp. 29–30. Self-published, royalties to Burntwood, Memorial Community Association.

18. *Fortean Times* magazine, January 2018, p. 36.

19. Roger Boar and Nigel Blundell, *World's Greatest Ufo Mysteries*, Octopus Books, 1983, p. 130.

20. Antony Milne, *Our Holographic World*, Empiricus Books, 2014, pp. 264–271.

## Chapter 16: Beware Fairies on the Road

1. *Chat It's Fate* magazine, November 2018, p. 51.

2. *Fortean Times* magazine, November 2018, pp. 27, 61–62.

## Chapter 17: Alien Black Cat Sightings

1. Janet and Colin Bord, *Modern Mysteries of Britain*, Grafton Books, 1988, p. 100.

2. See Merrily Harper, *Big Cats*, Heart of Albion Press, 2006.

3. Ibid., pp 24–25.

4. Bord, op. cit., pp. 1, 7–8.

5. Harper, op. cit., p. 167.

6. Somerset paranormal database.

7. Harper, op. cit., p. 2.

8. Internet: Nick Redfern, 'In search of the British Bigfoot' https://cryptomundo.com/bigfoot-report/british-bigfoot/'.

9. Peter M. McCue, *Paranormal Encounters on Britain's Roads*, The History Press, 2018, p. 91.

10. Harper, op. cit., p. 1.

11. *Fortean Times*, October 2018, p. 77.

## Chapter 18: The Wolf-like Apparitions

1. Peter M. McCue, *Paranormal Encounters on Britain's Roads*, The History Press, 2018, p. 102.

2. Merrily Harper, *Big Cats*, Heart of Albion Press, 2006, pp. 34–37.

3. *Fate and Fortune* magazine, September 2018, pp. 18–19.

4. *Fortean Times* magazine, December 2016, p. 21.

5. Ibid., June 2018, p. 77.

6. *Fate and Fortune* magazine, September 2018, pp. 18–19.

7. *Fortean Times*, Christmas, 2018, p. 73.

8. John Harries, *The Ghost Hunter's Road Book*, Letts & Co, 1968, pp. 68–69.

9. David Clarke, *The Ufo Files*, Bloomsbury Publishing, 2012, p. 38.

10. John Harries, op. cit., p. 122.

11. www.westmorlandgazette.co.uk.

12. Harries, op. cit., p. 154.

# Chapter 19: The Car-Chasing Orbs

1. Theresa Cheung, *An Angel Spoke to Me*, Simon and Schuster, 2011, pp. 120–122.

2. Tony Dodd, *Alien Investigator*, Headline Books, 1999, p. 84.

3. Ibid., pp. 86–88.

4. Paul Devereaux, *Earth Lights Revelation*, Blandford Press, 1990, p. 97.

5. John Harries, *The Ghost Hunter's Road Book*, Letts & Co, 1968, pp. 42–46.

6. Alfred Budden, *Ufos: Psychic Close Encounters*, Octopus Publishing Group, 1999, p. 142.

7. Surrey paranormal database.

8. *Fortean Times* magazine, February 2017, p. 29.

9. Arthur Shuttlewood, *The Warminster Mystery*, Neville Spearman, 1967, p. 145.

10. Ibid., pp. 40–42.

11. Brad Steiger, *Real Ghosts, Restless Spirits, and Haunted Places*, Visible Ink Press, 2002, p. 78.

12. Arthur Shuttlewood, *Warnings from Flying Friends*, Partway Publications, 1968, pp. 61–63.

13. Shuttlewood, *The Warminster Mystery*, op. cit., p. 147–148.

14. Wiltshire paranormal database.

15. Budden, op. cit., p. 130.

16. Ibid., pp. 130–131.

17. Hertfordshire paranormal database.

18. Ibid.

19. *Fortean Times* magazine, September 2017, p. 29.

20. David Clarke, *Supernatural Peak District*, Robert Hale, 2000, pp. 131–132.

21. See Facebook, 'Indominable', 23 January 2018.

22. Jenny Randles, *The Ufo Conspiracy*, Barnes and Noble, 1987, p. 160–161.

23. See *Phenomena* magazine, October 2009.

24. Budden, op. cit., p. 122.

25. Ibid., p. 142.

26  See internet discussions of this famous Ufo event, sometimes known as the 'Rendlesham Forest affair'.

27. *Chat It's Fate* magazine, August 2018, p. 35.

28, Jenny Randles, *Supernatural Pennines*, Robert Hale, 2003, p. 203–205.

29. *Fortean Times* magazine, September 2018, p. 77.

30. Roger Boar and Nigel Blundell, *The World's Greatest Ghost Stories*, Octopus Books, 1983, p. 37.

31. Ibid., pp. 64–66.

32. Ibid., p. 36.

33. *Fortean Times* magazine, April 2018, p. 27.

34. Tony Dodd, *Alien Investigator*, Headline Books, 1999, p. 207.

35. Ibid., pp. 205–208.

36. Marc Davenport, *Visitors from Time*, Greenleaf Publications, 1994, p. 115.

37. Budden, op. cit., p. 128.

38. Ron Halliday, *Ufo Scotland*, Black & White Publishing, 1998, pp. 187–188.

39. *Mail on Sunday* supplement, 2 September 1997.

40. Halliday, op. cit., pp. 210–213.

## Chapter 20: The 'Car Stop' Phenomenon

1. Arthur Shuttlewood, *The Warminster Mystery*, Neville Spearman, 1967 p. 135.

2. Timothy Good, *Earth: an Alien Enterprise*, Thistle Publishing, 2013, pp. 51–53.

3. See *Daily Express*, 18 January 2018.

4. Brinsley Trench, *The Flying Saucer Story*, Universal-Tandem, 1973, p. 106.

5. Arthur Shuttlewood, op. cit., pp. 59–61.

6. Clive Harold, *The Uninvited*, a Star Book, WH Allen & Co Ltd, 1979, pp. 20–24.

7. Essex paranormal database.

8. Shuttlewood, op. cit. pp. 132–133.

9. Peter M. McCue, *Paranormal Encounters on Britain's Roads*, The History Press, 2018, pp. 133–134.

10. Peter Hough and Jenny Randles, *Mysteries of the Mersey Valley*, Sigma Press, 1993, pp. 88–89.

11. Albert Budden, *Ufos: Psychic Close Encounters*, Octopus Publishing Group, 1999, p. 180.

12. Roger Boar and Nigel Blundell, *The World's Greatest Ufo Mysteries*, Octopus Books, 1984, p. 129.

13. Jenny Randles, *The Ufo Conspiracy*, Barnes and Noble, 1987, pp. 138–139.

14. Jenny Randles, *Men in Black*, Piatkus Books, 1997, pp. 105, 175.

15. Internet: 'The High Bentham Incident, 2005'; Jenny Randles, *Encounter* magazine, March 2016, pp. 128–130.

16. *Fortean Times* magazine, September 2018, p. 77.

17. Mark Davenport, *Visitors from Time*, Greenleaf Publications, 1994, p. 48.

18. Brad Steiger, *Strangers from the Skies*, Universal-Tandem, 1966, 1970, p. 75.

19. Hilary Evans, *The Evidence for Ufos*, Thorsons publishers, 1983, p. 74.

20. *Fortean Times* magazine, April 2012, p. 46.

21. Evans, op. cit., p. 78.

22. *Fortean Times* magazine, August 2018, p. 74.

23. Boar and Blundell, op. cit., pp. 31–32.

24. *Fortean Times* magazine, April 2018, p. 27.

25. David Clarke, *The Ufo Files*, Bloomsbury Publishing, p. 164.

26. Jenny Randles, *Time Storms*, Piatkus Books, 2001, p. 23.

27. Boar and Blundell, op. cit., p. 34.

28. Randles, *The Ufo Conspiracy*, op. cit., pp. 22–23, 29.

29. McCue, op. cit., p. 107.

30. Ibid., p. 108.

31. *Ufo Data* magazine (UK), March–April 2007, pp. 33–34

32. Hough and Randles, op. cit., pp. 94–95.

33. *Fortean Times* magazine, December 2016, p. 25.

34. Jenny Randles, *The Ufo Conspiracy*, op. cit., pp. 73–74.

35. *It Happened to me: Real-life Tales of the Paranormal*, vol. 3, Dennis Publishing, p. 57.

36. *Fortean Times* magazine, June 2015, p. 37.

## Chapter 21: UFOs – The Police Get Involved

1. Andy Gilbert, *Credible Witness*, ISBN: 978-11-326-92772-1,2017, p.2. Self-published, royalties to Burntwood Memorial Community Association.

2. Jenny Randles, *Time Storms*, Piatkus Books, 2001, pp. 153–154.

3. Roger Boar and Nigel Blundell, *World's Greatest Ufo Mysteries*, Octopus Books, 1984, p. 27.

4. Dr David Clarke, *The Ufo Files*, Bloomsbury, 2012, pp. 75–78.

5. Brinsley Trench, *The Flying Saucer Story*, Universal-Tandem, 1967, p. 165.

6. Gilbert, op. cit., pp. 87–89.

7. Clarke op. cit., p. 87.

8. Boar and Blundell, op. cit., p. 120.

9. Ibid., p. 122.

10. Gilbert, op. cit., pp. 86–87.

11. Tony Dodd, *Alien Investigator*, Headline Books, 1999, p. 6.

12. Ibid., pp. 13–17.

13. Ibid., pp. 63–64.

14. *Fortean Times* magazine, July 2016, p. 29.

15. Dodd, op. cit., pp. 56–57.

16. Ibid., pp. 20–21.

17. Ibid., pp. 15–18.

18. Ibid., p. 164.

19. Jenny Randles, *The Ufo Conspiracy*, Barnes & Noble, 1987, p. 70.

## Epilogue

1. Michael Goss, *The Evidence for Phantom Hitchhikers*, Coronet, 1984, p. 20.

2. *Fortean Times* magazine, February 2015, pp. 40–45.

3. *Fate and Fortune* magazine, September 2015, p. 19.

4. W. B. Herbert, *Railway Ghosts and Phantoms*, BCA Books, 1992, pp. 149–150.

5. Ibid., pp. 88–91.

6. *Fate and Fortune* magazine, June 2018, p. 26.

7. Jenny Randles, *The Ufo Conspiracy*, Barnes and Noble, 1987, p. 136.

8. Frank Edwards, *Flying Saucers – Here and Now*, Bantam Books, 1968, p. 48.

9. *Fortean Times* magazine, March 2014, pp. 52–53.

10. Ibid., July 2014, p. 26.

11. Ibid., February 2015, p. 75.

12. Herbert, op. cit., pp. 245–246.

13. Ibid., pp. 254–256.

14. Phil Whyman, *Dead Haunted*, New Holland Publishers, 2007, p. 15.

15. Colin Wilson and Rowan Wilson, *Strange but True*, Paragon Plus, 1995, pp. 419–420.

16. Aniela Jaffe, *Apparitions and Precognition*, University Books, 1963, p. 45.

17. Peter M. McCue, *Paranormal Encounters on Britain's Roads*, 2018, pp. 8–10.

18. Wilson and Wilson, op. cit., p. 427.

19. Herbert, op. cit., pp. 101–102.

20. See Chris Balzano and Tim Weisberg, *Haunted Objects*, Krause Publications, 2012.

21. Ibid., pp. 60–61.

22. *Chat It's Fate* magazine, February 2017, p. 28.

23. Albert Budden, *Ufos: Psychic Close Encounters*, Octopus Publishing Group, 1999, p. 197.

24. *Fortean Times* magazine, December 2018, p. 27.

25. Brian Inglis, *Coincidence*, Hutchinson, 1990, p. 47.

26. Anil Ananantswamy, *New Scientist* magazine, 29 September 2018.

27. Brad Steiger, *Real Ghosts, Restless Spirits and Haunted Places*, Visible Ink, 2003, p. 359.

28. Antony Milne, *Our Holographic World*, Empiricus Books, 2014, p. 14.

29. McCue, op. cit., p. 73.

30. Ibid., p. 73.

31. Alan Radnor, *Paranormal or Normal?*, Lennard publishing, 1989, p. 145.

32. See Joseph P. Farrell, *Secrets of the Unified Field*, Adventures Unlimited, 2008.

33. Ibid., pp. 128–131.

34. Ibid., p. 131.

35. Milne, op. cit., pp. 264–272.

36. Ibid., p. 254.

37. *Nexus* magazine, December 2013–January 2014, pp. 48–52.

38. Ibid.

39. Budden, op. cit., pp. 189–195.

40. See Bruce Gernon and Rob Macgregor, *Beyond the Bermuda Triangle*, New Page Books, 2017.

41 *Fortean Times*, April 2014, p. 75.

# Index

Note: Individual towns, villages and urban areas are not listed separately, but can found in the listed counties where they are located.

Printed in Great Britain
by Amazon

20501416R00254